BULLY IN SIGHT

How to predict, resist, challenge and combat workplace bullying

Overcoming the silence and denial by which abuse thrives

Tim Field

1996

First published in Great Britain in 1996

Success Unlimited, PO Box 77, Wantage,
Oxfordshire OX12 8YP, UK

© Tim Field 1996

The right of Tim Field to be identified as the author of
this work has been asserted by him in accordance with
the Copyright, Designs and Patents Act 1988.

British Library Cataloguing in Publication Data
A catalogue record for this book is
available from the British Library.

ISBN 0 9529121 0 4

Typeset using FrameMaker® in New Century Schoolbook.

All brand or product names are trademarks or registered
trademarks of their respective companies or organizations.

Printed in Great Britain by
Wessex Press, Wantage, Oxfordshire.

To

Susan

who survived the
double whammy of widowhood of
a partner being bullied
then
a partner writing a book
but
never gave up

and

Michael and Fiona
who will inherit my world

'Did you see that girl?' he asked, looking at me. 'She is a classic example of psychological violence. This is what the human need to control others leads to when taken to the extreme. The old man and woman are dominating the girl totally. Did you see how nervous and stooped she was?'

'Yes,' I said. 'But it appears she's about fed up.'

'Exactly! Her parents have never let up. And from her point of view she has no choice but to lash out violently. It is the only way she can gain some control for herself. Unfortunately, when she grows up, because of this early trauma, she will think she has to seize control and dominate others with the same intensity. This characteristic will be deeply ingrained and will make her just as dominating as her parents are now, especially when she is around people who are vulnerable, such as children.

'In fact, this same trauma no doubt happened to her parents before her. They have to dominate now because of the way their parents dominated them. That's the means through which psychological violence is passed down from one generation to another.'

Contents

Tables

Figures

In memory of

Andrea Adams

Pioneer, Saviour, Inspiration

Acknowledgements

Although I alone am responsible for writing this book, many people have helped and supported me during a traumatic time when I was acquiring first-hand the knowledge and insight imparted in this book.

In that respect, a great debt of gratitude is due to Denise Lewis, Doreen Newman and Ann Williams for their kindness, friendship, faith and support.

For help with the onerous task of editing, my thanks go to Jacky Kennedy for her tireless patience and sensitivity. For help with the even more onerous task of proof-reading, I am deeply indebted to the expert eye of Bert Newman.

For advice on legal aspects, I am indebted to Brian Barr, solicitor, of Antony Hodari & Co, 89-95 Oldham Street, Manchester who specialises in personal injury, especially resulting from bullying and harassment; to Bill Reynolds of Independent Advocates, PO Box 714, Buckingham, who is a specialist in industrial relations and employment law and a professional representative; to Lyn Jones; and many others.

My thanks also go to other friends, colleagues, and acquaintances for their roles, direct and indirect, in the writing of this book, including Peter Agulnik, Roger Allinson, Chris Ball, Elaine Bennett, Anthony Bolland, Stan and Irene Burden, Amanda Campbell, Vanessa Cob, Mike Coleman, Evelyn Cook, Cary Cooper, John Cunningham, Gordon Dinnis, Roger Dobson, Christine Dry, Rosalie Everatt, Fay Fielding, Robert and Elizabeth Fell, Nick Fisher, Martin Friend, Pauline Gleeson, Paul Gosling, Aynsley Grant, Annette Griffiths, Tony Hazell, Tim Hutchinson, Christina Jones, Jane Kalnins, John Kavanagh, David Kinchin, Jonathan Lambert, Diana Lamplugh, Susan Morgan, Yve Norton, Terry Oxley, Colin Parsons, Dan Poynter, Christina Rogers, Charlotte Russell, Janet Samuel, Anita Sharma, Suzanne Simcox, Julie Stone, Sheryl Sullivan,

Jenni Watson,   Nicola Venning,   Mark Whitehead, Lyn Witheridge, and all those who I have forgotten to include. Also to all my former work colleagues whose kindness and support at a time of crisis substantially aided my recovery.

Special thanks are due to Andrea Adams for her work in identifying and bringing workplace bullying to society's attention, and for her support in my time of need. Perhaps she feels she can be more effective and influential in helping the human race overcome its bullying habits from where she is now.

Thanks also to the countless people who have called or written to share their horrific experiences.

And finally, to my wife and children for their patience, tenacity, love and support during the most difficult time of our lives.

Whom does this book help?

Bully in sight: how to predict, resist, challenge and combat workplace bullying furnishes valuable insight into the underlying reasons why humans often behave badly.

The knowledge revealed and insight shared will benefit everyone, especially:

- any employee who has a line manager
- any employee responsible for managing other people
- anyone who feels they are being or have been bullied
- anyone who feels they may be bullying others
- anyone who is involved, or potentially involved, in bullying, either at work or at home, either directly, as a bully or victim, or indirectly as a a friend, colleague, witness, of someone who is being bullied
- personnel officers responsible for employees' safety and well-being
- human resources officers responsible for implementing or carrying out company policies with regard to employees' conditions
- equal opportunities officers and those responsible for ensuring fairness for all
- welfare officers with interest in, or responsibility for, employees' or clients' mental or physical health, wellbeing or recovery
- counsellors and therapists, especially those dealing with the effects of bullying
- occupational health professionals with responsibility for the health of employees
- union officers responsible for arbitration or resolving of disputes or relations between all levels of workers and managers
- workers' representatives
- anyone involved in arbitration of disputes, strikes, differences of opinion, etc

- training officers with responsibilities for courses in personal development and effectiveness
- doctors and GPs who see patients with stress-related illnesses, depression or other mental health problems
- psychologists and psychiatric professionals with an interest in, or responsibility for, mental health care, treatment, or research
- those working to combat harassment, discrimination, prejudice, persecution, oppression, abuse, etc
- anyone involved in setting up, organising, running or participating in committees, workshops, work groups, etc, whether in business, local authority, government, non-profit-making organisations, charities or other voluntary bodies
- parents teaching children interpersonal skills, encouraging behavioural maturity, building confidence and instructing young people how to take care of themselves in the world
- teachers who need to be aware of bullying, its causes, and how to handle the behaviour
- anyone in a teaching or caring role with responsibility for young persons' development
- anyone entrusted with the care or guardianship of others, for example nurses, social workers, carers, prison officers, etc
- anyone involved in community care whose clients may be victims of bullying
- police and other law enforcement officers who may be involved in disputes or legal processes
- solicitors, barristers and anyone in the legal profession
- those working at or for tribunals and courts
- any person who at any time in their life needs to interact or work with another human being

Aims and Objectives

The aims and objectives of this book are as follows:

- to raise awareness of bullying such that everyone knows, understands and can recognise bully behaviour
- to share the benefit of my own experience, knowledge, research and insight into bullying behaviours
- to surmount the denial by which bullying is sustained
- to provide practical advice and guidance to those who
  - are being bullied
  - use bullying behaviours
  - are tasked with resolving disputes involving bullying
  - provide support and counsel to anyone involved in bullying
  - are responsible for the safety and wellbeing of employees or other people in their care
- to inform, educate and guide employers and others with respect to
  - the disadvantages, costs and penalties of allowing or encouraging bullying to continue
  - the benefits of eliminating bullying
  - the development of policies, procedures and strategies for tackling bullying
- to provide hope, encouragement and inspiration to those suffering through bullying
- to give all sides involved in bullying a fair hearing as a precursor to tackling and overcoming the behaviour
- to encourage a formal diagnosis of the symptoms of being bullied
- to stimulate further research into bullying and to encourage the application of ensuing knowledge to other forms of abuse, harassment, violence, conflict, etc
- to bring about change in society on a global basis for the benefit of all mankind as my contribution to the survival of the human race; fortune favours the bold...

Author's note

Whilst every effort has been taken in the preparation of the material in this book, the author shall have neither liability nor responsibility to any person or entity with respect to any loss or damage caused or alleged to be caused directly or indirectly by the information contained herein.

The purpose of this book is to educate and entertain. It does not seek to recommend any particular course of action, rather to outline options and likely outcomes. The book does not constitute a definitive or authoritative statement of the law; the information is offered as strategies you might like to consider and should not be held as expert.

Addresses and telephone numbers in the resource section at the end of the book are believed correct at time of going to press, although the publisher cannot guarantee that they will not change in future. Whilst the author believes in their credibility and professionalism, no guarantees can be offered in respect of individuals or organisations or their respective services referred to herein.

In all matters the services of a qualified competent professional should be sought.

Health warning

This book contains detailed accounts of bullying behaviour which in the majority of cases displays considerable consistency and predictability. People who have experienced bullying may wish to seek support at the time of reading due to the unpleasant memories that may be evoked. The PTSD symptom of flashback and replay is discussed in chapter 8 "Symptoms and Effects".

Foreword
by Diana Lamplugh OBE

It never occurred to me that I could be bullied in the workplace, but I was. For a whole year and a bit I endured the experience of losing confidence, self-esteem and hope. It took me considerable courage to leave and look for another job.

This episode came flashing back to me when one weekend I found my youngest daughter weeping and distraught when she came to stay.

"I don't want to go back", she said, "my boss goes on and on, she belittles me in front of everyone else; she shouts at me; she tells me I'm no good, day after day. I cry when I get up and feel I cannot possibly go in, but I also feel I cannot leave as no-one else would employ me."

Helped by us and also her friends, who had all suffered similar experiences, we gradually built up her confidence and persuaded her to seek another post. She slowly began to realise that the problem was in fact not her problem but rather her boss's problem. It was her boss who was an ageing person who was growing out of touch. My daughter was as bright as a button, full of innovative challenging ideas. She was in fact a threat and as such "had to be put down".

Now having met so many victims of bullying, I am convinced that it is widespread, has many facets and is deeply destructive. It can also destroy the workplace itself. Slowly and surely it can change the whole ethos of an organisation. For the victims of workplace bullying life can be unbearably lonely. If you are able to speak about it, no one seems to hear or care.

Now there is help. This book can act as a supporting friend who truly understands the problems and feelings. Reading this book can help you retain your perspective. It also gives you many practical strategies.

Andrea Adams was the first and much-loved campaigner

on this issue. After her most untimely death, it is to Andrea's credit that such good people are now intent on carrying out and building on her work. As devoted followers, The Suzy Lamplugh Trust will also do our part; running Conferences, commissioning research and putting together resource packs.

Tim Field, himself a victim of workplace bullying, has produced a meaningful, heartfelt and dynamic book which is also an easy read. There is no doubt that there is still a long way to go. We have few statistics and much to learn. However this book will further the essential work and give encouragement and courage to so many people.

Diana Lamplugh OBE
17 October 1996

Preface

Humanity has always been beset by bullying, and until recently, society has tacitly accepted the practice. With the excesses of the behaviour being increasingly visited upon employees throughout the workplace, details of the abuse are now causing people to question this acceptance. At the time of writing, whilst there is disquiet, discomfort and a growing recognition of the need for change, society as a whole still does not understand how to tackle and overcome the problem. The purpose of this book is to impart insight and enlightenment to enable everyone to contribute to the understanding and eradication of the behaviour.

I am grateful to everyone who has talked to me, supported me and provided information in my pursuit of this quest. I am particularly indebted to the several hundred people who have shared details of their horrific experience with me; underneath, all these cases show a remarkable consistency. It is my hope that the information in this book will enable future generations to lead secure, safe and fulfilling lives in a workplace far removed from that of today, without the constant threat of harassment, discrimination or bullying to terminate careers, impair health, impede and destroy lives and livelihoods

All the material in this book is based on or derived from actual events. Some of the quotes have been included verbatim, others have been edited slightly to preclude identification of specific individuals, employers or situations. A few quotes have been distilled from perhaps several hours of conversation.

One person deserves special mention. Andrea Adams worked tirelessly to raise awareness of bullying at work, giving freely of her time to offer advice and support to individuals who were experiencing the behaviour first-hand. Her seminal work entitled "Bullying at work: how to confront and overcome it" (Virago, 1992) marked a milestone in alerting society to the unacceptability of bullying; the book has been a life-saver for many people, including myself, and is recommended as companion reading. It is Andrea to whom principal credit must be accorded for first identifying, then labelling the practice now known as bullying at work. It is sad that Andrea lost her battle against cancer in November 1995, but her inspiration lives on. The best memorial to her life and work will be the ultimate conquest of workplace bullying; in the forefront of that quest is a Trust which bears her name.

This is the first of a series of books I am planning on human behaviour which look at why we are the way we are, why we behave the way we do, and our responses to the ways other people behave towards us. The aim is to promote awareness and understanding of the importance of maturity of behaviour skills, and provide advice and guidance on developing communication, interpersonal, behavioural and assertiveness skills. I also plan to dispel the myth that we can never be anything other than what we are now.

With this in mind, I have decided, after much thought, to use the word "victim" for the person who suffers at the hands of a bully. For variation, I occasionally use the words "target", "sufferer" and "experiencer". After reading this book, I hope I shall have convinced all "victims" of bullying that the state of victimhood is not a permanent one, but with insight, knowledge, enlightenment, support and encouragement, plus the desire to learn, grow and evolve, the frame of mind known as "victim mentality" results primarily from never having learnt or been taught to withstand the unpleasant behaviours of other people. Overcoming the states of "victim" and "vulnerability" are topics I shall explore in future books.

Whilst recognition, especially of weaknesses and failings, can be painful, the achievement of the long-term goal of enlightenment, awareness and advancement eclipse the transient and brief discomfort of change. The techniques of psychological self-defence require constant practice but are simple to learn. One need never suffer in this way again.

Tim Field
Oxfordshire, UK, 1996

Introduction

Bully in sight: how to predict, resist, challenge and combat workplace bullying examines the widespread, growing, topical but still touchy subject of bullying at work. In Part 1 the nature and reasons for bullying are explored and revealed, as are the methods and tactics commonly adopted by bullies. The difference between "bullying" and "management" is highlighted, and the causes of the recent rapid rise in the incidence of bullying are scrutinised. The horrific yet largely unrecognised psychological injuries sustained by the victim are explored in detail, as are the costs to individuals, families, employers and State. Part 1 concludes with some suggestions as to why bullies choose to behave in the way they do and offers one answer to the perplexing question of why the bully chooses to see the victim as a threat when no threat exists.

Part 2 looks at the many ways in which bullying can be tackled, from developing assertive behaviour, to confronting and challenging both bully and employer. The current legal position is summarised, and the book concludes with some ideas for tackling bullying on a global basis.

The book has been written to be read from cover to cover and whilst there is a logical flow from beginning to end, the book can subsequently be used for reference, each chapter furnishing insight into a particular aspect of bullying at work. Some of the longer lists have been included for completeness, to help identification and as an aid to research.

Bullying is not a gender issue, and, having consulted widely, I have addressed the author's perennial problem of the non-gender-specific pronoun by using "he", "him", etc throughout the book. I have rejected the inelegant "he/she" and the clumsy "s/he", as well as the use of "he" and "she" in alternate chapters. Unless otherwise stated, "he" includes both "he" and "she", etc. This book has no academic aspirations or literary pretensions, nor do I pursue political correctness; I seek merely to uncover a persistent and unpleasant form of abuse which commonly masquerades as management. Many of the books that have been used for research are listed in the resource section.

The author, whose own experience of being bullied led to a nervous breakdown, now works with and advises many people from all walks of life on workplace bullying and how to tackle and overcome the behaviour. This book tends to focus on the more serious end of the spectrum, although each of us will recognise some the behaviours in ourselves and others.

The main focus of *Bully in sight* is pathological bullying as exhibited in the workplace, however much of the information is relevant to other instances of bullying, including domestic, family, social, political and other arenas. A number of adjacent and related areas are also alluded to, including child abuse (with which workplace bullying has many parallels), other forms of abuse, harassment, stalking, conflict and violence. The climate of the 1990s workplace is also appraised as the origin of the increase of the incidence of bullying. With bullying such a seemingly ingrained and instinctive habit of human beings, reference is also made to historical and spiritual angles.

Bullying at work is about the repeated daily use of most of the behaviours described in this book, combined with abuse of power, gratification of the individual through the destruction of others, and denial of rights and opportunities.

Until recently, society has largely condoned bullying, either actively through encouraging and justifying its use, or passively by ignoring it. As the horrific consequences of abuse now emerge, such resolute consent is now being questioned.

My aim in writing this book is to reveal, perhaps for the first time, what goes through the bully's mind, how he thinks, what he thinks, and why he thinks the way he does. It is my belief that awareness and understanding of bullying will lead to a significant step forward in human evolution.

Definition

Bullying at Work

"He" and "she" are synonymous.

Bullying occurs when one person, typically (but not necessarily) in a position of power, authority, trust, responsibility, management, etc, feels threatened by another person, usually (but not always) a subordinate who is displaying qualities of ability, popularity, knowledge, skill, strength, drive, determination, tenacity, success, etc. The bully has conditioned himself, or allowed himself to be conditioned, to believe that he can never have these qualities which he sees readily in others.

Displaying high aggression and lacking appropriate interpersonal skills, the immature behaviour skills of the bully are insufficient to fulfil the duties and responsibilities of the position into which he has been, or allowed himself to be, recruited or promoted. The nature and demands of the position may have changed over time, perhaps without being realised. If in a position of management, trust, etc, the bully is also unable or unwilling to accept responsibility for the physical and mental wellbeing of those in his charge.

Insecurity and a lack of confidence cause the bully to desire to control the individual using aggressive physical and psychological strategies. The bully seeks to increase his confidence, not by raising his own, but by bringing the other person's down to below his, so that, in relative terms, he can feel good about himself. This process is repeated on a regular basis and becomes both addictive and compulsive. Through fear, domination is established, leading to disempowerment of, and loss of confidence by, the individual.

In order to avoid having to face up to, tackle and overcome his own shortcomings, the bully seeks to project his own failings on to other people whilst at the same time actively abdicating responsibility for the consequences of his behaviour on others. If necessary, the bully abuses his position of power, or calls on those with power, to achieve these ends.

The bully's behaviour is exacerbated by his own predominant behaviour style, also by stress, change, uncertainty, financial pressures, the prospect of failing to meet budget targets, lack of resources, and being bullied himself. Once initiated, it is stimulated by the victim's apparent low assertiveness, indecisiveness and approval seeking through the need to be valued.

Part One: Bullying defined

1   A human conduct

"After several months of uninterrupted bullying, I was a quivering wreck. Unable to eat, unable to sleep, terrified of going to work - and all because of one individual, unfit to be allowed out on his own, let alone be in a position of management."

Employee

"We don't have bullying here. It's not a problem."

Senior manager (in the same company)

Being bullied is an unnecessary hell. It destroys individuals, wrecks families, devastates lives and livelihoods, and costs both employers and the State dear. It does not "toughen people up", instead it weakens, disempowers and destroys. It does not aid survival, instead threatens our existence. It does not promote long-term growth and prosperity, but favours short-term expediency at the expense of the long term. And, as with other forms of violation and trespass, only those who have suffered it fully appreciate the sheer awfulness of daily unremitting abuse that has no answer, no reason, no value and no end. In the last decade of the twentieth century, workplace bullying is, in my view, the second greatest social evil after child abuse, with which there are many parallels.

Bullying affects everyone. Employees, colleagues, friends, partners, children, family; company, customers, clients, suppliers, even shareholders and investors through diminished profits and lost opportunities. No one escapes the effects of bully behaviour, whether direct or indirect, transferred or otherwise.

Bullying is widespread. Surveys suggest that over half the population has experienced or witnessed bullying at some time in their lives. Even this figure may be conservative.

"I always thought the purpose of going to work was to do work, not to spend one's entire time fighting off the

unwelcome attentions of more senior employees. All my
attempts to give excellent service to customers and
contribute to the profitability of the company were
thwarted by the immature behaviour and non-existent
interpersonal skills of my abusive managers. What these
people thought they were achieving was beyond me."

Whilst those on the shop floor have always been at risk of
being on the receiving end of unpleasant behaviours of
workmates and supervisors to such an extent that it is an
"accepted" practice and one "just has to put up with it", the
epidemic of bullying that is sweeping the workplace now
potentially affects everyone from shop floor to executive level.

The popularity, membership and influence of unions has
declined since the Thatcher years, with many of these bodies
still licking their wounds after the effects of swingeing anti-
union legislation. The exponential rise of workplace bullying
is now encouraging many to believe that the pendulum has
swung too far in favour of employers, and that a better
balance is needed. Whilst many firmly believe in the
necessity of reform initiated by Mrs Thatcher in the 80s, the
Iron Lady's rolling stone of progress, combined with
recession, has turned into an avalanche laying waste
everyone and everything (employees, business, the economy)
in its path. In the absence of measures to halt the
destruction, the havoc may only subside when this grim
reaper runs out of harvest. To be fair (as the government is
keen to emphasise) this phase of economic evolution - or is it
devastation? - is common to all industrialised nations.

Recession, ruthless cost-cutting, mergers, and a host of
other reasons have caused whole layers of management to
disappear in the blink of an evolutionary eye, with the few
staff that are left often having to take on the burdens of their
precipitately departed colleagues. The upshot is that almost
everyone in the workplace is at risk of abuse, with perhaps
the sole exception of those few at the very top, for whom
telephone-number salaries, bonuses and share options are
now de rigueur. "He's [97% of chief executives are male] being
paid £x a year for running that company, now that this
hospital is subject to market forces, I should be paid the
same" said one hospital trust chief executive, oblivious to the

immorality of his greed, and choosing to overlook the fact that his anticipated bonus alone would pay the salaries of three nurses. With this type of leadership now commonplace, it's little wonder that many of those lower down (but eager to be further up) covet the same bounty, especially when seeing the ease with which such gluttony is gleaned. If behaving like that brings results, what better than to do the same? The message is clear, even if unspoken: to get on in this organisation you have to behave like those at the top.

Pressures in the workplace are now running at such sustained high levels that otherwise normal, intelligent, rational and apparently harmless individuals are being ensnared in a temper of aggressive management and ruthless cost-focused attainment. Where an individual might formerly have been regarded as "perhaps not the most brilliant manager" - particularly in respect of people skills - but otherwise tolerable, the unending demands of daily survival - especially meeting ever-tighter budget targets - cause that person's behaviour to deteriorate into that of a heedless and brutish bully. The family man - or woman, for bullying is not gender dependent - with photographs of smiling offspring appropriately adorning the desk becomes a monster making the lives of those in his or her charge intolerable to point where breakdown, burnout, ill-health retirement and unfair or constructive dismissal have cut regular retirement age in many cases by up to half.

Most cases of bullying occur when a manager uses the opportunity of position to bully a subordinate. Although less common, the behaviour can be visited on peers, or in rare cases, on superiors; the effects are equally injurious and destructive. Abuse of power often comes into the equation, although this seems to facilitate rather than initiate the process. Bullies generate their own power and their hold is examined in chapter 5.

"Management" and "bullying" are distinct behaviours, although the two are commonly confused. A bully usually likes to think of himself as a "manager", despite his inability to manage. The primary purpose of "managing" is to motivate staff, minimise cost, maximise profit, achieve targets, etc. However, the primary - indeed sole - purpose of "bullying" is to make the bully feel good - it is the gratification that the bully gains from hurting others which is the motivating factor. Bullies can only feel good about themselves by making others feel bad, and the position of management is the means to this end. A bullying manager (sic) is often a dead weight carried only by the loyalty (to the employer) and hard work of those prepared or forced to cover for him; as such, the bully is a liability to himself, to his staff and to the employer.

Purpose of management	Purpose of bullying
• attainment of tasks • achievement of goals • control of resources • utilisation of staff • fulfilment of obligations • attainment of targets • optimisation of production • provision of best service • minimisation of cost • maximization of income	• gratification • survival

Table 1: Difference between management and bullying

In the playground, as in darkened streets, run-down areas and war zones (which some might see as playgrounds for adults), the hurt which bullies inflict is mostly physical; in the controlled environment of the workplace, the pain is inflicted mainly at the psychological level, eg through criticism, where the injuries are invisible to the naked eye. Invisible, that is, until one learns to interpret the symptoms.

> *"Each day going to work was like going to war - the office was a battle zone where a group of managers would take it in turns to humiliate and denigrate staff. I would not have believed that this type of behaviour could happen in a civilised society on a daily basis and be accepted had I not seen and experienced it myself."*

In addition to abuse of position and power by the bully is the denial of the right of the victim to earn their living through employment. The predictable pattern of a bullying relationship invariably ends with the victim being hounded out of their job, with physical and mental health impaired and professionalism discredited. The iniquity is often compounded by the withholding of a suitable reference, or provision of a deliberately bad one, plus the difficulty of explaining to a prospective employer the circumstances surrounding previous termination of employment. Many then become trapped in the treadmill of repeated job applications knowing how little chance there is of success. Months, perhaps a year or more, of recuperation may be necessary before the challenge of gainful employment can be faced again. In today's climate, the longer one stays out of the job market, the harder it is to get back in - if at all. Meanwhile, the bully continues to draw salary, frequently gaining promotion in the meantime.

Table 2: The unacceptable nature of bullying

- abuse of power
- intrusion of self
- violation of rights
- betrayal of trust
- imposition of will
- betrayal of confidentiality
- breach of loyalty
- defamation of character
- trespass of freedoms
- denial of right to earn a living
- obstruction of opportunity to work
- destruction of the individual

At the moment of dismissal, when health, self-confidence and self-esteem are at their lowest, the aggrieved victim is faced with a legal system that is unfriendly, slow, expensive, and which, at present, does not recognise the inequity of bullying. Ministerial platitudes of "we believe the law as it presently stands is adequate to address the circumstances described" serve only to display the speaker's or writer's ignorance and lack of interest in the injustice of occupational intimidation.

Bullying, especially on a regular basis and for the perpetrator's pleasure, can be regarded as a form of psychological rape because of its intrusive and violational nature. Bypassing or piercing the outer defences of assertiveness and behaviour skills, the inner self - including self-esteem, self-worth and self-confidence - is penetrated by a regular and unrelenting trespass of threat, intimidation, provocation and guilt.

> *"I was bullied severely over a period of three years and eventually dismissed on a trumped-up charge. The dismissal and appeal hearings were a foregone conclusion. A year later, having been let down repeatedly by the legal system, I still feel like I've been accused of a crime whilst the real criminals are off gallivanting about, probably bullying someone else. My only 'crime' was to take pride in and enjoy my job."*

At the moment, the onus is on the victim to seek justice, redress, compensation, etc. The parallels with rape are strong, but in bullying, the victim is also expected to find, identify, arrest, charge, prosecute and convict the offender largely by their own efforts and whilst recovering from the experience unaided, using a legal system that is unsympathetic, uninformed and often itself hostile.

> *"At my appeal hearing, I was made out to be the bully, everything I said was twisted round and used against me. I was made to feel a liar and encouraged to believe that I had made everything up; in short, I was made to feel as if I was the one that was guilty."*

As any victim of bullying will tell you, the perpetrator appears to be untouchable. Acts of regular verbal, psychological, professional and occasionally physical abuse go on unchecked and unpunished, the bully secure in the belief that basic etiquette, accepted rules, procedures and the law do not apply to him. Acting with impunity, his assumption and presumption of immunity to prosecution is rarely misplaced. Frequently, everyone knows what's going on, but no-one seems to be able to do anything about it.

So how can this be going on? Is it true? Are large numbers of people really being bullied every day of their working lives? How can so many people be suffering so much without society being aware? The same questions were asked when Esther Rantzen and others lifted the taboos surrounding child abuse in the 1980s. An appalling catalogue of horror was revealed to the disbelief of everyone bar the abusers and their victims. Presumptions of its incidence were, if anything, underestimated. Even today victims now in adulthood still stifle their secret nightmare fearing the wrath of disbelief.

As evidence mounted, so did the disbelief, horror, then denial; children went from "imagining it" and "fantasising" through "heard it from a friend", "got it from television", "making it all up", "must be mistaken", culminating in "must be lying". This is a familiar pattern when people, and society, are forced to face up to a persistent unpleasantness in their midst which has hitherto gone unchallenged. You may already have a feeling of déjà vu.

As a rule, children have a sharper, albeit less mature, sense of justice and fair play and are frequently more honest than their adult counterparts. The exception to this juvenile honesty are children who have already started to exhibit bullying behaviour, who seem to have missed out on learning how to tell the difference between fact and fiction. When pressed to answer, such a child makes up an excuse on the spur of the moment, perhaps genuinely unaware of whether it is true or not. If it seems to suffice, the behaviour is reinforced, and henceforth the child truly seems unable to differentiate between the two. This practice is commonplace for a very young child, and can be regarded as fantasising or confabulating rather than lying. It is a normal and natural part of early development, and most children either grow out of it, or learn to use it only as appropriate.

Children are also surprisingly conservative when it comes to defining rules and making decisions, especially when in a group (for example a classroom) mediated by a mature leader. In anticipation of the impending responsibilities of adulthood, their probity is precocious - especially when they themselves are affected by those decisions.

In child abuse, the abuser is mostly a parent, family member or other responsible adult or authority figure into whose legal duty of care the child is entrusted. In workplace bullying the abuser is usually a manager, and when the abuse is revealed, the employer, personnel and legal system express disbelief, horror and denial that such a horrific act could be taking place in their midst. Nevertheless, abusers of all types must be caught, revealed and made accountable for the injuries their behaviour causes to their victims. In the workplace, the injurious effects extend beyond the physical and psychiatric injuries and encroach upon the employer's credibility, reputation, financial performance and profitability.

Taboos

Taboos often serve to sustain bad behaviour, aiding perpetrators in the pursuance of their perversion whilst abetting the rest of us to get on with our lives without having to think about troublesome consequences. Until it happens to you, that is.

In addition to taboos, there are several reasons why adult bullying has maintained a low profile. These include:

Embarrassment: for a grown-up to admit that he or she is being bullied is, to say the least, embarrassing. With society still largely believing that only weak people can be bullied, can you imagine anyone, especially a man, confessing over a pint at the pub "I was bullied at work today"? Echoes of childhood resurface, the unpleasantness of immature interpersonal and behavioural skills is rekindled. Guilt, shame and a sense of failure stir. Would *you* admit to your partner or friends that you are being bullied?

Secrecy: most bullying occurs in private; there are no witnesses, no records and no forensic evidence. It's your word against theirs - and if "they" are in a position senior to you, which is usually the case, the odds are stacked against you. When witnesses are present, bullies are such nice, charming people. Aren't they?

Fear: bullies maintain their dominance through fear. In the workplace, this means fear of losing one's job, position, status, livelihood. No sensible person is going to risk those whilst revealing their apparent inability to stand the heat. Outside the workplace - and occasionally within - the bully's grip is strengthened by the use of intimidation and threat, both psychological, and, in some cases, physical. The latter manifests itself most often by shouting at and humiliating the victim in front of others, although physical assault is occasionally reported.

Recognition: bullying - or rather its effects on the individual - are often seen but not recognised. Symptoms, particularly of stress, are misdiagnosed, or misattributed. Rationalisations abound, for example "he's having a tough time at work/home with boss/partner/kids", "there's a personality clash", "she's not cut out for this type of work". The real cause goes unseen and unrecognised.

Perception: words which strike fear in the heart of a demoralised victim appear little more than "common sense" or "a bit on the assertive side" to others ignorant of what is going on. A coded language evolves, its meaning known only to those involved. To outsiders the person being bullied appears to have lost their sense of humour, can't take a joke, or is "too sensitive".

Fear of taking action: when or if it is recognised, colleagues are often afraid to do anything about it. If they show support for the person being bullied, they might attract the attentions of the bully as well - or instead. This type of fear can be called secondary bullying.

Disloyalty: it is currently not socially acceptable to "blow the whistle" on another individual, even when you're 99% (or more) certain of what is going on. It can be represented as disloyalty, with all the guilt and fear which that entails. No-one likes to "shop" a colleague, especially when the only evidence is circumstantial and anecdotal.

Ignorance (not knowing what to do): here, bullying is recognised for what it is, but colleagues are paralysed both by fear and ignorance. Society has, until recently, not faced up to, understood, and evolved strategies and procedures for tackling bullying, so many individuals don't know what to do. Most organisations have not yet extended their personnel and grievance procedures to cover bullying, and labelling it, like harassment, as a specific, clearly identifiable and unacceptable behaviour.

Cowardice: society condemns cowards, and to be seen to run away from the problem is likely to be interpreted as cowardice. In fact, cowardice is the simple recognition of one's inability to overcome adversity in the face of overwhelming odds. The victim knows that he must stand up to the bully (that is, act bravely) but is unable to summon the courage to do so. He becomes trapped in the "I have to but I can't, I can't but I have to" syndrome. This applies increasingly to the job as well. Admonitions from well-meaning colleagues or partner make things worse. The upshot is that the victim puts up with the abuse, thereby increasing stress further.

> *"Despite being in the job for several years, my manager still couldn't do his work properly. I was constantly correcting his mistakes and covering for him when dealing with customers - for which I was frequently reprimanded ... the only thing that seems to be rewarded by my employer is incompetence."*

Tacit approval: lack of disapproval, procedures, unwillingness or hesitation by the employer to tackle - or even acknowledge - bullying is taken as tacit approval by the bully to carry on. There is no punishment for the behaviour, no reward for altering their behaviour (indeed the reverse is common) - so why change the habits of a lifetime? If it's an acceptable management style within the organisation, why do anything different? In this sense, assumption of right (which includes a lack of respect for the rights of others) is a widespread human failing whose counterparts include smoking and dog fouling.

Absence of anti-bullying policy/climate: bullying can only be successfully addressed by a clear statement of employer policy which is adopted, implemented and followed enthusiastically and wholeheartedly **from the top down**. If any manager - or director - shows hesitancy or unwillingness, however slight, this is seized upon by the bully as tacit approval to continue.

Mental illness: bullying increases stress levels dramatically, and the common consequences of high stress, particularly negative stress, are symptoms of depression. Because depression acts mainly on the brain, it attracts the term "mental illness" which causes the spectre of insanity to loom large in peoples' minds. No-one wishes to admit to suffering "mental illness", even though, in mild form, it is so common that it should perhaps be considered as normal. People keep quiet, hoping it will go away. Sometimes the bully does; more often, he does not. Mental illness, or rather the psychological and behavioural symptoms arising from bullying, are discussed in more detail in chapter 8.

Example: the culture and climate of a company is consistent throughout all levels. If employees are happy, contented, outgoing and cheerful, this is likely to be the preferred behaviour style of the director and senior management. Similarly, if individual managers behave badly, their staff will begin to emulate these characteristics. In the short term, bad behaviour has at least twice the effect of good behaviour. For example, a satisfied customer, on average, will tell between four to six friends or colleagues about the good products or services they have received or experienced. A dissatisfied customer will tell between eight to twelve people, twice as often and for twice as long.

Good managers work long and hard to build relationships, establish trust and respect. A poor manager who takes over will undo his predecessor's good work quickly and with little effort. A subsequent good manager will have to work twice as hard for twice as long to re-establish the good working relationships and productive, happy atmosphere.

Bad habits are easily learnt and quickly replicated. Bad management, bad culture, bad news.

Acculturation: this is the greatest danger - over time, through acclimatisation and becoming accustomed to the company culture, bullying comes to be seen as normal. It then requires an event of significant magnitude - such as legal action, violence, or even suicide - to shake the workforce - at all levels - out of its complacency, acquiescence and denial.

Where does bullying happen?

Although awareness of bullying is rising in terms of its effect in the workplace, the behaviour is endemic to the human race, and can occur wherever two or more persons interact. People spend one-third of their adult life in the workplace, so, given the pressures of money, time, competition, etc within and between companies and organisations, the behaviour naturally manifests itself readily here.

Bullying is rife in the private sector, where the recession has bitten deep into profitability. Staff cuts are now an everyday occurrence, with those that are left often having to take on the work of their departed colleagues. Increased customer expectations, ever more stringent quality standards (often without corresponding investment), and insatiable City demands aggravate an already depressed situation.

Bullying is sweeping through the public sector, where savage short-term cost-cutting programmes have slashed resourcing to the bone - and sometimes beyond. The intention of better financial management for schools, hospitals, etc has resulted in greater administrative burdens with reduced resources. Simultaneously, customers', clients', patients' and parents' expectations of quality and service have been heightened through the imposition of "charters". The result is rocketing stress for the fewer employees charged with achieving publicly quoted targets. Objections and warnings of industrial action by overworked employees are met with appeals to their professionalism, such as "By this action you will be putting patients lives at risk". More about guilt later. Consequently, "I'm now doing the job of two or three people" is an increasingly common clue to the true cost of this policy.

The two professions most badly affected by bullying seem to be teaching and nursing (closely followed by social services). In addition to the causes outlined above, these occupations have both a keen vocational element and a strongly hierarchical management structure. Vocational professions attract those with strong empathic skills, whilst a career in management is inviting to those who feel drawn to positions of power. When the skills of the latter are inadequate to manage the former in a climate of creeping commercialism, artificially heightened expectation and the threat of inspection, the potential for conflict is high.

In the privatised sector, or those organisations in the throes of privatisation, financial pressures in the form of profit targets have raised pressures to hitherto unimagined levels, bringing out the worst in managers whose qualifications are often in anything but management.

Even the voluntary sector is groaning under the strain. Gone are the days of elderly and genteel ladies selling second-hand items to raise much-needed cash for local worthy causes. With an average of seven charity shops in each small town, and more in the cities and larger conurbations, competition for supporters' pennies is cut-throat, with shop managers under enormous pressure to achieve predetermined targets. The National Lottery has aggravated the problem with its potential for making people instant multimillionaires, further diverting funds away from traditional methods of - and reasons for - giving.

The result
...is stress, and the consequence of stress is to behave in ways inappropriate to the needs of the situation in which people find themselves. GPs often now spend so much time dealing with stress-related illness that some have written to employers asking what is going on.

Bullying happens in all walks of life. It occurs in companies and organisations, large and small, at board, section, department, group and shop-floor level, in committees, arbitration bodies, even in organisations devoted to stamping out bullying. Only people-free zones are immune.

It happens wherever circumstances are opportune, eg where there are restricted resources (especially when coupled with high expectations), high stress, poor interpersonal skills, lack of behavioural maturity, low confidence (but perhaps high determination), charged emotions, frustration, resentment, lack of direction and uncertainty, to name a few; these are discussed further in chapter 10.

Bullying takes place anywhere there is control, persuasion or the need to influence; in particular, behaving as a bully, as well as proneness to being bullied are a feature of people with low confidence and esteem. Even people with apparently high outward self-confidence can fall victim. For some the experience is so demoralising that they never fully recover.

Background
Wherever two or more humans meet with the purpose of working together, whether as equals or in a superior/subordinate role, bullying can occur. One wonders how humanity has survived, but in the distant future bullying - and our growing awareness of it - may be seen in its rightful context, as part of the human species' evolution to a more mature and spiritually enlightened existence.

Bullying is now recognised for what it is - a waste of individuals' talents and skills, a threat to survival. Raising a person from birth to adulthood in Western society costs a very large sum of money, taking into account education, administration, health care, self-development, transport, maintenance of the family, plus personal costs such as food, clothing, shelter, warmth, hobbies, etc. Why then does society waste that investment by allowing - even complicitly encouraging - one individual to destroy another - or several others - through bullying in the workplace? And why do we squander human potential by intimidating, harassing and oppressing our colleagues when we are supposedly on the same side?

As awareness of the scale, intensity and urgency of the problem becomes apparent, people are realising that it is no longer acceptable to have to be in possession of the psychological equivalent of a karate black belt in order just to carry out their job in the workplace. One's work is sufficient challenge on its own without having to fend off the unwelcome advances of an immature, overbearing boss or colleague.

Until recently, coping with aggressive managers and colleagues was seen as an essential part of surviving in a tough, competitive world. A necessary learning experience, and if you couldn't hack it, you were a wimp, there was something wrong with you. If you can't stand the heat, get out of the kitchen. Pursued over the long term, there would soon be no-one left to do the cooking. No shortage of people to state what needs cooking though.

For centuries, the State has needed fighting men to ensure its survival. Officers to give orders and have the means to ensure they are obeyed. Men to carry out those orders, regardless of their sense. As society has become more "civilised", these inherent qualities of "toughness" have transferred from the battlefield to the workplace. Whilst this may have been appropriate for society's survival in the post-war years, the new millennium heralds a change in attitude from a hostile, ruler-based "do as I say" to an empathic, caring "how can we work together to achieve common goals?"

Some see bullying as a hangover from our alleged cave-people origins - another manifestation of the "fight or flight" syndrome. Under threat, the human body gets ready either to fight or to run. The modern equivalent, in our hierarchic, workplace-dominated, highly organised and sedentary lifestyle, is to react instinctively according to our levels of behavioural maturity, self-confidence and interpersonal skill.

Viewed from a distance, humans could be seen to be making the transition from physical - fight or run - to psychological - do we dominate or accept dominance? The key lies not in our physical survival, but in our feelings of self-worth, self-esteem and self-confidence. Slaying animals, fighting rival tribes, weathering the elements are taken care of; we can pop down to the local superstore for our joint of meat or nut cutlet, use the law to protect ourselves, and centrally heat, air condition, and otherwise pamper ourselves in sumptuous, if superfluous, comfort. Knowledge, thought, cooperation and brain power are the new (or maybe not so new) survival skills for providing the means to pay the bills - and survive. It is a measure of society's progress, and perhaps part of mankind's journey from the physical to the spiritual. Whilst this may seem far-fetched or out of place in a book about bullying, many victims have reported that the trauma caused by bullying has required not only a period of physical recovery, but initiated questions regarding purpose and meaning of life, sometimes leading to spiritual enlightenment. If this applies to you, then books such as *The Celestine Prophecy* and *Embraced by the Light* might help you make sense of the events in your life (for details see the resource section at the back of this book).

So what stimulates bullying? One cause is the adversarial basis of society, engendered by our education system - there's only one right answer, by implication all others are "wrong". We grow up obsessed believing there's only one way, one answer, constantly looking to "teacher" for confirmation that we've got that right answer. The attitude is epitomised by exams, tests, quiz shows ("no, that's not the answer I'm looking for"), and so on. These all trade on the belief in superiority - if you've got the "right" answer, you've passed, you're in, you're accepted. The wrong answer (not the one the other person believes is correct) and the benefits of membership are denied. Thus we grow up constantly trying to prove "right", and in so doing establishing superiority - but heedless of the fact that a superior person has no need to establish superiority.

Whilst all these factors may provide opportunities for bullying to break out, and breed, it can happen to almost anyone. It is irrelevant whether you are a company director or a cleaner, academically qualified or not, male or female, white or black, abled or disabled. Being different is an attraction for the bully, but to understand why a person is picked on in this way, we need to look at the underlying behaviour styles and motivations.

Being bullied at work is a situation that most individuals cannot handle by themselves. Well-meaning advice from colleagues, such as "Why don't you stand up for yourself", or misplaced sympathy, such as "Well, he's not worth worrying over", provide no comfort, and, ironically, may make the victim feel worse. Similarly, suggesting a no-blame approach may - without insight, training and support - be seen as insulting, like telling someone experiencing depression to "pull yourself together", or advising a person who has just broken their leg that what they need is "a good run round the park". Only when the bully has been brought to account and reparation made can most victims of bullying allow themselves the luxury of feeling sorry for the bully whose circumstances cause him to behave in the way he chooses to.

There is nothing wimpish, cowardly or weak in seeking help. It is a sign of strength to know when it is appropriate to solicit counsel. To maintain dominance, bullies employ highly selective memories, stack all odds in their favour, and regularly move the goalposts; in short, they cheat. You need support to make the playing field level.

A question that is frequently asked is "where do we draw the line between tough management and bullying?" There is a subtle but important difference. In the former, the focus is on achieving targets or tasks in hand; however managerially clumsy, the self-confidence of the participants is not addressed. In the latter there is an intention is to reduce a person's level of self-confidence. It is this distinction - the disparity between *intent* and *content* - which warrants the tag "bullying".

What does it achieve?

Criticism, which is how bullying most commonly presents itself, is self-defeating. In bullying the criticism is usually unjustified - so how can it possibly achieve any good? Dale Carnegie, in his best-selling book "How to Win Friends and Influence People", makes plain the pointlessness of fault-finding and negative feedback. Written in 1936, it should be compulsory reading for all.

In the short term, an employee can be threatened into doing almost anything - especially if the threat is linked to their job security. No sensible person is going to take the risk of jeopardising their livelihood - and that of their family if they are the breadwinner - for a minor disagreement with their boss. After all, their boss is a senior person, and therefore more experienced, capable, professional, wise, knowledgeable, etc. Isn't he?

It comes as a surprise to many people to realise that in the case of a bully, the answer is - probably not. He is likely to have reached his position more from the ability to persuade his superiors that he is the right person for the job, rather than his actual ability to do the work entailed by the job.

"I spent many years working for a large scientific research and development organisation. It struck me that those scientists who were mediocre at their job stayed in that role. Those who were good at their job were soon promoted into management positions. All too often, they did not show the same enthusiasm and ability for management that they showed as scientists."

We know from the work of American psychologist B F Skinner that on animals reward is far more effective than punishment. The same is true for humans. People move away from what displeases them and toward what accords pleasure. A carrot is deemed beneficial, worth earning, but a stick is to be avoided at all costs. People work harder, longer and more productively when there is a reward. If there is no reward - or worse still, if there is only punishment and pain - people learn to avoid the behaviour/task/situation that invokes that outcome.

In the workplace, reward traditionally comes in financial form; however, the effect diminishes and after a while, pouring more money (reward) at a person starts to have the opposite effect. What really rewards - and motivates - people is the pleasurable feeling that comes from being made to feel

valued and worthwhile. This gives meaning to their lives,
they look forward to going to work, and will give above and
beyond the call of duty.

The key to understanding why the bully needs to criticise
is to recognise the role of behavioural maturity and self-
confidence. By criticising, the bully is letting others know
how badly he feels about himself. He has little faith in his
subordinate because he has little faith in himself. This
fundamental rule holds true for all aspects of our self, and is
worth expounding:

> You can never have more faith in anyone else
> than you have in yourself. You can never trust
> others more than you trust yourself. You can
> never respect others more than you respect
> yourself. And ultimately, you can never love
> others more than you love yourself.

Perhaps the most important aspect of criticism is what it
reveals about the person who uses it. Criticism is a way of
avoiding facing up to one's own failings; it is much easier to
find faults in others than in oneself. By projecting one's own
shortcomings on to others, one can feel good - at least in
relative terms - by knowing that you have judged and found
others to be less worthy than yourself.

Related to criticism is blame, which is a means of
abdicating responsibility for addressing one's own failings by
transferring or projecting them on to another individual. If
the recipient is absent, or unable to defend themselves, or
one's position of power can be abused to impose the criticism,
satisfaction is increased.

The effects of bullying

Whilst the short-term effects are to get the job done, the
medium and long-term outcomes elicit the opposite effect -
both on the individual and on the employer.

Bullying causes stress, and the body's response to stress is
varied and vast, ranging from aches and pains to frequent
illness, headaches to irritability. It may be that many serious
illnesses and disorders, especially those linked to the nervous
system or immune system are also activated either by stress,
or the sudden release from stress.

From the company's point of view, there is absenteeism, high staff turnover, low morale, poor productivity, and poor relations between people, be they staff or customers.

If the bullying continues unchecked, and the victim, unwisely or through lack of knowledge, does not seek professional help, then the body's ultimate reaction is predictable. The brain - which is the principal bearer of stress, reaches the point where it has had enough, and a mental breakdown occurs. This traumatic event is more common than one imagines, although society's taboos discourage the true tally from being discerned.

Bullies have a knack of pushing people to the edge, then drawing back at the last moment, perhaps with unexpected praise. Eventually, they make a misjudgement and go too far.

When you're pushed over the edge it is the natural and normal response of the brain to close down temporarily. A consequence of such breakdown is reactive depression, from which recovery takes months, and often, years. In serious cases, where professional help is not sought, or the diagnosis is inappropriate, the person may never fully recover. The employer needs to realise that in the majority of cases, after a breakdown, the useful working life of the individual - in that organisation at least - is over, and the investment in recruitment, training, experience, etc is lost.

People who are being bullied take that stress home with them. Some overtly pass it on to the family, others try desperately to keep it to themselves. That act of suppression ironically makes things worse, both for the individual and the family. The result is the same, and the family experience the same bullying behaviours, expressed unwittingly, to the detriment of all. It is likely that bullying represents a major cause of family break-up. If you're not happy at work, then you're unlikely to be happy at home.

Common excuses

"Only weak and inadequate people are bullied."

The two most common reasons - by far - for attracting the attentions of a bully are being good at your job and popular with people (selection criteria are discussed in chapter 7). Bullying is about projecting one's own weaknesses and failings onto others. Only a bully has the insensitivity to make a statement like this, and in so doing, unwittingly confesses to their own weakness and inadequacy.

"People respect toughness."

Firmness, assertiveness, fairness, trustworthiness, leadership, yes. Bullying is none of these. Bullying is about gratifying the self through hurting others.

"You're too sensitive."

Also conscientious, industrious, reliable, honest, trustworthy, imaginative, creative and a host of other virtues. The person who produces this statement as a justification for bullying is demonstrating their insensitivity and prejudice. Most wars and conflicts are caused by the insensitivity of one or both parties.

"You take things too personally."

This is denial of consequence of behaviour on others; the bully is openly but unwittingly admitting their insensitivity.

"You're over-reacting."

Just as a person who has been hit over the head with a blunt instrument would not be considered as "over-reacting" when they report a fractured skull, a person who has been bullied should not be regarded as "over-reacting" when they report the severe psychiatric injuries. The full effects of bullying experienced by the victim are described in chapter 8.

"You're just behaving irrationally / emotionally."

Irrational/emotional behaviour is one of the symptoms of bullying. This statement is an attempt by the bully to divert attention away from the *cause* the other person's behaviour by focusing on the *effect*. Pursue the cause of the irrational/ emotional behaviour - who is causing this person to react in this manner and why?

"It's her time of the month."

Ditto. It is important to distinguish between symptoms of PMS, which are transient and predictable, and the symptoms of bullying, which are a reaction to the behaviour of the bully and continue regardless of time of the month.

"It's about time for her menopause."

Ditto.

"Teaches you to be a man."

Tough luck if you're female. Bullying is about gratification of the individual through hurting others. What it does teach you is that there are a lot of nasty and insensitive people in the world who work hard to deny the consequence of their behaviour on others. It also teaches you how to be a bully and the extent to which society allows you to get away with it, should your conscience be insufficiently developed to allow it.

"This sort of thing happens, doesn't it?"

It certainly does, and employers must understand and accept their moral and legal responsibilities when it occurs.

"It's all your fault."

Admission of insensitivity, denial of responsibility for consequence of behaviour, also projection, etc. Read on.

"It's only a bit of horseplay."

By trying to justify and excuse what they have done, the person saying this is admitting to their behaviour and tacitly acknowledging its adverse effect on others.

"You have to be tough to improve the performance of staff."

People move toward what gives them pleasure, comfort and satisfaction, and away from what does not. The effect of the attitude expressed here will be disenchantment and alienation.

"The more I criticise people, the more they know what they need to change."

Ditto. Read Dale Carnegie's "How to win friends and influence people".

"This way we get rid of those who aren't pulling their weight."

The people most likely to be bullied are those who are best at their jobs, often working above and beyond the call of duty. Those most likely to bully are those least competent at their jobs. So what do you end up with?

"It's a clash of personality."

Technically, it's a clash of behaviour styles, but it is the bully's behaviour which is reprehensible and unacceptable.

"You'll come out of this a stronger person."

Having read this book you'll understand what has happened to you, who is the cause, and why; you may thus be empowered to take appropriate remedial action.

"By leaving you're running away from the problem."

Choosing to leave is an acceptable, and sometimes only, solution to a problem which is (a) not of your making, (b) not under your control, and (c) waged by people who choose to cheat, lie, deceive and exhibit a host of other reprehensible behaviours.

"You're being negative."

You have foolishly dared to disagree with the bully or drawn attention to the absurdity or illogicality or the bully's way of managing, or have had the temerity to point out the foolhardiness, impracticability, short-sightedness and inequableness of management's plans for change and will now be subjected to the behaviours described in this book.

"You've got an attitude problem."

This claim is so vague and lacking in substance that in choosing to use it the bully is drawing attention to the fact that they have nothing else on which to base their case. So why does the bully choose to say this? Projection? Distraction? Diversion? Denial?

Euphemisms

"It's just strong management."

Bullying has nothing to do with management; it is about gratification of the individual by projecting weaknesses, failings and shortcomings onto others as a way of avoiding having to face up to, tackle and overcome faults in oneself.

"Serious review by management for not doing their job particularly well."

Old attitudes and prejudices die hard.

"Stringent management regime to identify and rectify weak links."

QED - quod erat demonstrandum - or should that be quod erat desperandum?

Traditional remedies

"I want you two to shake hands and let bygones be bygones."

The person saying this is revealing that they know nothing about bullying; if in a position of management, that person is also denying and abdicating responsibility for the duties of their position.

"Forgive and forget."

Ditto. Perhaps - but only after justice has been done.

"Try to build bridges."

Ditto. Perhaps - but only if there is genuine reciprocation.

"All grievances and other such staff matters are dealt with by the line management."

In at least 80% of cases, the line manager **is** the bully, and bullies only survive (and thrive) if they have the support (passive or active) of their manager.

"We don't have bullying, we're one big happy family here."

As families are one of the most fertile breeding grounds for conflict, division, resentment, argument and bad blood, the metaphor may be rather closer to the truth than intended.

"We'll see if we can move you to another department, perhaps you'll fit in better there."

Oh dear.

Why does it happen?

Bullying is a behaviour which everyone has the capacity to exhibit; all we need is for the circumstances to be appropriate. Whereas most people display bullying behaviours infrequently and intermittently, the bully is a person who exhibits the behaviour almost all the time, and who seems to derive satisfaction from doing so.

In the workplace, one criterion for choosing to bully is stress brought about by an inability to fulfil the responsibilities of one's job, the reasons for which include:

- being promoted beyond ability - or desire
- being shunted into a job by the employer, regardless of need, desire, aptitude or ability
- the lure of more money from accepting higher office, without understanding the attendant obligations

- the job is taken because it's the only way to get on in the company
- the job is taken because it's the only way of earning a salary commensurate with one's ability, experience, expertise, etc
- the requirements, duties and responsibilities of the job change over time, perhaps without being realised

Other reasons include:

- the hierarchical nature of management, combined with poor people-management skills
- low self-confidence, with opportunity for power over people
- lack of behavioural maturity, especially in the workplace
- financial stresses, eg privatisation, profitability, recession, high expectation combined with resource cutting
- fear engendered by uncertainty, particularly in times of change

Our behavioural maturity is determined primarily by our upbringing. On entering adulthood, we have evolved a degree of maturity based on our experiences, influenced by authorities with which our childhood has brought us into contact, but above all, our parents' skill in raising us, which in turn is determined by their behaviour skills. Parental skill levels are, of course, determined by their parents, and so on.

The degree of maturity required depends on the demands of the job - those in a position of power today were brought up 10, 20, 30, even 40 years ago. Now, change is so rapid that the older the manger, the more removed their upbringing will be from the interpersonal and behavioural demands of the modern workplace and the greater the challenge of adapting.

What we can do?

Most of the behaviours involved in bullying seem to be allied to self-protection and self-defence, which are part of the instinct for survival. They also seem to act as initiators and sustainers of the human body's fight-or-flight mechanism, frequent sustained activation of which is often implicated in stress and stress-related illness. Whilst bullying behaviours were necessary for survival in earlier harsher times, the relative comfort, ease and security of modern society has diminished their usefulness, and in some cases made them redundant. Ironically, the daily battle for survival has now transferred to the workplace, where the enormous pressures of financial privation, change, uncertainty and insecurity are the new threats to survival.

Bullying needs to be tackled at all levels and from all angles and by society as a whole. In schools, success in tackling bullying has come where the whole school - from the head down - actively adopts an anti-bullying climate. The no-blame approach, when implemented and backed - wholeheartedly - by the head and all teaching staff, has shown itself to be highly successful with young people who are still in their formative years.

In the workplace a different approach is required. Whilst children and young adults are still forming ideas and opinions - and, importantly, still developing and learning behaviour skills - grown-ups have cemented theirs. Once adulthood is attained, the brain becomes resistant to learning and adopting new behaviours, except by extreme circumstances (for example trauma), enlightenment (such as a "road to Damascus" experience), or wisdom won by the passage of time.

Employers must recognise the self-defeating nature of the phenomenon and the true cost that this inappropriate management style incurs. There needs to be easier recourse to law when necessary. And we need to educate ourselves - and our children - in the ways of improved interpersonal skills and greater behavioural maturity, so that the need to bully, and the lack of knowledge in knowing how to handle bullies, is purged.

Over the last two decades, precedents have been set, including discrimination (on grounds of disability, race, etc) sexual harassment (this is not the same as bullying, but shares the underlying lack of behavioural maturity), and child abuse. In each case, there was initial resistance and reluctance to act, but now respect for others, especially those who differ from society's currently accepted "norm", is incorporated into human knowledge and, where appropriate, enshrined in law.

It is time for bullying at work to join the list.

2   Education - a prime example

"How can you expect to instil decent values into young people while they're attending an educational establishment when the very principals are unprincipled?"

One of the worst affected professions is education, which possesses peculiar pressures in addition to the usual circumstances which stimulate bullying. Much of the following applies to other professions as well.

"It got to the point where I couldn't enter the head's presence without taking beta-blockers first. I remember thinking this was crazy but I couldn't think of any alternative or see another way forward. I can't understand how I let this go on so long, although as the only wage earner we were dependent on my salary. I've been off sick ever since, a career ruined and a lifetime of experience wasted. I daren't even think how the kids in that school are faring now."

Teachers have rights (enshrined in Education Acts) which place them at an advantage compared to other employees; unfortunately, head teachers, and heads of departments (actively or passively supported by the head teacher or principal) also wield power to such a degree that if so inclined, they can choose to ignore and overrule parents, governors, staff, education authority, etc with every expectation of getting away with it. This tendency seems to be increasing as Local Education Authorities devolve managerial power and financial responsibility to individual head teachers.

"Every night you're expected to work till at least 10 pm, some of my colleagues work regularly till after midnight, then the next day you're expected to stand in front of a class of thirty or more uninterested, disenchanted and often disruptive young teenagers. I can't see any prospect of improvement, and all the indications are that it's going to get worse - much worse. I'd advise anyone today

considering taking up teaching for a career to think very carefully indeed."

Without generalising or oversimplifying, the record number of teachers taking early or ill-health retirement reveals much about the effectiveness and success - or otherwise - of the government's education policy. It's easy to blame the government for the ills which beset society, but I resist this temptation, which I recognise as a denial of my responsibility for the circumstances in which I find myself. However, in the present circumstances, I am prepared to make an exception. Education is one of the few sectors where the government has direct responsibility; nothing ministers say or do can absolve them of that responsibility.

Whilst no-one can argue with the principle of getting better value for money, especially tax-payers' money, there are longer-term factors and considerations which may make immediate cost-cutting measures less attractive or appropriate when one puts apparent short-term "profits" into perspective.

"After more than two successful and enjoyable decades in a job I loved [teaching young children], I found myself, as a result of the bizarre bullying behaviours of a head teacher, in the invidious position of being coerced into taking ill-health retirement despite the fact that my GP, counsellor, a psychiatrist and a consultant all declared me mentally sound. The prospect of accepting pension and state benefits under false pretences at the insistence of my employer fuelled my sense of guilt, injustice, anger and outrage that this should be allowed to happen. My frustration was increased by the fact that no-one seemed to be able to prevent it, or take any action against it, and my anger multiplied by seeing the bully continuing to draw salary in post whilst subsequently destroying someone else. I am only slightly relieved to discover this is an increasingly common practice and that there are many individuals in the same boat."

A consequence of commercialism is that schools where pupil numbers are low (for example in small towns and villages) now find themselves in competition with each other for more sinister reasons: former friendly and cooperative rivalry has now turned into a battle for survival with the bottom line measured in livelihoods.

Resources cut beyond the minimum, imposition of league tables, increasing class sizes, the ogre of OFSTED, constant blame, increasingly limited prospects, the imposition of the National Curriculum and accompanying trolley-loads of documentation and paperwork, increased work and hours but reduced contact time with pupils, poorly maintained buildings (including "temporary" cabins) and more are a daily fact of life for those in the education sector and all contribute to stress.

> *"School A has an average of 17 pupils per class, whilst School B down the road has an average of 14. In order to improve standards and provide better service to children and parents, School B is closed and pupils transferred to School A. What is the resulting average number of pupils per class in School A? (answer at foot of page)*
>
> *Alleged selection test for DfEE ministerial recruits*

Schools, and therefore teachers, now seem to operate in a climate of "everything depends on position in league tables, and if anyone gets a poor result there's an automatic reprimand". Disturbing trends are appearing, including "bribing" potential students with cash-in-hand "awards" to attend a particular college because the anticipated higher grades they will achieve will move the college up the league table performance chart. Others have reported students being barred from taking exams if tutors feel that their anticipated pass grade will have an adverse effect on the establishment's league table position. Sometimes it seems as if pupils and students are regarded merely as a means to league table ranking and their education a cost to be minimised to meet political and commercial budget criteria. It seems churlish to point out that many of the world's most famous and successful people have left school without qualifications.

No appreciable increase

As shortcomings in government policy appear, teachers are increasingly being blamed for almost everything. Whilst superficially the concept of weeding out and eliminating poor teachers sounds sensible, closer inspection reveals an intent distinct from the alleged aim. What better way to divert attention away from the real cause of the failings within education than to blame "poor teachers"? Poor teachers indeed.

"I may be old-fashioned, but I'm sure that in my younger teaching days, schools used to tick over efficiently without the now-mandatory 'management team'. One has the uneasy feeling that the primary objective of these people is to secure their own position, and salary (which is often greater than the teachers), if necessary at the expense of those who are employed to do the real work of the school - to teach."

One of the instruments of diversion is OFSTED, the Office for Standards in Education. Whilst everyone agrees with the principle of raising standards, and the need to take action against those who are not competent to carry out their duties, the unceasing treadmill of cramming, assessing and testing gives one the uneasy feeling that responsibility for knowing how children are progressing has been taken away from those who know (class teachers) and handed to those who don't (government). Some heretics suggest that league tables have more to do with proving the effectiveness of government education policy than the stated aim of increasing parental choice and raising standards. Whilst I am sure that there are many inspectors who have a genuine desire to contribute to improving standards, and who carry out their duties fairly, thoroughly and conscientiously, the added stress of an impending inspection, with the disastrous potential of a profit-motivated ill-judged assessment of a single observation are hardly conducive to creating a climate of trust, support and enhanced performance and standards.

"Am I alone in thinking it perverse that anyone should want to make one's career - and money - out of finding fault with others? Am I a killjoy, or am I missing the point?"

Adding fuel to the fire of controversy are the high earnings potential for OFSTED inspectors. In some cases, these are alleged to amount to twice a head teacher's annual salary and three times a teacher's. Reports of higher potential income for failing a school have horrendous moral implications. Such iniquitous remuneration reveals the importance and true intent of inspection policy.

For the Chief Inspector of Schools to claim recently that a conveniently round total of 15,000 incompetent teachers (a figure more reminiscent of accountancy than competency) should be sacked invites one to ask whether the same fate should be visited upon incompetent inspectors and politicians. Who is to judge? Or inspect?

> *"Culling is no more likely to improve team spirit among teachers than it is among seals."*
>
> *Roy Hattersley*

The role of governors deserves highlighting. Governors are volunteers comprising teachers, parents and other interested parties who have a legal responsibility to ensure the school remains within budget, and take necessary action if this is not likely to be achieved. Having exhausted other means of curtailing resource expenditure, this now usually means making teachers redundant. In other words the government cuts funding for schools, then abdicates responsibility for making savings to the governors who are legally bound to effect the necessary redundancies. Any attempt to highlight the iniquity of teachers' and governors' plight with resistance is met with intimidation and guilt: "...in taking this action you will be harming the children's education."

> *"I am certain I was bullied into ill-health retirement because I was too expensive. Given the duplicitous nature of bullies, I could imagine a situation where a head teacher, having made savings equivalent to an experienced teacher's salary, could reasonably expect to ask for and subsequently receive a bonus on the basis of having met his preplanned cost reduction target for the year. If this were happening on a national scale, the implications are alarming, to say the least. Meanwhile, I*

*sit here, two years later, on a pension, still on benefit,
and still unable to even contemplate returning to work."*

Such are the financial stringencies of late that heads are
adopting some worrying trends in order to keep their school
solvent. Those that have come to light recently include:

- teachers working for half pay or less - sometimes for
  nothing - in order to keep their school from closing
- parents being asked to contribute "a certain amount" in
  order to pay the salary of a teacher who would
  otherwise be made redundant (the use of guilt in this
  type of situation is particularly disturbing, as are the
  potential consequences for those children whose
  parents either choose not to comply or who cannot
  afford to comply)
- commercial sponsorship, usually by way of collecting
  product wrappers or till receipts for the purchase of
  basic items of equipment
- sponsorship of a school through the "donation" of a
  large sum of money by tobacco companies and other
  patrons who could be deemed unsuitable (this is a
  moral issue and acceptance of such "donations" raises
  serious questions about the judgement of head teachers
  and governors - this has been described by opposition
  parties as "being as near to prostitution as you can
  get")

Teachers are unusual in that they are accountable to a large
number of people, including pupils, parents, governors,
colleagues, superiors, etc. In many cases, teachers have
reported that they have stuck it out, sometimes for years, in
order to protect the children from the unpleasant behaviours
- and often incompetent teaching "abilities" - of those above.
Professional ethics and personal morality are challenged and
the strain of remaining in this guilt trap inevitably takes its
toll.

*"It's far easier to deal with a class of disruptive children
than to deal with a disruptive head."*

Two of the most disturbing types of cases are worth special
mention. One is where the school professes a religious faith
and the bullying behaviours exhibited by senior staff and the

head are in direct contravention of the moral doctrines which they themselves advocate and decree. The other is where a senior member of staff makes repeated allegations of sexual misconduct, including implied abuse, without evidence, but (a) with the purpose of getting rid of a member of staff, (b) where the person making the allegation possesses the profile closer to that of a potential abuser, and (c) similar allegations have been made in the past about other members of staff, also without substantiation. More about projection later.

In the further education sector, lecturers are being coerced into signing new short-term contracts. Those that resist are being bullied into accepting, and there are disturbing reports that there exist unofficial "training" sessions for principals and other "management teams" on how to bully defiant members of staff into accepting the new working practices.

For schools in the independent sector, the financial necessity of maintaining or increasing pupil numbers adds to the burden. Many teachers operate under the threat of "lose two pupils and you're fired", which is hardly conducive to an atmosphere of learning. No-one is going to perform at their best under these conditions, but this type of threat is most revealing. The overall responsibility for promoting and managing a school, particularly in the independent sector, lies not so much with individual teachers, but with the Head and senior management of the establishment. Above all, it is a team effort. To dump responsibility for maintaining pupil numbers onto individual teachers with threats of this nature demonstrates both denial and abdication of responsibility. This is a recurrent theme in the way bullies operate. It is noticeable that such denial does not extend to refusing salary.

And all of this in an environment where children learn most by example.

3   What is bullying?

They are playing a game. They are playing at not
playing a game. If I show them I see they are, I
shall break the rules and they will punish me.
I must play their game, of not seeing I see the game.

Knots, R D Laing

The term "bully" describes a range of behaviours, from a persistent unwillingness to recognise performance, loyalty and achievement, to repeated critical remarks and humiliating and overtly hostile behaviour such as shouting at an employee in front of colleagues. The full spectrum ranges from a person whose communication, interpersonal and behaviour skills are poor, to those who are spiteful, vindictive and destructive and who use their position of power to practise these traits for their own gratification. In serious cases, bullies may resort to crime, such as fraud, to get rid of or embarrass people into leaving.

Whilst the information in this book is relevant to all bullying behaviours, the focus tends to be on the more serious end of the scale. Bullying is part of human behaviour, and everyone exhibits bullying behaviours from time to time; all we need is for the circumstances to be appropriate. Workplace bullying consists of the regular, usually daily, use of these inappropriate behaviours for the purpose of gratification at the expense of another individual. Bullies are people who demand respect for themselves whilst simultaneously denying respect to others, and who are unaware of the incongruity and unacceptability of their conduct.

Although based on behaviours exhibited in the workplace, and which include abuse of power, bullying behaviours are seen in the home, in relationships, in fact wherever two or more human beings come into contact. Although the particulars and outcomes may differ, the underlying reasons are often the same - desire to dominate, subjugate and eliminate, with insensitivity to the rights and needs of others, plus denial of responsibility for the consequences of the person's chosen behaviours.

Table 3: Bullying consists of...

> - refusal to recognise, face up to, tackle and overcome one's own weaknesses, failings and shortcomings
> - denial of responsibility for the consequences of one's actions and behaviour on others
>
> If the bully is in a position of management, control, trust, etc, then also...
>
> - refusal to accept the legal and moral obligation for the safety, care and wellbeing of the person(s) in their charge

The reasons why people choose to behave in this manner are discussed in detail throughout the book, but seem to result primarily from low self-confidence, low self-esteem and low self-worth combined with a particular predominant behaviour style, poor interpersonal skills and - perhaps crucially - low behavioural maturity.

It could be said that the desire to control, dominate and subjugate is itself an admission of inferiority, inadequacy, weakness and immaturity. Bear this in mind as you read on.

The process

A bullying relationship in the workplace almost always follows a predictable pattern:

> - There is a period of calm, from a few days to a few weeks, whilst a new manager settles in, or a reorganisation takes effect, or the dust settles after a predecessor has left, often on ill-health grounds, early retirement, dismissal or resignation. Often, the precise reasons for this person leaving cannot be ascertained. Sometimes a "management team" or "office manager" is appointed without consultation, adding an extra layer to the hierarchy and often pushing others down a level in the process. The appointees either have no relevant qualifications, or have a recently-gained "business degree"; in either case, poor people skills soon become apparent.
> - The bully selects, consciously or unconsciously, a target, usually a person in a subordinate position (a peer or superior will suffice if no underling is available). The principal criteria for selection are (a) the person is good at their job, often excelling, and (b) the person is popular

with people. Recognising instinctively that he does not have these qualities, and having convinced himself or allowed himself to be convinced that he can never develop these qualities, the bully chooses to perceive the individual as a threat.

> A period of constant criticism ensues in which the victim is subjected to daily psychological abuse, the purpose of which is to control and in the process of which confidence and self-esteem are destroyed. Most of the unpleasant behaviours (which are outlined below) take place behind closed doors with no witnesses. All attempts by the person being victimised to understand what is wrong, seek explanation for the manager's behaviour, put things right, start afresh, etc, are met with further hostility and an increase in unpleasantness, threat and intimidation on the part of the bully, and incomprehension and resentment by everyone else.

> After a while (this may be as little as a couple of months, or as much as a year or more), the effects of the bully's behaviour begin to show. Tearfulness, irritability, sullenness, anger, low morale, prolonged absence and other psychological and behavioural symptoms alert others to the presence of something untoward. As the bully begins to fear that the consequences of his actions are now being perceived by others, he seeks to justify his behaviour by publicly finding fault with and further humiliating his victim. Typically this involves picking on a minor indiscretion (eg two minutes late for work, raising one's voice to a patient who is deaf, making more than one spelling mistake in a thirty-page document) as the basis for giving the person a verbal warning.

> The individual is placed on a capability or competence procedure and subjected to inquisition, test, report, scrutiny, etc. If the employer does not have a suitable procedure for the purpose, the bully invents one.

> Reluctantly the person complies with the procedures, which are imposed using intimidation and threat, usually of disciplinary action; the implication is "unless you do exactly as I say, you will lose your job".

> The bully makes life as difficult as possible for the victim, setting them up to fail, catching them out on every possible occasion. Such incidents as are "revealed" become the basis by which the bully justifies his behaviour, an attempt to demonstrate his superiority through the other person's alleged inferiority.

> Sometimes a letter of complaint from other members of staff is conjured up. "We, the undersigned, object to so-and-so's behaviour etc." The letter may be to the bully, or to his superior; in the latter case, the bully's own signature may be conspicuously absent. It is likely that the composition of the complainants will be some supporters of the bully plus some innocent parties who have been threatened or coerced into signing. Alternatively, comments and "ideas for improvement" are importuned from customers, clients, etc, and these are "converted" into "complaints". The effect is to create fear, confusion, suspicion, mistrust, etc, as well as provide "evidence" for disciplinary proceedings. Any manager who encourages or supports this type of activity is revealing much about their own competency and fitness to manage.

> After a few weeks, perhaps as little as a fortnight, a trivial incident or minor indiscretion is identified, selected, contrived or invented which is nominated as the basis for disciplinary proceedings. Sometimes the initiating event is a response to provocation, or the victim stands up and asserts their right not to be treated in this way. The bully decides that the victim must now be got rid of, and the person being victimised is subjected to the full force of the employer's disciplinary procedures. The bully, with Jekyll and Hyde nature to the fore, will usually have convinced his management of his side of the story, and further encouraged management to use the personnel department as the tool for disposing of the recalcitrant employee.

> If the victim has the temerity to stand up for himself, and possibly fight back, the process is hastened, and the levels of threat, intimidation, provocation, harassment, victimisation, spitefulness and vindictiveness are

increased. Employment (and pre-employment) records are combed for any suitable oversight, omission, inaccuracy or indiscretion. A case is fabricated using words like "sub-standard work performance", "non-cooperation", "insubordination", "gross misconduct", etc. The terms chosen conveniently appear in the employer's disciplinary rules and procedures.

> If the victim is beginning to show symptoms of the enormous negative stress they are enduring, the mental health trap may be sprung (see chapter 8).

> At any time throughout the process, the victim may have a mental breakdown due to the enormous and unremitting negative stress that being bullied engenders. This will be seized upon as justification for the bully's course of action, demonstrating clearly the person's "unfitness", "instability", "mental health problems", etc. More about this later.

> The victim is eliminated, through dismissal, ill-health retirement, enforced early retirement, redundancy, obligatory resignation, etc.

> Occasionally at this time the bully runs to authority (eg senior management, personnel, police) and claims they are the one being bullied or harassed.

> The victim seeks justice through the tribunal system. As bullying is not addressed in law (yet), it is very difficult to prove, and the stress, cost and novelty of navigating the legal system extract a further toll on the victim's physical, mental and financial state at a time when their injuries are greatest and they are psychologically and physically at their weakest. For many people this is their first encounter with the law. The employer adopts one of two strategies:

   a) aggressive defence of the case, including use of corporate lawyers to threaten and intimidate the employee further (thereby ironically demonstrating precisely those behaviours of which they are accused and which they are denying). The threats usually consist of suing for costs (hundreds of thousands of pounds), portraying the person as a troublemaker etc thereby significantly reducing future employment prospects, etc;

b) adopting a "hands-off" approach, preferring instead to encourage the victim to take on the bully alone, hoping that the "the two of them will sort each other out" and that no action will be required by the employer.

> Messages of support flood in from colleagues past and present. Everyone wishes the victim luck, but few, if any, will stand up as witnesses - fearing, rightly, that they will be targeted next. Most are unaware or choose not to consider that they will be targeted soon anyway.

> Either the tribunal is lost, or a settlement is reached out of court. The amount of award is small, and a comprehensive gagging clause prevents the victim from speaking about the case.

> Everybody knows who the bully is, what goes on, the fact that it's happened before, and will probably happen again, but no-one seems to be able or willing to do anything about it.

> The victim retires to lick their wounds, wondering what on earth they did to deserve such appalling treatment. A period of convalescence begins which may last several years. With enlightenment, the person may be recovered sufficiently within a year to consider going back to work. Without the benefit of knowledge and insight, the person may feel blighted for the rest of their life. Some people report that it took five years before they began to enjoy their work again.

> The bully or employer refuses to provide a reference, or supplies a deliberately bad reference which is unusable.

> The bully is rewarded by promotion, recognition, bonus, increased responsibility or enhanced title or privileges. Sometimes the bully accords himself the reward, or encourages his supporters to initiate the reward process.

> In rare cases, where the employer is forced to concede that there "may exist the tiny possibility of a small problem", the bully is sent on a two-week mega-jolly which usually consists of an expensive management training course in the country. On return, all is

sweetness and light; frequent use of the latest management jargon is perceived by the bully and management as "improved interpersonal skills". The novelty wears off quickly and within two weeks normal service is resumed.

> After a few weeks, perhaps as little as a fortnight, the bully identifies a new victim and the cycle starts again. In some cases, victims overlap with the next cycle starting before the previous one is completed.

Whilst there are many variations, the basic process is almost always the same. Sometimes, if the bully has not contrived sufficient evidence for disciplinary action, or only has passive rather than active support from above, then the "answer" to the "problem" is to move the victim. This frequently incurs devalued status, reduction of salary, loss of responsibility, reduced promotion prospects, denial of opportunity to pursue chosen career, etc. The bully seems to derive pleasure from this. The move is documented on the employee's personal record and will require explanation at future promotion boards etc. Meanwhile, the bully remains in post, although in rare cases where the employer is compelled to take action, the aggressor may also be moved. It is noticeable that the direction of movement is almost always forward and upward for the bully, and downward for the victim. At this stage, the words reward and punishment may flit through your mind.

What to do?

The vast majority of bullying cases follow the process outlined above, and once begun, the tragedy is played out to its predestined conclusion. At all times, the victim is encouraged to believe they have no control over their situation. The inevitability is such that often for the victim:

- if you do nothing, it gets worse
- if you start explaining, supporting, defending, justifying etc, it gets worse
- if you stand up for yourself, it gets worse
- if you obtain support, it gets worse
- if you take action, it gets worse
- if you fight back, it gets worse

Serial bullying
Because of the repetitive and predictable nature of the process, the term "serial bully" might be appropriate. The presence of corporate bullying (see chapter 10) seems to encourage serial bullying.

Bully phases
The bullying process can be separated into two discrete phases:

a) Phase 1: subjugation and control
From selection of the victim up to immediately prior to full disciplinary proceedings, the principal aim of the bully is to establish control - to dominate, subjugate and deny the right to independence and self-determination; the victim *must* submit to the bully's will - or else...

b) Phase 2: destruction and elimination
At a certain point, the bully realises that total control over the victim will never be possible, and therefore the only way forward is to eliminate the offending individual. One trigger for the second phase is when the bully senses that the victim has realised what is happening and is starting to take defensive (or even offensive) action. Another trigger is when the victim's rebellious streak comes to the fore, perhaps fuelled by a sense of grievance, resentment, and injustice. A provocation becomes the victim's final straw, and a suitably assertive and aggressive reaction finally pierces the bully's thick skin. So hurt, perhaps for the first and only time in the conflict, the bully decides that the individual will never submit to their will, ergo the only option is to eliminate this victim before choosing another.

At the point of transition between the two phases, the combination of (a) the principal selection criteria, and (b) the realisation of inability to control, produces an irony which goes unnoticed by the employer and the bully: they cannot do with, nor can they do without, this person.

Bully behaviours
Whilst everyone occasionally exhibits some of the behaviours listed below, bullying is the continual and relentless attack

on other people's self-confidence and self-esteem using many
of the following methods regularly and repeatedly:

- constant criticism which cannot be justified or
  reconciled with reality, and which does not agree with
  the assessment of the individual, subordinates,
  colleagues, peers, former managers, customers, clients,
  patients, pupils, parents, etc
- refusal to be specific about criticisms
- claims of underperformance etc which do not square
  with the facts
- sidelining, overruling, ignoring, marginalising,
  dismissing as unimportant or irrelevant, people, ideas,
  opinions, work, performance, contributions etc
- removal of status and authority, especially in an
  underhand or devious manner
- demotion, real or implied
- the increasing of responsibility but withholding or
  diminishing or removing the necessary authority
- being tasked with additional responsibility, but not
  being informed
- exclusion from anything to do with the running,
  operation, workings or management of the section,
  department, organisation, company, etc
- isolation, cold-shouldering, snubbing, sending to
  Coventry, exile, quarantine, excommunication
- being singled out for special treatment, eg everyone
  else can be ten minutes late but if you're ten seconds
  late it's a disciplinary matter
- threats of disciplinary action for trivial or fabricated
  incidents, but refusal to discipline other staff for
  severely disruptive behaviour
- giving performance markings significantly lower than
  a previous manager
- giving performance markings significantly lower than
  documented achievements merit
- giving performance markings or annual appraisals
  which are significantly and adversely at variance with
  previous reports
- betrayal of trust, taking advantage of good nature,
  especially on a regular basis

- refusing to accord respect or acknowledge the rights of others
- humiliation by being shouted at, especially in front of others
- repeated behaviour which is demeaning, belittling, ridiculing, patronising, degrading, etc - especially in front of others
- deliberately undervaluing, downgrading, ignoring or minimising the value of any individual's contribution
- refusal to acknowledge performance, achievement, results, worth, value, success, etc
- deliberate and persistent undermining of professional competence
- making mountains out of molehills; twisting or distorting everything that is said
- focus on trivia - a big fuss being made over incidents and indiscretions which are insignificant or irrelevant
- refusal to clarify job description and function or put it in writing
- changing a person's job description without consultation, then imposing it without right of reply
- persistent unwillingness to make clear what is required
- reassigning work unnecessarily or unexpectedly, perhaps replacing it with inappropriate or menial tasks
- denial of right of the individual to undertake tasks for which they were recruited
- the removal of any authority which is necessary for a person to carry out their work
- the withholding of knowledge, information, permission, approval, consent etc that is necessary for a person to carry out their duties
- the withholding of support at times of necessity
- denying one individual the resources or equipment necessary to fulfil the requirements of the job, whilst allowing others the resources and equipment as and when requested
- refusal to communicate, periods of silence, perhaps for weeks or even months at a time

- limiting communication to memo, email or via a third party in lieu of speaking directly
- being overburdened with work, often unnecessarily, perhaps with unrealistic conditions and deadlines
- the setting of impossible objectives, or changing them without good reason; being set up to fail
- the setting of tasks, whilst refusing to be specific about timescales, then criticising for not completing the work "on time"
- demanding that work be redone or repeated, especially when it's satisfactory or complete
- imposition of non-tasks or work which is unnecessary
- withholding or refusing to assign or delegate work, then criticising for non-completion of the same work
- the imposition of unrealistic deadlines, and changing them at short notice, or without notice
- sabotaging, interfering or impeding performance for the purpose of later criticism
- significant (adverse) difference in appraisal markings over previous years
- making claims that third parties agree, concur or support the bully's point of view, especially with respect to criticisms or alleged shortcomings
- adverse comments made to or through a third party
- claims of complaints about a person but refusal to substantiate or confirm in writing
- encouraging members of staff to spy, snoop, eavesdrop or snitch on others
- any behaviour whose intent is to make you feel useless
- being isolated in an office by being forced to sit apart from colleagues, eg in a remote corner
- snide remarks, jibes, name-calling, use of offensive nicknames or any behaviour which is childish, immature, petty and inappropriate
- back-stabbing, back-biting, sniping, mud-slinging, slagging off
- teasing, taunting, pestering, mocking, ridiculing
- behaviour which is inappropriately aggressive and indicative of lack of self-control, eg thumping the table, stamping one's feet, jumping up and down, shouting,

screaming, having a temper tantrum, going purple in the face, especially with intent to intimidate or frighten

- holding meetings, the purpose of and attendance at is significantly at variance with what you have been led to believe
- refusal to minute meetings or attempts to deny opportunity to take minutes of meetings or producing minutes that are inaccurate and one-sided, especially in matters of grievance and discipline
- meetings, hearings, appeals etc run like interrogations
- attempts to deny representation, eg in disciplinary meetings
- claims of misconduct, breach of discipline etc but refusal to formalise or put in writing
- being difficult with respect to requests for allocating shifts, flexible working hours, etc
- being difficult with respect to handover of shift where communication is essential, eg nursing care
- in contiguous shifts or job share, selecting only the "nice" or "easy" jobs and leaving another to do all the unsavoury tasks
- being difficult over or denying requests for annual leave, withholding approval until the day before, giving the employee a deliberately hard time on the day prior to the holiday
- contacting employees at home on holiday or sick leave with "urgent" work or unreasonable demands
- denying or being difficult over compassionate leave to attend to seriously or terminally ill relatives, especially in contradiction of agreed procedures
- denying or being difficult over compassionate leave following bereavement
- denial of training, or unacceptable limitations on training required for a new job as a precursor to criticising a person for being unable to do the job
- denial of ongoing training opportunities, refusing to give approval until the very last moment, or withdrawing approval at short notice
- regularly interrupting meetings, procedures, classes etc with apparently "important" business

- inappropriate praise
- frequent changes of mind, reversal of decisions with little or no notice and without explanation or reason
- plagiarism, taking undeserved credit, but never accepting responsibility when things go wrong
- deceit, lying, cheating, duplicity, hypocrisy, deception, deviousness, fabrication
- the use of ulterior motives, hidden agendas, etc
- harassment of any kind
- the use of foul, obscene or offensive language
- inappropriate remarks, comments, aspersions, suggestions etc about a person's gender, race, colour, beliefs, sexual orientation, background, upbringing, etc
- jokes of a sexist, racist, ageist or similar nature whose objective is to humiliate
- regularly being the butt of jokes or "black humour" where the intention is to humiliate or intimidate
- arranging formal or social occasions, then inviting everybody and deliberately excluding you
- regularly displaying the need to score points off others
- talking about an individual, in their presence, using the second or third person
- a room falls silent as you enter
- people whispering about you in your presence or behind your back
- gossip, whispers, insinuations, innuendo
- regular intrusion of a person's personal and intimate zones by touching, caressing, holding, grabbing, "demonstrating" or using another individual as an "example" or "guinea pig", or other objectionable and socially unacceptable behaviour
- the use of threat or implied threat
- provocation in any shape or form
- the use or threat of violence, assault or intimidation
- regular use of sarcasm without consent
- regular use of guilt to coerce, manipulate and control
- being coerced into regularly undertaking work of a higher grade but without recognition or remuneration
- any form of coercion which disregards the rights of the individual

- two-facedness, saying one thing to a person's face, something else (especially the opposite) to others
- contact with higher authority (eg head of personnel) without reference, notice, or anything in writing, especially in relation to allegations
- the misuse of power to ensure another's removal, dismissal, etc
- abuse of the disciplinary procedures to get rid of people
- the appointment or promotion of "chosen" individuals by default or via the back door without due consultation
- nepotism with denial of opportunity for others to compete on an equal footing
- any form of dirty tricks campaign
- the use of nasty, spiteful, vindictive or vengeful behaviours
- being the subject of a witch hunt, any form of persecution, victimisation, oppression, etc
- spreading malicious rumours, falsehoods to discredit
- telling tales
- the use of innocent third parties (eg pupils) to carry intimidating messages or carry out unwelcome actions on behalf of others
- the use of innocent third parties to fabricate complaints
- malicious or ambiguous letters sent to home, partner, family or friends
- ordering of unwanted goods or services with malicious intent on behalf of the victim, eg taxi at 4 am, visit at home by funeral directors, train tickets to Coventry, books on rats, unresolved crimes or other intimidatory topics
- anonymous telephone calls to yourself or members of your family, especially at unsocial hours
- the monitoring of telephone conversations
- interference with, interception or "loss" of items of mail
- the presence or display of any weapons, approved or unapproved, licensed or unlicensed on work premises with intent to intimidate or threaten
- the use of fraud or other criminal behaviour to entrap, swindle, trick, ensnare or embarrass

You will notice how childish and immature some of these behaviours are. For example, screaming and stamping one's feet are more reminiscent of a 3-year-old being denied sweets in a supermarket; telling tales and sending someone to Coventry is junior school behaviour.

One of the great challenges in pinning down bullying behaviour is the difficulty in differentiating between, say, poor interpersonal skills, and bullying. As in all dealings involving human beings, common sense must prevail. Some of the criteria you can use to identify a bully include:

- **intent** - the intent of the behaviour is to demean and belittle in order to gratify the self
- **regularity** - the behaviours are exhibited repeatedly

Other yardsticks include:

- does the bully's behaviour have anything to do with achieving objectives, meeting targets, improving service, cutting costs, or increasing income?
- is the bully's behaviour consistent?
- is the bully, through choosing to behave in the way he does, projecting his own failings on to others as a way of avoiding having to face up to them?
- is the bully acting at all times out of self-interest, despite attempts to portray the opposite?
- is the bully abdicating responsibility for fulfilling the duties and responsibilities of his position?
- is the bully denying responsibility for the consequences of his behaviour and actions on others?

How do bullies get away with it?

One of the hardest parts of coming to terms with a bullying experience is understanding how bullies get away with it, especially given the repetitive nature of their behaviour. The main reasons seem to be:

- ignorance (choosing not to see)
- unenlightenment (not understanding what bullying is, how it goes on, how to address and resolve a bullying situation)
- disbelief
- denial
- acquiescence
- not wanting to get involved

- unwillingness to challenge for fear of being picked on next
- unwillingness to put one's own job, career and promotion prospects in jeopardy
- unwillingness to act decisively for fear of making a wrong judgement
- not wanting to rock the boat
- not wishing to upset the status quo
- freewheeling to retirement, not wishing to jeopardise pension rights, etc
- people in authority being frightened of the bully
- tacit approval by refusing to take action
- unwillingness to take action for fear of skeletons in the closet
- being unable to perceive or comprehend amoral behaviour
- being taken in by the bully's lies and then rewarding the bully by promotion
- willingness by the bully to abuse their position of power
- willingness by the bully to abuse the disciplinary procedure to eliminate their victim

Denial

Society's recognition, acceptance and understanding of the horrors within its midst seem to be characterised by four principal stages, and only when the final stage is surmounted can the abuse (both effects and causes) be addressed, tackled and overcome. This action of the self-protection system appears to be the means by which human beings safeguard themselves; it is the human survival mechanism, particularly in the context of living together as a social species.

Firstly, there is innocence, inexperience and uninformedness, a pleasurable state of naivety; a status quo. We carry on with our lives without having to concern ourselves with all the problems of the world. The first threshold is traversed when we hear or see or experience an event or report which piques our interest; the purpose of investigation is not so much intellectual as to evaluate of the level of danger the perceived event represents to our personal safety and security.

Table 4: States and thresholds

State 1:	naivety
Threshold 1:	inquisitiveness
State 2:	ignorance
Threshold 2:	impatience
State 3:	disbelief
Threshold 3:	resentment
State 4:	denial
Threshold 4:	anger
State 5:	enlightenment, change, betterment

Typically, if no immediate danger is perceived, we choose to ignore the event, to pretend not to see it, to pass by on the other side, to dismiss (perhaps with a perfunctory "that's terrible") then forget it, as it has little or no relevance or threat to our daily life. There are too many other pressing problems to worry about. However, if the event does not go away, but continues to intrude, impatience sets in; how dare this matter interrupt our daily routine, how dare it threaten our cosy ordered existence.

Further information or evidence which becomes progressively harder to shrug off brings about a state of disbelief. "How can this be going on?" "No, I don't believe it." We choose to discount the evidence of our eyes or ears, fearing that acknowledgement means change, possibly to our detriment. We look but still choose to pass by on the other side.

If the event intrudes yet further, resentment builds: "No, I'm not going to let this interfere with my life." "It's not my problem."

Finally, when the perceived danger refuses to go away, but threatens to have intrusive consequences, a state of denial ensues. Often, it is easier, less demanding and more convenient to deny that something nasty exists rather than face up to it, with the upheaval of change that such admission entails. Denial is the ultimate mechanism by which we protect ourselves from all the nasty things going on around us, including (and especially in the case of bullying) those of our own making.

Lives and routines may be inexorably and irrevocably challenged and changed, the comfort of practised and ordered existence overturned in an uncomfortable and indeterminate period of adjustment. Our self-protection mechanism operates at full stretch, bolstered by a barricade of anger. Only when this ill temper is surmounted are we sufficiently motivated - or forced - to accept the event, to begin to understand what is happening and start the process of adjustment. And only when transition is complete can the benefits of the new state of enlightenment, acceptance and understanding be appreciated.

Statements such as "Why didn't we tackle this before?" will be familiar to those who have conquered denial in previous causes. Rape, discrimination, sexual harassment, child abuse, now workplace bullying - it's as if society is picking off and ticking off these violational abuses one by one; perhaps the next millennium will be one of enlightened and pleasurable existence after all. In the meantime, there is much to do and we must not be complacent.

4   The bully

"The resentment that criticism engenders can demoralise employees, family members and friends, and still not correct the situation that has been condemned."
                                  How to Win Friends and Influence People
                                                              Dale Carnegie, 1936
                                                              Cedar Books, 1991

Bullying can be defined as "behaviour which consistently undermines another's confidence, reducing feelings of self-worth and self-esteem". The behaviour may be deliberate, as in a planned campaign, or may arise out of the bully's own immaturity of behaviour skills and lack of self-confidence, exacerbated perhaps by his own susceptibility to stress.

As children we are not taught how to value ourselves and our performance appropriately and accurately. This combination leads, for many people, to a belief that other people's opinions are more important than our own. Whilst this may not be a handicap in everyday life, when bullying arises, this shortcoming becomes critical.

For people who have worked hard and are used to trusting those they work with, it comes as a shock when your manager displays behaviour inconsistent with his hierarchically superior status. We are all human, have the occasional bad day, and make mistakes. With bullying, the 'off days' and 'mistakes' happen with increasing frequency and regularity, and we become aware that the person's judgement, especially about us, our work or our behaviour, is inconsistent with our own perceptions and feedback from colleagues and, perhaps, customers and clients. It's now that our own levels of confidence take on a greater importance. Are we sufficiently alert to recognise that the feedback we are receiving is at variance with the feelings and observations of ourselves and others? Do we have sufficient faith in ourselves to override our bosses' opinion of us? And if so, for how long can we carry on without support in this type of management environment?

The ability to trust one's own judgement is severely tested, with the bully employing a subtle but effective technique. A criticism is made, or a shortcoming highlighted, in which there is a grain of truth. When analysed, it is perhaps only 5% true. Unfortunately, inexperience and low confidence in the area of receiving and responding to criticism mean that the assessment is perceived as 95% accurate. If we are inclined to suffer feelings of guilt - and people who are prone to being bullied seem to be born with their predisposition to guilt set too high - the criticism is reinforced to a degree which only the greatest maturity can override.

The bully often adds guilt to the criticism, for example *"I'm disappointed"*, *"...letting me/the side/the department/ the company down..."*. He also injects his own insecurity which is then transferred to the victim. On the surface, all sounds credible, but over time, one has the growing suspicion that something is awry. The bully is adept at minimising discrepancy, and "open discussions" will often elicit statements of support which confuse, with the result that guilt is intensified.

Criticism, especially when unjustified, and from a supposed 'elder and better', needs to be handled with maturity and assertiveness. Without these, our reaction can contain more emotion than sense. Bullies then feed on the immature emotional response as justification for making the criticism. Only high assertiveness combined with strong nerves (high self-confidence) can rebuff such superior censure.

A characteristic of a manager unable to fulfil the duties of the job is a random element in decision making. There is long and tortuous argument over small, unimportant issues, but when a bigger issue presents itself - perhaps the spending of a large sum of money on a product or service whose benefit is not clear - the decision is waved through without a second glance. This inappropriate level of attention warns alert observers that the manager lacks ability, but for victims of bullying the authorisation may come as a welcome respite, especially if they are the beneficiary. It may also be mistaken as support and approval.

Such unpredictability permeates the bully's behaviour, resulting in confusion and irritation amongst staff. Whilst mostly negative, the odd positive behaviour appears on rare occasions when the bully feels good about himself. Most of the time, the bully feels frightened, insecure, afraid that he will be 'found out', and consequently seems to exude a form of paranoia; it's as if the bully chooses to believe that the victim is putting on an act and plotting against him to usurp his position. In the majority of cases, the opposite is the case. Ironically, in most cases, the bully has sufficient skills to undertake his job successfully, but chooses not to apply them.

Pressure from above is another common cause of bullying; the company may be having difficulty competing, and profit forecasts are low - or negative. Or resources and funding may have been cut again. The insecurity of senior staff is communicated down the management hierarchy through aggressively over-assertive behaviour. People react to this treatment in various ways; they can either pass it on and bully their own staff, or they can absorb it, protecting staff from the harmful effects of negative management.

Characteristics of the bullying manager

Bullying exists in different degrees, and we will all recognise some of the following characteristics in our own behaviour - they are part of the human instinct for survival. What distinguishes bullies is their need, propensity and compulsion to exhibit these behaviours on a regular basis.

A person who exhibits bully behaviour regularly cannot be trusted. Despite assurances and appearances, their word cannot be relied on, for many reasons.

Short-term thinking: this applies to the past, as well as the future. Credit (which is scarce) for work well done is quickly forgotten, swamped by the demands of the present.

"He switched on and off like a tap and didn't know what he wanted longer than it took him to think of it."

The bully is preoccupied with the now and immediate future, yesterday is gone and has no further relevance. Quick fixes abound, there is no long-term thinking or strategic planning. The attitude is "if there's a problem, let's fix it quickly. If it needs fixing again next week, we'll worry about it then". Anything to assuage the needs of the moment.

"My manager took me to task regularly for taking time to ensure that applications were scrupulously accurate. I

Table 5: Bully characteristics

• Cavalier attitude, especially to safety	• Misrepresentation
• Delegation and dumping	• Mood swings
• Differing values	• Need to assert authority
• Divided loyalty	• Negative language
• Duplicity	• Opportunism
• Envy	• Plagiarism
• Evasiveness	• Poor judgement
• Failure mentality	• Poor listening skills
• Fait accompli	• Resoluteness
• Favouritism	• Rigidity
• Focus on the victim	• Self-importance
• Frequent moves	• Selfishness
• Humourlessness	• Shifting goalposts
• Inability to cope with failure	• Short-term thinking
• Inability to plan ahead	• Short-term memory
• Inconsistency	• Spinelessness
• Indecision	• Steadfast self-reliance
• Ingratitude	• Taking credit
• Insatiability	• Trivialising
• Insensitivity	• Untrustworthiness
• Insincerity	• Unwillingness to accept responsibility
• Interference	• Unwillingness to acknowledge
• Imposition	• Unwillingness to apologise
• Jekyll and Hyde persona	• Unwillingness to communicate
• Know-it-all attitude	• Unwillingness to cooperate
• Lack of competence	• Vindictiveness
• Lack of contingency planning	
• Lack of foresight	

knew that each time a mistake occurred, however small, the person would appeal and the appeals process consumed considerable resources - and it was muggins who was always lumbered with all the extra work. It was all to do with achieving targets of the number of claims processed, but ignored the amount of work involved. As long as she reached her target, that was all that mattered. Everyone regarded her behaviour as ignorant, short-term and selfish, but she was in charge

*and always had her way. It's no wonder there was a high
turnover of staff."*

Gradually, the bully acquires a reputation for superficiality,
becoming renowned for short focus and inability to see in
depth. A mature approach is to analyse and understand the
problem, then produce a permanent (proper) fix, but this
takes time, patience and resources. It's not worth the effort,
and there's the likelihood that the pay-off will be collected by
someone else, especially if it's months or years downstream.

Allied to the short-term focus are an **inability to plan
ahead** and **lack of foresight**, the consequence of which is an
absence of contingency planning and a resultant
**inability to cope with failure, omission and the
unexpected**. Responses in these circumstances tend to be
random and ill-considered.

Short-term memory: this goes with short-term thinking.
A bully is often unable to remember what he said a few
minutes ago, and this infuriating habit makes the person
impossible to deal with. Some people liken this to the
"goldfish mentality" on the basis that the fish is incapable of
thinking beyond about five seconds; others might think that
comparing bullies to goldfish is insulting to goldfish.

Where the bully's memory does function, it is highly
selective, choosing only to remember the "good" bits - those
which make him feel comfortable - and forget the "bad" bits -
those which evoke feelings of insecurity and low self-
confidence. Consciously - or unconsciously - the bully prefers
only those facts which gratify the self; such is history re-
written. Having a conversation with a person who exhibits
this behaviour can feel like kicking a dead whale along a
beach. One suspects that the whale is not very happy either.

Untrustworthiness: the bully will say one thing to your
face, but something else behind your back. This may range
from a minor misrepresentation to an outright lie. Over time,
however, discrepancies become apparent. This disingenuous
behaviour can be the hardest to deal with, as you are in the
position of having to decide who is telling the truth, and who
is being economical with it. A reliable indicator of maturity is
the congruity of what people say and how they behave.

Most bullies are accomplished liars and their behaviour suggests that they genuinely believe what they say, even when faced with evidence in their own handwriting to the contrary. It's possible that this inability to tell the difference between fact and fiction, or truth and lie, stems from the short-term focus; when put on the spot, the bully makes something up - anything - to get them out of the fix they're in at that moment. This aspect of bullies is particularly disconcerting, especially in a managerial context.

Selfishness: everything the bully says and does is for himself. Even acts and gestures which are supposedly for the benefit of others can often be perceived, on closer examination, to derive their motivation from the bully's sense of self-preservation and betterment.

The bully spends most of his time either covering his back or gaining something for himself, usually at another's expense. Once this selfish streak is recognised, the bully's loyalty can also be reassessed, and employers need to be aware that the bully may be lining their own pocket, sometimes literally, but usually by way of maintained or enhanced position and secured salary at the long-term expense of the organisation.

Poor judgement: in manner and content, the bully's urge to criticise their victim is a revelation of poor judgement. The nature of the censures is unsound, decisions are suspect, judgement is flawed; by choosing to behave in this manner, the bully is demonstrating unfitness to hold position.

Poor listening skills: in conversations, the bully seems to listen only to those parts of the conversation which he finds either gratifying or on which he can pick or trip you up. Bullies are generally not good at conversation and in interactions will usually be either (a) silent and aggressive, or (b) dictatorial, holding the conversation and only letting you speak briefly when it suits them, or (c) effusive, fulsome and self-centred. There is a tendency to come away feeling that, despite your efforts, communication has not taken place.

Focus on the victim: because the bully fears exposure, and their memory is 'unreliable', it can be very hard to pin such a person down. It's like nailing jelly to a tree. The bully steadfastly refuses to be specific, shifting his ground continually, hopping from item to item, flitting from topic to topic, avoiding any area of conversation which they fear will lead to their unmasking. The spotlight is always on the victim. Attempts to discuss unsatisfactory behaviour of the manager, or his unacceptable treatment of others, evoke retaliation by nit-picking and highlighting trivial mistakes that the other person has made. The bully becomes obsessive about catching people out, and when backed up with guilt, the result is highly effective.

Trivialising: when a specific issue is raised, and objections to talking about it overcome, the bully changes tack and resorts to the "you're too sensitive" approach. The emphasis moves from behavioural to personal, the transaction from adult-adult to parent-child. The victim, who may not register this stratagem, is encouraged to feel that they are making a fuss over nothing, that the issue under discussion is not worth wasting breath on. As an isolated example, this may be true; as part of a pattern of behaviour, its significance is by no means trivial. Other exhortations include "where's your sense of humour?" - although the bully fails to observe his own deficiency in that department.

Insatiability: it is not possible to satisfy the bully - however hard you work, however good your work, whatever success you achieve - nothing is enough for the bully. He will always demand more, pick holes in anything, and if there are no holes, invent some. Ironically, the greater success you achieve as a result of the bully's tirades, the less satisfied he becomes. Nothing breeds criticism like success, indeed criticism can be a reliable indicator of achievement. The bully's fear of other people's success is an admission of their own lack of self-confidence, an acknowledgement of their own feelings of low self-worth.

Unwillingness to acknowledge: people thrive on feelings of wellbeing, usefulness and value; absence of these daily lubricants wears down resolve and grind away at self-confidence. Attempts to obtain assurances of worth and merit are futile, as praise requires the bully to acknowledge other people's virtues, and by implication, their own dearth. The inability to give due praise, recognition and approval seems, in some cases, to be so deep-rooted that it could be perceived as a mental infirmity.

Envy: bullies are usually envious and privately covet what others have in preference to recognising and realising their own strengths. Bullies have convinced themselves, or allowed themselves to be convinced, that they will never be able to have those qualities which they see readily in others. This self-limiting belief seems to form the basis of resentment. Ironically, the bully often has more than enough skills to perform their job satisfactorily - sometimes brilliantly - but through lack of self- confidence is condemned to a life of envy and self-prescribed failure. Envy is seen most clearly in the bully's reason for selecting a victim - being good at one's job and popular with people are the two principal qualities that attract the bully like a wasp drawn irresistibly to a honey pot.

Failure mentality: bullies have conditioned themselves - or allowed themselves to be conditioned - to failure. They are convinced they will never fulfil their dreams, and that they can never be as successful as other people. Paradoxically, in the bully's mind, the sense of failure is as dominant and inevitable as their determination to avoid it, and can only be slaked by confirming failure in others. The bully's fear of success becomes apparent when faced with the achievements or impending success of others. Many victims respond to the bully's criticisms by working harder, thereby achieving more and becoming even more successful; the bully responds with increased criticism - and so on.

Differing values: in seeking to establish their true value and thereby feel worthy, the victim quotes their record of achievement. Tasks completed, jobs performed, success attained, clients satisfied, feedback from delighted customers. Faced with this undeniable evidence, the bully changes tack again and alters the value of each undertaking. When he undertakes a task, the value is high; when their subordinate does it, the task is easy, elementary, of low value, unremarkable, just par for the job, not worth mentioning.

Ingratitude: bullies rarely, if ever, express gratitude. To do so requires the acknowledgement of the achievements or kindness of another, which reminds the bully of their lack in this department.

Lack of competence: whilst most bullies exhibit many characteristics with a high degree of predictability, in the area of competence there is more variability. The most dangerous types of bullies seem to be those at the silent aggressive end of the scale. With better memory, longer focus and modest analytical skills, they can be devious, manipulative and scheming. The female of this breed is one to be particularly wary of.

In many cases, the bully demonstrates poor ability, lack of competence, or occasionally, outright incompetence, and is often being carried by the person or persons whom they are bullying. Another consequence is that the department in which the bully works, or is in charge of, is often highly dysfunctional, disorganised and inefficient. Staff spend considerable amounts of time covering their backs, discussing the behaviour of the bully, or looking for ways to escape. The bully is regarded as a disruptive influence.

In some cases the degree of competence is linked to stress in that a person who is acting like a bully through being under enormous pressure is the type of person whose behaviour might be more passable under favourable working conditions.

Taking credit: when the bully needs to present himself to his peers or superiors - or wants to impress anybody, especially outside his immediate environment - then he may stoop to plagiarism. Select some good work, add a title, perhaps an introductory sentence, then brandish it as if it's all his own work. Nothing is guaranteed to cause loss of respect more quickly or completely than stealing others' work and presenting it as original.

"My boss persistently plagiarised other peoples' ideas and work. On one occasion, he lifted several paragraphs from one of my reports by breaking into my computer system. There was no attempt to disguise the text. When I tackled him about it, he said he thought that 'I wouldn't mind'. His 'latest idea' always conveniently materialised after someone else had suggested it."

Shifting goalposts: the bully is obsessed with control. Free-thinking individuals have been universally despised by tyrants throughout the ages - especially if they *act* independently as well. By constantly shifting the goalposts, a person can never achieve their tasks, failure is guaranteed, and control is imposed.

> *"After a year of being bullied, in private, with no record, I finally received an admonishment in writing. It contained a clue that I wasn't to spot until several months later. When I did, it unlocked the secret of how my boss was thinking. It said "You have not lived up to my expectations in fulfilling your role in...". At the time, I was so stressed up that I didn't think to insist that he define his expectations. Had I done so, and stuck to my guns until he did, I would have unmasked him sooner. He never did define them, nor has he since. I could never live up to them, because he made them up and altered them as necessary. In my opinion, they were a fantasy, concealing his insecurity and nourishing his need to control and dominate."*

Insensitivity: perhaps the bully's worst trait, focusing on the personal side of peoples' nature. Hurtful remarks, unjustified criticism and sarcasm testify to little or no idea of consequence, no consideration for others' feelings. The bully is impervious to the callousness of his words. Only a bully can turn people against him without recognising the effect of his words and behaviour on others.

Insincerity: a consequence of insensitivity and lack of empathy combined with selfishness. Attempts to be friendly are often random, infrequent and in stark contrast to the bully's behaviour the rest of the time; such endeavours are consequently perceived as superficial. Apparent caring gestures, when examined closely, often have more to do with covering the bully's back than any genuine concern for others. "How are you feeling?" is more likely to mean "How am I likely to be affected by how you're feeling?". The bully's insincerity often peaks when any of those under his control and dominance experience bereavement or severe ill-health of a person close to them. Without a sense of care, the bully often, unbelievably, goes out of his way to make life especially difficult for those going through a painful time. In such situations, the bully's insensitivity graduates to callous indifference; the word malicious is often appropriate.

Jekyll and Hyde persona: in private, and behind closed doors, bullies can be vicious, spiteful, intimidating, threatening. In public, with witnesses present, they can be innocence personified. This duplicitous behaviour is very hard to unmask, although perceiving and drawing attention to intent rather than content is a start. This aspect of bully behaviour is one of the hardest to counter and is the principal reason why many bullies are able to hoodwink their employer into supporting them.

Mood swings: bullies are often reported as exhibiting wild and unpredictable swings of mood - one moment charming, cooperative and agreeable, the next aggressive, disagreeable and critical. Friendly and cheerful one day, ignoring or cutting you dead the next. Sometimes this occurs on predictable days (for example after the weekend), at other times on a seemingly random basis. Whatever the cause, the bully shows a poor self-control and a lack of professionalism in allowing events in their personal life to affect their managerial duties and responsibilities.

Inconsistency: judgements and decisions which are often poor and unsound, are frequently overturned or reversed, often without explanation or justification.

Cavalier attitude, especially to safety: probably part of their overall insensitivity, bullies show a relaxed attitude to safety. Whilst fine words are forthcoming when subordinates point out the potential for accident, action is notable by its lethargy, or absence. Once again, platitudes abound, but risks and dangers are played down, often to the disbelief of those whose safety is at risk. It is almost uncanny how such people get away without serious mishap for so long. Overtime must be a way of life for the bully's guardian angels - perhaps they're on performance-related pay.

Delegation: the bully sends mixed signals when it comes to delegation. On the one hand, everything is delegated, which means the bully doesn't have to learn anything new, or get his hands dirty. Not being actively involved also makes it easier to distance himself from consequential shortcomings, failures and disasters. On the other hand, there is an unwillingness to let people do things their own way, within agreed parameters or targets - the bully is always there, peering over peoples' shoulders - both literally and metaphorically - checking that everything is being done strictly according to plan - his plan. Often, the amount of supervision is inversely proportional to the manager's ability to manage. Constant interference of this type, which confirms subordinate's suspicions of their manager's inexperience, inability, and lack of knowledge, kindles resentment and leads to a rapid decline in respect, morale and loyalty. Employees divert their energies into avoiding their manager's attentions and secreting their work, leading to a further deterioration in their manager's behaviour.

The bully jumps on trivial mistakes and deviations, especially anything which may incur cost or lead to departure from predetermined budgets - anything which risks exposing him to his peers or superiors. In behaving like this, the bully is disclosing his insecurity, his inability to let go - and in doing so, revealing his unfitness to fulfil the responsibilities of the job. He is happy to dictate to others how the work should be carried out - but is unwilling to lead by example. The bullying manager has no faith in subordinates' judgement, regardless of the facts - but then he cannot trust others more than he trusts himself.

Occasionally, the bully may be tempted to display his leadership skills in a bravado of example. Loudly proclaiming this is "how it should be done", subordinates are subjected to an inappropriate and embarrassing exhibition of managerial competence - or incompetence, for the bully frequently displays the lack of skill for which he castigates others.

Dumping: the difference between a leader and a bully is that a leader will delegate, whereas a bully dumps work onto anyone he thinks he can get to do it. Some define this as the difference between delegation and abdication. As subordinates become resistant to this type of management (sic), the bully increasingly picks on those who are least able to say no. Often, dumping is accompanied by threats, both direct and implied, usually to job security, advancement, promotion, etc. As long as staff can be "persuaded" to accept more work, there is no need to recruit more staff. In the short term, this keeps costs down, and if an individual experiences burnout through being permanently overburdened, then the associated costs are not borne by the individual manager's budget, but come under the aegis of "sickness" and ill-health". The question of cause is neatly side-stepped.

Delegation is also characterised by the bestowal of the appropriate amount of authority which is needed to complete the task. Dumping is usually accompanied by little or no authority, and frequently by its removal or denial; as such it falls into the category of being set up to fail.

Dumping is also a form of control - overload a person with work and they are less likely to have time to think about what - or who - might be the genesis of their plight. People quickly learn that if asking questions is met with more work, the easiest way to avoid more work is not to ask questions.

Occasionally, the bully uses the opposite ploy of refusing to allocate any meaningful work to their victim. Underload can be as harmful as overload, especially to the type of person who normally likes to be fully occupied.

Interference - occasionally, to reinforce control, the bully jumps in and insists that a particular task be performed *his* way - regardless of how inexpedient, ill-judged and ill-timed that may be. Often, the bully has no knowledge or previous experience of the task. Reluctantly, subordinates comply, cursing under their breath. Half way through, the bully walks away with head held high, smiling broadly, safe in the knowledge he has made a significant contribution to the running of the department or project - as well as demonstrating once again his leadership skills. Anticipating the praise and honour that will be forthcoming as a result of his noteworthy contribution, the bully is too pleased with himself to be aware of his trail of devastation and the damage limitation exercise now hastily being initiated in his wake.

Imposition - in another hapless attempt to demonstrate leadership (or rather, superiority), and to boost flagging self-confidence, the bully occasionally feels it necessary to wade in and insist that a particular action be taken, regardless of the need or appropriateness of that action. Where third parties are involved, such as customers, clients, suppliers, etc., the irrelevance of the edict has uncomfortable and frustrating consequences for all concerned - except the bully, whose insensitivity blinds him to the embarrassing nature of his action. Frequently, staff are placed in the invidious position of having to comply with orders when both they and others affected are fully aware of the stupidity of the prescribed course of action.

"Having worked hard over a period of years to provide some of the best levels of customer support in the world in this field, my boss arbitrarily decided one day to change the terms and conditions under which customers received support. This was imposed half way through a year and meant customers would have to pay extra for certain services which were included as part of their existing agreement which was a legally-binding document. My protestations about the unacceptability of this practice were overruled and I found myself in the invidious position of having to justify my bosses' decision to irate customers. The potential cost-saving was minute compared to the long-term damage to customer relationships. I could also see that when customers came to renegotiate their contracts my boss would have moved on. He was prepared to risk several thousand pounds of business in future years - plus adverse publicity - for the sake of potentially saving a few tens of pounds in the current financial year. This blinkered short-term thinking was in contrast to his fine words in public about commitment and service to customers."

Need to assert authority - on random occasions, the bully feels an urge to assert authority, to demonstrate and confirm "who is in charge". The victim is coerced into taking a course of action, the completion of which will earn "approval". The task is usually menial, pointless, unnecessary, but obligatory in order for the individual to continue to exist in their present position, particularly with respect to the relationship to their aggressor. In this context, authority is a euphemism for control and dominance. Once the person has jumped through the requisite hoop, thus gaining a full appreciation of who is master, they can go back to getting on with their job - until the next time.

Paternal adviser - occasionally, the bully will swop into a parental caring mode in a vain attempt to give their juniors some benevolent advice and guidance which will benefit them as they make their way in the world. Unfortunately, this caring mode is expressed with equal degrees of immaturity as their leadership skills, as can be gauged from the wording used: "you should do this...", "you ought to...", "what you need is...". On examination, each has a dictatorial and self-centred undertone.

Fait accompli: the bully fears that if he discusses an impending change or decision or item of work with his subordinates, he will be unable to persuade them or get his way. A situation is engineered such that the decision or course of action has already been determined, but the case is presented to staff as if the decision has yet to be taken - and can therefore still be influenced. The ensuing "discussion", offered to employees in the guise of choice, far from being a discussion, takes place only to communicate what has been decided. The bully confidently expects others to be taken in, but people always see through the charade, especially when it happens repeatedly. The bully, being insensitive, is unable to see that others see through him. A challenge brings forth the claim that everybody who needs to be has been consulted, but can you find anyone who has been?

Steadfast self-reliance: the bully sees their role in life as to lead, manage and organise others. They are over-convinced of their superiority, steadfast in their belief that their performance is everything it needs to be, and that there is little, if anything, left to learn. It is an arrogance and pomposity which clouds judgement. Bullies see help as both a threat - they may reveal themselves unwittingly to a third party - and as a sign of weakness - and a manager cannot be seen to be weak. Ironically, they are unable to appreciate their own strengths, preferring preoccupation with their perception of others' strengths.

Self-importance: to justify - and advertise - his position of responsibility and influence, the bully adopts an inflated sense of his own importance. The desire to prove and exhibit superiority is strong, but derives from low self-confidence, and inner consciousness of undeservingness stokes insecurity. In meetings the bully will always dominate, lead the conversation, put on their best show, especially if outsiders or superiors are present. Bullies have mastered the gift of spontaneity, always producing fine words at the right moment. What jolly decent chaps they appear to be.

Know-it-all attitude: revelation, discovery, insight, research or reports are often met with a dismissive "everyone knows that" or "it's hardly new", etc. Despite claiming foreknowledge, the bully's scholarship only becomes apparent after being informed, and the bully is often able only to regurgitate, not add or develop. The know-it-all attitude, which has an air of "there's nothing anyone can teach me", is closely allied to plagiarism, self-reliance and self-importance. However, in a small number of cases, the bully really does know it all - these can be the most dangerous types of bully.

Unwillingness to apologise: the bully never makes mistakes, at least he can't see any. Such unwavering self-righteousness is in stark contrast to their subconscious beliefs. On rare occasions, when there is something to be gained for himself, he may make a big fuss of apologising over a trivial event. A great show is enacted, often for the benefit of a third party; if the victim(s) can be embarrassed in the process, so much the better.

Only a mature individual can admit to making a mistake, especially a serious one. Assertiveness training teaches that we have a right to make mistakes, but with that right goes an obligation to accept responsibility for the consequences of our mistakes. Bullies abuse this right by denying and abdicating responsibility for the consequences of their behaviour on others.

The more serious the mistake however, or the longer it has been perpetrated or left uncorrected, the greater the maturity required to acknowledge the error. This mature approach is more likely to evoke forgiveness, especially once the heat of the moment has cooled. Unfortunately what is more likely to happen in bullying is that threat levels will be turned up and the individual who has dared to draw attention to the failing is persecuted into oblivion. The victim limps away with their tail between their legs, battered, dejected, dismissed, suffering severe psychiatric injury in the brutal wielding of power, beaten and alone in a society that has yet to recognise the dynamics and injustice that such a conflict provokes. The original mistake is buried and forgotten; the bully lives to fight another day.

Unwillingness to cooperate: bullies have poor cooperation skills, which necessitate the ability to share and trust. Cooperation may also help others achieve their aims and objectives, complete their tasks etc, which are anathema to the bully's own objectives of feeling good through others' discomfort.

Unwillingness to communicate: ditto, also the withholding of information is a tool of control. The victim is set up to fail by having their task made unnecessarily difficult through not having the requisite knowledge or information to hand. Information which is devolved tends to be minimal and carefully filtered.

Negative language: when bullies do communicate, their vocabulary is almost exclusively negative. The emphasis is always on what hasn't been done, rather than what has. The focus is on the 1% (or less) error rather than the 99% perfection. If there are no errors, omissions or oversights at all, some will be invented. Bullies often cannot bring themselves to say a good word about anything or anyone, but in choosing to talk in this way, they reveal a lot about themselves. Sometimes when faced with undeniably satisfactory performance, the bully is reduced to portraying success as failure in that they "did their job too well".

Evasiveness: a consequence of the unwillingness to communicate and cooperate, also a sign of insecurity. Evasion and shifting goalposts make it more difficult for the victim to achieve targets, complete tasks, etc, as well as helping keep attention away from the cause of the victim's difficulties.

Misinterpretation: everything the victim says and does is misinterpreted, distorted and twisted to suit the bully's purpose, which is to portray the victim to other people (for example superiors) as worthless, unreliable and untrustworthy. In fact, precisely those attributes which the bully possesses, but is unwilling to acknowledge.

Duplicity and divided loyalty: the bully behaves as if he has blind faith in his management, and this becomes apparent whenever there are staff issues such as redundancy. With few interpersonal skills and an inability to handle people matters, management policy is recited perfunctorily. Corporate-speak becomes the order of the day, and loyalty to the company - or the company line - is conspicuous.

In the same way etiquette demands that words like "toilet" (and all activities therein) be couched in metaphor, a plethora of euphemisms has emerged to enable weak managers to avoid the word the R word - redundancy. Downsizing and other euphemisms (more are explored in chapter 10) are trotted out, with the bully impervious to the fact that staff see straight through the linguistic guile. Through company-approved terminology, duplicitous behaviour is exhibited, staff are assured that "all is well" and "everything possible is being done" to avert the situation. In some cases, managements have shown themselves so weak and lacking in self-confidence that whole departments have been fired, with staff given only 30 minutes to collect their belongings and be escorted off site.

Bullies are ruthlessly **cost-focused**; people are incidental, units of resource to be allocated and reallocated like a piece of machinery. Flog it hard for six months, then get rid of it. If it (sic) breaks down before the planned end of useful working life, that's unfortunate but an acceptable price for achieving budget targets. All the while, bullies are full of platitudes, redolent with reassurance; finally, however, their true characters will be revealed. Such is duplicity defined.

So fearful is the bully that he may be called upon to tell staff of their impending severance that he may unwittingly divulge his loyalty. Whilst appearing to subordinates to be loyal in the following order

staff - customers - company - management - self

and whilst appearing to his management to be loyal to

company - management - customers - staff - self

closer inspection reveals

self - management - company - customers - staff

Bullies are often so insecure that their behaviour suggests that they would prefer to omit customers and staff altogether.

Frequent moves: a common way of climbing the management pole is to hop from position to position, like scaling a vertical face by using adjacent hand and footholds wherever they present themselves. Such sideways advancement precludes continuity, is opportunist and consistent with short-term thinking; but a predestination to this crab-like progress up the rocky shores of management is also beneficial in an organisation which is encountering frequent and rapid change. Anything as long as its forwards and upwards. A bonus for the bully is that they are always able to move on before being found out. Found out for their behavioural immaturity, found out for their lack of knowledge, found out for their insecurity. Found out for the way they treated their subordinates.

Opportunism: whilst many employers encourage managers to move departments regularly to "broaden their experience", regular changes of position can also indicate a less salubrious reason. Move on before someone finds you out. The interests of self are paramount.

Resoluteness: bullies see themselves as leaders, and recognise that decisiveness is a key component of leadership; the bully therefore confidently takes decisions wherever necessary. Unfortunately, such decisions as are taken are ill-informed, amount to little more than random guessing, and on examination, often show that there has been no consideration of the long-term consequences. In this sense, rather than being a leader, bullies exhibit characteristics more akin to a tyrant, or ruler, one who governs by dominance in preference to example. The ruler believes that a change of mind can be interpreted as weakness, therefore resolutely refuses to change his mind, even in the face of overwhelming evidence to the contrary. Only when impending disaster threatens the security or dominant position of the bully will a change of mind be forthcoming - and then presented in a manner calculated to depict the bully in the most informed, caring light. Funny how these decisions always seem to benefit himself, his friends, peers, or management - with the costs falling on subordinates.

Indecision: although bullies by nature like to be decisive, and enjoy demonstrating their decision-making mastery, they are simultaneously terrified of making a wrong or bad decision which will incur wrath from above. This dichotomy confuses subordinates who sense inconsistencies between their manager's words and behaviour. Promises and assurances prove repeatedly to have little or no validity. Staff become uneasy and lose faith in their leader, who, sensing erosion of control, tries harder and harder to maintain his grip, to which staff react by having even less faith. And so on.

Rigidity: bullies think rigidly, for there is safety in sticking to the plan; it is a manifestation of loyalty to superiors and to the employer, particularly with respect to budgets. Nothing talks louder than the bottom line. Adherence to a predetermined and agreed budget is paramount, and apparent or anticipated deviations are stamped on. In the area of sales, variations are notoriously seasonal, even in supposedly non-seasonal products and services; customers' and consumers' spending power and patterns fluctuate according to the time of year, to the weather, to school and other holidays, and to diverse events, both national and global. The flexibility that these fluctuations demand bring out the worst in nervous managers, who lack the confidence to allow others to function freely, whilst fearing wrath from above if targets are missed. This is further evidence of inability to think long term.

Spinelessness: in the bully's mind, there is a confusion between loyalty and obedience. He wants to be loyal to his management and to the company, but in order to maintain respect from staff, must appear to be loyal to them too. Because the bully is primarily interested in the self, decisions will always be made which ensure the survival (and if possible, prosperity) of self. When ordered to do so by his management, unpleasant actions involving staff (for example redundancy) will always be obeyed; but to maintain good relations with staff, promises and assurance will have been made, giving employees the impression that their manager is on their side and will stand up for them in the face of adversity. When it comes to the crunch, the manager will do what he is told rather than what he has promised his subordinates.

Unwillingness to accept responsibility: when there is reward, prestige, or superiors to impress, responsibility is grasped and held high for all to see. When things go wrong - it's always someone else's fault. A popular poster of the six phases of a project hangs on employees' walls; the bully is

---

Six Phases of a Project

1. Enthusiasm
2. Disillusionment
3. Panic
4. Search for the guilty
5. Punishment of the innocent
6. Praise and honour for the non-participants

---

unaware of his caricature. This abdication of responsibility is common throughout the bully's behaviour, an unwillingness to acknowledge, face up to, and accept responsibility for the consequences of his actions. This aspect alone has important moral, ethical and legal implications for the degree to which criminals can claim to be, or can be held to be, responsible for their crimes. Bullying has the added complication that it is not illegal - yet.

Humourlessness: the bully lacks a sense of humour, being unable or unwilling to laugh unselfconsciously - except when the "joke" is at another person's expense. Such vacuous humour is a disguised form of criticism.

Favouritism: people's strategies for coping with bullying vary. Most put up with it, hoping it will go away; some move department, or leave; but some embrace the behaviour. It's often recognised as the "best way to get on" in the company. Recognising this, the bully "rewards" this group with favours, ranging from sharing knowledge (which is partially or wholly withheld from other members of the department) to promotion, either real or cosmetic. By imitating their manager's behaviour, favoured status is procured, and information "shared" on a regular basis. Other employees see this as "informing", and soon realise that knowledge, intelligence, titbits and gossip are being disclosed, sometimes with an economy of truth. Fictional details may also be added. The bully gains a distorted view of his staff, tailored to what he wants to hear. Thus a department becomes divided, with mistrust endemic. Who is informing? Who is leaking information? Who is telling tales? Who cannot be trusted? Who is the agent? Who's the snitch?

Tone of voice: a giveaway for an alert observer, the tone of voice that a bully uses when dealing with staff yields insight into what's really going on inside his head. A simple comment such as "That's great" can be a sign of genuineness, a congratulatory pat on the back, fashioned to further feelings of value and wellbeing. An alternative tone of voice laced with sarcasm denotes insincerity and indicates that the bully is really thinking the opposite.

Non-verbal behaviours: these disclose discrepancies between inner feeling and outward expression. Research suggests that, in Western cultures at least, we rely more on gestures, expressions and posture in conversation than on the words spoken. When we feel uncomfortable, we are detecting a discrepancy between verbal and body language; for most of the time, we make up our minds using the latter.

When a person tells a lie, or is economical with the truth, they often touch their nose or cheek. This is a modified form of the child's habit of putting hands over the mouth when telling an untruth. By adulthood, the behaviour has been refined so that only the fingers, or tip of a finger, make contact with the face, usually the nose or cheek.

Reluctance to make eye contact can also be a sign of insincerity, as well as lack of interest. There are many other reasons for a person not looking you in the eye, such as shyness, anxiety, lack of awareness of appropriate amount of eye contact, etc, so as with all non-verbal gestures, should only be interpreted in conjunction with other signals.

Avoidance of eye contact can also mean lying, hiding, withholding or some "economy". You may also be witnessing a deceit. This is especially pertinent when a person maintains eye contact for significant periods, but breaks it whilst certain topics are discussed.

When a bully is fearful of colleagues "seeing through" him, tactics are employed to avoid eye contact as much as possible. On the other hand, a person seeking dominance and control may respond with an aggressive, challenging stare. Significant deviation from average eye-to-eye contact for two-thirds of the time during any interaction when combined with other bullying characteristics should ring warning bells. When dealing with a bully, more may be revealed more through the eyes than through the lips.

Bully behaviours

The bully's feelings of insecurity are exhibited through his behaviours. To an informed observer these describe and define his innermost thoughts and feelings, revealing inadequate maturity, lack of interpersonal skills, low self-confidence, etc.

The bully's hold is sustained using a number of techniques, including:

Threat: threats are an aggressive behaviour to strengthen dominance and control, a show of force to frighten and subjugate. The implication is that something nasty will happen if you don't do as you are told. Threats are particularly effective on children, who lack the maturity to handle their plight. Unfortunately, most children do not receive tuition in how to handle threatening behaviour, and this juvenile innocence is carried into adulthood, only to reappear when a similar situation flares up.

Threats can be overt, such as in the statement "*You'd better do this - or else*" - or, more usually, implied, such as "*If you do/don't do this, I can't be held responsible for the consequences*". Here, the implication is that the hurt will be inflicted by a third party, perhaps working in partnership with the bully. The insinuation of misfortune or damage to job security or career progress rarely fails to achieve its intended result. The effectiveness of threat is increased if the ultimate outcome, real or implied, is derived by the thought processes of the victim, rather than stated explicitly. Guilt boosts dramatically the efficacy of this strategy.

Implied threats are more effective, as they also reinforce their victim's fear that they are on their own, alone, with no-one to stand up for and protect them. Prolonged use of this behaviour induces feelings of paranoia, the individual becoming convinced that "they will get me". From here it is only a small step from believing that punishment is a deserved consequence of inadequate performance, to regarding punishment as inevitable regardless of performance. Dangerous stuff, especially when stoked by low self-esteem and low self-confidence. But what makes threat particularly effective is...

Guilt: the state of believing that we have done something wrong, and are therefore liable to - and deserving of - punishment. Whether this be punitive, or simply withdrawal of privileges or rights, guilt emphasises how undeserving our actions have rendered us. Whilst guilt keeps us on the straight and narrow by reinforcing the negative consequences of straying, setting our tolerance of, or to, guilt at an inappropriate level has a disproportionate effect on our self-esteem and levels of self-confidence.

We learn the behaviours that induce guilt before we can walk. A baby's cry encourages its mother to attend to its needs immediately, but the terrible twos are an age when the value of guilt is tested to obtain more than the basic necessities of food, warmth and comfort. By the age of five, guilt-inducing behaviours are perfected and used instinctively to fulfil needs and wants, regardless of the effects of the behaviour on others. It is now that parents must call on their own maturity of behaviour skills to ensure that their infant grows through childhood and adolescence to emerge with an appropriate knowledge and understanding of the power of guilt.

Most people attain adulthood without this insight, and although exhibiting a mature understanding of the nature of right and wrong, set their guilt levels either too high or too low. Guilt is the most effective way of controlling others, and its repeated success, reinforced regularly, ensures that it remains a potent weapon in our armoury of interpersonal (lack of) skills.

The bully, observing the value of guilt in maintaining supremacy, only has to hint at the unpleasantness of consequences (especially to job security) and subordinates succumb. Bullies know that you can get anyone to do almost anything by using guilt. What they overlook is that everyone will feel bad about it - especially the person using guilt.

Aggression: this behaviour, a standard sign of insecurity and low confidence, can overcome even modest levels of assertiveness, and being overtly unpleasant, feeds on embarrassment and humiliation. The bully is impervious to his behaviour, often making a complete fool of himself in front of witnesses. Once overt aggressive behaviour is demonstrated, then professional help is needed urgently, for the bully has revealed a dangerous side to his nature.

There is one approach to aggression which has been demonstrated time and time again - even as I write this book - not to work. You do not appease aggressors - appeasement encourages them and makes their behaviour worse. Appeasement is an overt acknowledgement that you are giving control over the situation to the bully. Bullies love appeasement - they see it as a green light to carry on with their behaviour, as well as enabling them to get away with murder.

I believe it is peace for our time ... peace with honour."
Neville Chamberlain, 1938

Procrastination, indecision and meekness in the guise of negotiation prolong an appropriate response, as democracy deliberates and reflects with measured coolness. A cautious and considered approach is required to avoid giving the aggressor, by attacking the wrong target or causing civilian casualties, a propaganda bonanza with consequent justification to continue the aggression. In a classic Catch-22 trap, appeasement is viewed by the bully as approval for his behaviour, confirmation that his strength is sovereign in a world of weakness, as well as furnishing him the opportunity to make further gains. Response to aggression must considered but authoritative, forceful and rapid but not knee-jerk. In a national or international context, this means combined force. Beneficial application of a short, sharp shock will teach the aggressor that his behaviour is not acceptable, and that further excursions and incursions will be dealt with quickly and efficiently.

Aggressive tyrants and despots, who are bullies on a world stage, threaten the stability of society, testing the limits of tolerance and exploiting weaknesses and loopholes. In the workplace, aggression must be handled using a combined response, with the threat of disciplinary action and recourse to law if necessary. Hesitation, consultation and review encourage, rather than discourage, the bully.

A characteristic of bullies, however, makes swift action difficult. They are aware of their rights as an individual, and will assert them authoritatively. Also, they can switch behaviours so that they appear to be the victim, inducing doubt - even sympathy - in observers. "Perhaps he's not such a bad chap after all...", "Perhaps we've been a bit harsh" are familiar phrases which cause hearts to sink and anger levels to rocket. A successful reprieve, and, the status quo having been restored, within two weeks (or days) old habits and behaviours resurface, the momentum of justice has been lost and battle restarts.

Dominance: hierarchically, the bully feels compelled to keep subordinates at arm's length. Whilst occasionally welcoming them into the territory of his office, a distance is maintained, and an absence of rapport, a subtle feeling of not being "in" registers in the subconscious and results in an unease that is hard to put one's finger on.

The bully has good reason to be wary. His behaviour is framed to keep people from drawing near. Too close, and people might see through the paper-thin veneer of propriety. Psychologically too, lesser creatures must be kept at bay, for fear of piercing the mosquito net that shrouds his insecurity.

An anxious manger is in constant fear of being ousted or replaced by a junior employee, a humiliation which must be avoided at all costs. Therefore, the bully adopts behaviours designed to ensure that subordinates remain where they are. Should promotion be unavoidable, their "unsuitability" ensures that any upward move is made in a diagonal direction away from the department. At the same time, the bully mounts a public display of his role in bringing about this advancement for one of his staff. The perceived threat removed, the bully has more time to focus his attention on other menaces.

Power: knowledge is power, and bullies believe that by giving away knowledge, they are giving away power. A willingness to delegate responsibility but with a corresponding unwillingness to delegate authority is an unmistakable indication of the insecure manager. Conversely, a confident manager ensures that delegation includes sufficient authority to empower staff to determine and take action independently within an agreed framework.

The bully exhibits many behaviours and habits which to the enlightened onlooker betray lack of confidence. Expensive training courses, management pep-talks and corporate networking all provide opportunities for acquiring the latest jargon, which then creeps into conversation. Buzzwords are dotted throughout dialogue, and corporate-speak is mimicked from management meetings; all are designed to heighten the sense of self-importance, but in reality disenchant an increasingly reluctant and disillusioned audience.

Another sign is the manager who always has to have the latest executive toys. Electronic diaries and organisers, the latest lap-top personal computer and the like all aid aggrandisement and authority. Closer inspection however reveals superficial use, a short life quickly superseded by the next fad. Replace it before you're asked to explain it, justify it, or, worst of all, demonstrate the value of it.

Such executive gadgets (or rather, toys) are often placed strategically on the manager's desk. A cynical observer might say these are the only things on his desk, which provides another clue. Few people are so well organised that their desk remains clear; perhaps it is because they are not actually doing anything.

The bully's language also reveals his thinking; words like "character" are trotted out, although what the bully means by "character" is unclear. Phrases like "this is how I learnt, it never did me any harm" are also heard, as well as "it's tough at the top". Such macho natter is more indicative of testosterone than intelligence.

"If there's a problem with an employee, then the real problem is not with the employee, but with the

employee's manager, or the manager's manager. Either
the problem has not been spotted, or it has but no action
has been taken. Whatever the reason, the responsibility
of a manager is to ensure that there are no problems
with staff for whom he is responsible. This holds true
right to the top."

Employee performance cascades down from the top, and with
this in mind, the true mettle of a company - or rather its
senior management - can be discerned. Look closely at the
senior figures - and ask employees for their view as well - and
the style of management becomes clear. Similarly, look at the
workforce - once again, asking them what they think of their
management - and you will also gain a clear view of the
average   interpersonal   skill   levels   throughout   the
organisation.

Managerial ability tends to be consistent throughout a
company, permeating its products and services. Whilst there
may be pockets of excellence or frightfulness, over time,
standards   equalise   and   an   organisational   culture
impregnates the workforce. There's an old story about never
travelling on an airline that has coffee stains on the foldaway
tables. The same management team that has failed to
organise the simple task of cleaning the craft in between
flights is responsible for maintaining the airframe, servicing
the engines, and training the pilots.

Projection: as suggested already, the bully chooses to
behave in such a way as to project their own shortcomings,
weaknesses and failings on to others as a way of avoiding
facing up to them in themselves. Once alerted to this, each
unpleasant behaviour or act of criticism can be seen as a
revelation or admission.

5   The bully's hold

"Behaviour reveals all"

The bully uses a variety of methods to maintain his grip on individuals over whom he has, or wishes to have, control. Hierarchical position, such as that of manager, confers real power, but bullies can also exert their own power from a peer position, as well as from a station of subordination. Studies suggest that as many as 90% of cases of bullying are of a manager on a subordinate, with around 8% peer-to-peer, and the remaining 2% subordinate on manager.

One of the holds that a bullying manager has over employees is that of "underperformance". An employee's performance is often appraised on the basis of managerial opinion and assessment, with few hard facts and little or no real data to back up those views. Under these conditions, the manager claims that the member of staff is "not doing their job", "not up to scratch", "not meeting expectations", etc, but the justification for such opinions is difficult or impossible to discern. The evidence is usually to the contrary, which is why the bully feels it necessary to dismiss defensive testimony as "not relevant". It's now that shifting goalposts come in handy. When combined with guilt, the result is total control. Statements such as "I promoted you on the basis that I believed you could do the job - you're not going to let me down are you?" strike fear into the heart of the unwary, and the implications of demotion, removal, loss of job etc, not to mention embarrassment, shame, guilt, blow to pride, combined with general job insecurity in an employers' market ensure the bully's objectives are met.

The technique of claiming "underperformance" has the added advantage that it can encompass almost any aspect of the individual's position, presence or performance in the workplace - provided that an insinuated failing is never actually specified.

People who are being bullied show remarkable tenacity, resourcefulness, determination and resistance - in fact, precisely those characteristics which may have attracted the bully's attention in the first place. To counter this resistance, the bully employs a number of tactics to weaken position and resolve. These include:

- imposition of limits on the number of hours that may be worked, thus forcing people to have to work harder in the time that is available, as well as increasing the probability that tasks cannot be completed
- setting limits on the amount of overtime that will be eligible for payment - this puts employees in the difficult position of either risking not completing their work, or going for completion but working long hours without remuneration
- using threat and guilt at the slightest sign of dissidence - or using threat and guilt anyway

If a bully senses that any member of staff cannot be controlled, or may be difficult to subjugate, or is in any way a threat to the bully's survival (for example by challenging him for his job), then a more comprehensive plan of subjugation is adopted. The process, which was described in detail in chapter 3, draws on the following ploys:

- subject the individual to constant criticism, fault-finding, etc
- increase the threat level
- marginalise, sideline and isolate - steadily decrease the amount of say the victim has in the affairs and running of the department
- undermine the person's position, remove status, perhaps through "reorganisation", "rationalisation", "efficiency", etc
- ignore and humiliate the individual in meetings with other (controlled) victims present
- move the victim under someone who is controlled
- appoint to a more important but dead-end position
- appoint to a project or position which has a finite life and no obvious succession
- promote to a more important job in a less important area
- pile on the work; justify by claiming "underperformance"

- set tasks which are impossible to achieve, then claim underperformance
- make all tasks unnecessarily complex, then claim underperformance
- withhold information necessary for the individual to complete the tasks in hand, then claim underperformance
- repeat the above

When the bully's behaviour is analysed, the true purpose of criticism becomes apparent. It is for control, and has nothing to do with performance or the improvement thereof. Once this is understood, it becomes clear that the alleged criticisms, shortcomings, faults, etc have no validity, and that in choosing to persist with such behaviour, the bully is unwittingly admitting that their judgement is unsound. It also becomes clear that this style of "management" has nothing to do with the aims and objectives of the employer, despite claims to the contrary.

The 10% or so of cases of peer-peer or subordinate-manager bullying in the workplace tell us that the hold that bullies exert over their victims is not just an abuse of hierarchical power. Rather than a cause or prerequisite, managerial superiority is merely an advantage which facilitates the process.

The bully's hold seems to comprise:

a) dependency - the victim becomes dependent on the bully to allow them to get through each day without their life being made hell (this is additional to the dependency a subordinate has on their manager to give satisfactory appraisal for career advancement)

b) approval - the victim feels compelled to seek approval and acceptance in advance of every action in order to forestall or preclude criticism

c) loss of control - the bully's behaviour steadily deprives their victim of any feeling of control over their situation

d) isolation - the victim is encouraged to feel that they are alone, they are the only person in the world who feels like this; colleagues are turned off or warned off

e) amoral behaviour - the bully will lie, cheat, deceive and generally behave in such an obnoxious manner as to imply no scruples, no principles, and no conscience; the bully often acts beyond the bounds of decency, etiquette, civility and the law as if these standards do not apply to him and with the expectation - normally fulfilled - of not being called to account

f) fear - is used by the bully to disempower, who then reinforces the hold by encouraging their victim to believe that any action which does not meet with the bully's approval will automatically qualify that person for disciplinary action which may result in loss of job

(In the wider political context, dictators will imprison, torture and murder those who disagree, or even commit genocide, all the while believing this to be acceptable behaviour.)

The bully can exert this hold because:

i) the absence of an anti-bullying policy creates a climate where bullying is regarded as acceptable

ii) those in authority either

a) refuse or show reluctance to implement an effective anti-bullying policy, or

b) implement an ineffective anti-bullying policy, perhaps as a window-dressing exercise

iii) when alerted to the actions of a bully, those in authority either

a) back the bully (active approval), or

b) refuse to take action (passive approval)

iv) in most cases, the bully will abuse their position of power to sustain their behaviour, or call on those with power to support them

v) when challenged or investigated, the bully uses their Jekyll and Hyde nature to elude detection, instead diverting attention away from themselves by portraying their victim as the person at fault

vi) the bully lies convincingly to sustain this travesty

vii) the victim feels helpless (especially, as is often the case, they have not learnt the skills of psychological self-defence) and powerless (due to the inability or unwillingness of those in authority to take appropriate action), especially as the bully reinforces the hold using the threat of loss of employment

viii) with society adopting an uncaring and unsympathetic approach which is tantamount to denial and even complicity, the victim has no-one to turn to, and feels isolated, trapped, paralysed, vulnerable, and alone

Eventually, the victim becomes dependent on acceptance and approval from the bully not only for their work and performance, but for their prosperity, advancement, survival and ultimately existence; approval to live, be, think, act and remain independent from the behaviour of the bully.

In the same way that an abused child dreads the approach of their abuser, so the bullied person begins to shudder at the prospect of encountering their tormentor. The child abuser's strategy is phrased along the lines of *"You've done something which you know to be terribly wrong and if the police find out, you'll go to prison and you'll never see your mummy and daddy again"*. No wonder a child faced with this prospect is too terrified to tell anyone. The bullying manager's hold is phrased along the lines of *"You have not performed satisfactorily in your job and if anyone finds out you'll be subjected to disciplinary proceedings, you'll be embarrassed, shamed, fired and may never work again"*. With insecurity rife and prospects for re-employment (at least for permanent, full-time positions) at an all-time low, no wonder a subordinate in this position is too fearful to tell anyone.

Because workplace bullying is played between adults, the bully counters any growing sense of realisation by playing the "To gain my approval..." game. It starts with an apparently innocuous "In order to gain my approval, you must satisfy the following (my) criteria...", then moves on to "...you must pass this test...", graduating to "...you must jump through this hoop..." and ultimately reaching "...you must do as I say (or else...)". The game is, of course, a con as approval will never be forthcoming, regardless of what is achieved. In the majority of cases, the criteria have little or nothing to do with fulfilment of the duties and responsibilities of the job or position, but have everything to do with the control that the bully is imposing. Recognition of this differentiation is the start of perceiving the *intent* behind the *content* of the bully's behaviour. When tackling a bully, it is the intent on which you must remain focused.

In denying others the right to independent existence, the bully displays an arrogance and contempt for the rights of others, thus demonstrating unfitness to exercise those views in the first place. Victims find themselves constantly looking over their shoulder, for ever on guard against the unremitting and unwarranted verbal and other behavioural attacks to which the bully subjects them on a daily basis.

Conflict (be it personal, domestic, regional, governmental, international, etc) involves the desire to control, manipulate, subjugate and if necessary destroy others. Defence involves the assertion of right to self-determination and a refusal to surrender to the unacceptable demands of the bully. Whilst the victim is happy to walk away from an initial confrontation and get on with their job and their life, the bully feels compelled to overcome the resistance as if it represented a threat to their survival.

A war of attrition then ensues in which the hold is imposed using the tactics of criticism and humiliation etc as described in chapter 3. Repeated criticism makes a person feel increasingly self-conscious whenever the bully is near; if the bully is a manager, the deferential attitude of "What did I do wrong" begins to assert itself. The person being bullied finds themselves constantly on alert in a manner similar to a soldier in a combat zone whose recognition of a single sound may make the difference between life and death. This hypersensitivity is one of the principal components of Post Traumatic Stress Disorder as suffered by war veterans, and can take years to wear off. Without help and support, it may never fully subside. This state also goes towards explaining the unusual and sometimes erratic behaviour of people who have been bullied after they have left the bullying situation. The fight or flight instinct is constantly active despite the absence of threat. From being a normal reaction in an abnormal situation, it becomes an abnormal reaction in a normal situation.

In many cases, a form of "coded language" or double-speak evolves, whereby only the bully and the victim understand the hidden meaning within the communication. Without insight or knowledge of what has been going on, third parties remain ignorant of the threat behind the facade. Words, phrases and statements (whether verbal or in writing) which on the surface sound innocuous have an intimidating and threatening ring designed to remind and reinforce the control the bully is exerting. Superficial pleasantries can be used openly in the presence of others who remain blissfully unaware and ignorant of the power play being performed before them; the presence of witnesses appears to intensify the hold, especially when the bully appears to be such a charming and upright person.

Physical bullying

In certain situations, pain is inflicted to reinforce the message, for example the use of corporal punishment. Whilst adults can resort to the law to safeguard themselves from any form of physical violence, many children still do not qualify for this protection. In many cases, the vicious beatings administered to children in educational institutions have more to do with gratification of the person who chooses to assert control using an instrument of pain, to the extent that such unnecessary violence, often on an intimate area of the child's body, could be construed as a form of sexual abuse. This ugly discipline, which is commonly and erroneously confused with self-discipline, is evidence of a person's immaturity and inability to lead other than by fear, and as such certifies the individual unfit for office. Institutionalised violence of this nature is anathema to every natural instinct to nurture, educate, and build self-discipline and self-control.

Violence can be physical or psychological; with the former now widely criminalised, there seems to have been a trend to the latter, which is still largely unrecognised or denied. Those who regularly advocate solutions which involve the use of violence are admitting that they enjoy causing harm to others, despite vehement denials. People derive pleasure from seeing others "get what they deserve". Advocacy of savage "remedies" in the name of legal or religious justice is especially perturbing, showing a lack of understanding of the difference between revenge and controlled aggressively assertive behaviour for the assertion of the rights of the individual. Who, however, on hearing the details of a dreadful crime such as serial murder, has never felt the lust for revenge? Would it have been possible to have stopped Hitler without using aggression? How many victims of bullying, having lost their job, their income, career, perhaps marriage and house, has not, on seeing their bully still in post and starting on their successor, not thought of taking "matters into their own hands"?

The bully's hold can be seen as a combination of threat and intimidation backed up by repeated violence (physical or psychological), combined with isolation and the denial of justice in the absence of moral, practical and legal support. Bullying can only be defeated by strong defences, mutual support, legal protection and exposure of the bully in a climate of unacceptability with policies and procedures in place to deal with the behaviour when it arises.

Maintaining the hold without being uncovered

There are many reasons why bullies maintain their hold without being uncovered; these include:

- practice: bullying is compulsive and addictive, so people who bully have usually perfected the skills through a lifetime of practice
- turning up the threat level to silence people
- by appearing to be successful (to their boss at least); bullying is a successful short-term strategy and because it brings the required results, the bully is often promoted or moved on within 1-2 years, which is just short enough for people to tolerate. (*"I'm just keeping my head down until he moves on - it shouldn't be long"*)
- the Jekyll and Hyde nature of bullies enables them to pull the wool over people's eyes; bullies often spread untruthful but convincing rumours about others - this is part of tactic designed to isolate their victim by turning others against them
- lack of knowledge and understanding in society; although bullying has always occurred in the workplace, the tag "workplace bullying" was only ascribed in the early 1990s
- denial - people are unwilling to acknowledge or recognise something nasty going on in their midst, especially if they are involved
- by promoting either like-minded individuals, or individuals who are completely controlled

- the type of person who is bullied is by nature reluctant to name names or identify an individual against whom disciplinary action may be taken - who wants to be responsible for another person losing their job? This forgiving nature is part of the guilt mechanism.

Maintaining the hold indirectly

Bullies are cowards and often recruit other people to do their dirty work. Typically, the coterie consists of an assortment of willing accomplices who enjoy the benefits of patronage in return for doing what they're told, plus a number of less willing conscripts for whom resistance means death, at least in the professional or security of employment sense. There are a number of advantages to this strategy:

- the cohorts act as both smoke-screen and defence screen - the arch-bully stays in the background
- the arch-bully can sit back and take life easy
- there is safety and strength in numbers
- the underlings can be used to divert attention away from the arch-bully
- the conspirators can back each other up when a complaint is made, especially when it's one word against another
- if there are investigations or recriminations, one of the coercees can be sacrificed for the survival of the others; scapegoats are dispensable, there are usually plenty more from which to recruit

Personal life

In many cases, bullies have as much turmoil and dissatisfaction in their personal lives and relationships as they exhibit towards others in the workplace. Inability to form lasting friendships, troubled relationships, difficulty in relating to members of the opposite sex, dominance of or by spouses, dislike of or lack of interest in their own children, unusual or obsessive behaviours, bizarre attitudes to sexual and related matters - all are regularly reported by those on the receiving end. "Their life is in an appalling mess" is a phrase that comes up repeatedly.

Some bullies have events in the private life that they would prefer not to reveal. Whilst an individual's right to privacy must be respected, when that person's behaviour causes distress or injury to another, the incidents in the bully's life which cause them to choose to behave in the way they do now may need disclosing.

Denial and projection are regular features of bullying behaviour. It's as if bullies can't bear to look at themselves, for the picture they see is so ugly. Only by displacing or projecting that ugliness onto others can the self-loathing be assuaged.

Conscience

A word frequently used to describe the bully's behaviour is "unconscionable", and in many cases it would appear that the bully is a person whose conscience is immature and intermittent; in serious cases, it seems that the bully has no conscience. Given that many bullies seek, and operate from, a position of power, the implications are disturbing.

Compulsive lying

Most bullies can be or are described as compulsive liars and exhibit this habit with such consummate skill that others, especially peers, superiors, and those in authority are frequently taken in by it.

On closer examination, it often appears that the bully genuinely believes what he says, and even when confronted with evidence to the contrary *by his own hand*, will continue to lie and deny everything. It could be that the very short-term focus which such people exhibit causes them to make up anything on the spur of the moment in order to get themselves out of the fix they are in, but are unaware that the hole they are digging themselves is getting deeper. Distressingly, the deeper the hole, the more aggressive their behaviour becomes.

It has long been recognised that lying is an essential survival skill to which everyone resorts on occasion; however, with most people, this is restricted to the odd white lie which is not intended to hurt, or is used to avoid hurt. Similarly, most people can tell the difference between truth and lie, know when they are telling a lie, and may feel guilty afterwards. Bullies seem not to have acquired this faculty.

In some ways, the short-term memory and spontaneous lying are reminiscent of the confabulation demonstrated by casualties of Korsakov's syndrome, where amnesia causes the sufferer to make up a past to fit the present circumstances. The person is unaware of the fabrication, and often seeks no gain, other than to maintain a consistent reality. However, whereas in Korsakov's the cause is usually attributed to brain damage caused by alcohol abuse and vitamin deficiency, the bully's motivation for choosing to behave in this way has more to do with self-interest and survival - if necessary, at their victim's expense.

Psychopathic personality
In discussions with victims of bullying, the designation "psycho" crops up regularly (as does, especially in these cases, the word "evil"). Although the term is used loosely and in a lay sense, the definition of psychopathic personality often fits closely the style of behaviour exhibited by bullies. The following description of psychopathic personality is given in "The Oxford Companion to The Mind", edited by Richard L Gregory, 1987, and is summarised here by permission of Oxford University Press.

A psychopathic disorder is defined by the Mental Health Act as a "persistent disorder ... of mind ... which results in abnormally aggressive or seriously irresponsible conduct on the part of the [individual]". The Act considers psychopathic disorder to be a form of mental illness, and one might be tempted to suggest that when the bully springs the mental health trap, that this too could be an unwitting projection.

The key features of psychopathic disorder include:
- a person unable to conform to the rules of society
- inability to tolerate minor frustrations
- tendency to act impulsively or recklessly
- incapacity for forming stable human relationships
- failure to learn from past experiences, however unpleasant

There is still much debate about what precisely constitutes psychopathic behaviour, but Lord Chief Justice Parker defined it as "...a state of mind so different from that of ordinary human beings that the reasonable man would term it abnormal". His opinion, he continued, applied to a person's acts, his ability to distinguish right from wrong, and his capacity for exercising will-power to control his behaviour in accordance with rational judgement. This definition raises tantalising questions when juxtaposed with the principal behaviours exhibited by bullies:

- constant criticism which has no relevance, basis in fact or justification with reality
- Jekyll and Hyde nature
- compulsive lying (or confabulation)
- the desire to humiliate and embarrass
- the compulsion to control, dominate and subjugate
- obsession with elimination once the bully realises that subjugation is not possible
- inability or unwillingness to recognise effects of behaviour on others
- lack of remorse, other than perhaps an insincere and expedient moment of regret when publicly called to account
- the repetitive and cyclic nature of the behaviour in the eradication of one victim after another

In short, the bully appears to lack the inner controls which are normally developed during childhood and adolescence. Worryingly, the bully also gives the impression that he (a) doesn't know any other way of behaving, (b) cannot accept that there are other and better ways of behaving, and frequently (c) doesn't wish to know of any other way of behaving. In this respect, one cannot help but notice superficial similarities with individuals who have certain types of right (brain) hemisphere syndrome and who are unaware that they have a problem.

A demonstration of this type of behaviour can be seen when the bully demands respect and consideration *from* others whilst simultaneously refusing to accord respect and consideration *to* others; in disclaiming this responsibility, the bully always wants to have his cake and eat it.

Whether there is brain malfunction, or whether it is simply the self-protection mechanism out of control (for example the perception of threat where no external threat exists), or whether there are other agencies at play, the underlying cause of the need to bully awaits formal identification and further research.

Favourite bully sayings

"You know you're being bullied when you're told you're going to fail."

Whether you're experiencing bullying, or supporting someone who is, or witnessing it, the following examples will help you perceive the bully's intent and enable you to discern what the bully is really thinking:

The bully says...	The bully means...
Trust me	I'm wholly untrustworthy
We've had initial difficulties with you settling in here	I've had initial difficulties with you settling in here
You've never got on with...	I've never got on with...
I've been very careful to protect you	I've been very careful to protect myself
I thought we had an excellent working relationship	I'm using guilt to make you doubt both yourself and your view of me
I'm only thinking of your own interests	I'm only thinking of my own interests
I only called this meeting because I was concerned about your health	I only called this meeting because I was concerned about your health and that people might start asking questions about who or what is causing the symptoms you are displaying
The pupils/patients/customers are saying...	I'm coercing/encouraging the pupils/patients/customers to say..., *or* I'm imagining the pupils/patients/customers are saying...

Table 6: Bully sayings

The bully says...	The bully means...
I've had a complaint made against you	I've made up a complaint about you, *or* I've coerced someone into making a complaint about you, *or* I've asked one of my cronies to whip up a complaint about you, *or* Someone has made a comment which I've twisted into a complaint about you
We get on so well	I need to believe we get on well, *or* I need to portray our relationship to third parties as normal as a way of denying that I bully you
It's in your own professional interests for you to move...	It's in my own survival interests for you to move...
We can sort this out informally between you and me	I want to be sure no-one else becomes aware of what I am doing to you
We can sort this out together	I want to sweep this under the carpet
I'd like to put this episode to bed now	The sooner I can sweep this under the carpet the better

Table 6: Bully sayings

Bully profile

By studying the behaviour of bullies, it is possible to derive a profile of the typical bully, with the principal variations. These are shown in the table below.

Facing up

If the bully is in the position of having to apologise for their behaviour, and promise not to do it again, then by definition they do not have the maturity of behaviour skills to fulfil that promise. If they did, they wouldn't be in the position of having to apologise in the first place.

The bully: general qualities	Variations	
	Introvert type	Extrovert type

aggressively assertive
see themselves as leader
interested only in self
self-important
greedy, selfish
not people-oriented
insensitive
thick-skinned
uncaring
unsympathetic
unable to value
budget-focused
untrustworthy
two-faced
inconsistent
lacking conscience
insecure
superficial
cowardly
short-term thinker
short memory
spontaneous
tough, rigid, hard-nosed
dictatorial, bullying
dominant
power-oriented, climber
taker
single focus
impulsive
self-reliant
focus on effects rather
  than causes
unimaginative
non-creative
plagiarist
punitive
vicious
vindictive, spiteful
critical, sarcastic
uses guilt openly
lacks sense of humour
attitudes:
  follow me
  look up to me
  do as I say
  do it now
	silent aggressive
	over-assertive
	manipulative
	plotting
	scheming
	devious
	cunning
	terse
	silent
	listener
	watcher
	unwilling to
	  communicate
	unwilling to
	  cooperate
	unresponsive
	can think longer
	  term
	better memory
	better analytical
	  skills
	eye for detail
	less obtrusive
	attitudes:
	do exactly as I say
		overtly aggressive
		outgoing
		extrovert
		likes to be centre of
		  attention
		talks about self
		talks a lot
		hogs conversation
		arrogant, vain
		pompous
		false
		short memory
		forgets quickly
		attitudes:
		  like me
		  watch me
		  praise me
		  admire me
		  adulate me
		  worship me

Table 7: Bully profile

Ironically, the bully may possess the requisite skills to fulfil the requirements of their job, especially with respect to people. More often than not they could do it easily if they put their mind to it - but they choose not to.

This attitude is nourished through their own managers' lack of interest or unwillingness to acknowledge bullying. Such apparent acquiescence is taken as tacit approval for the behaviour to continue.

"After I got my promotion, I was staggered by my boss's attitude when he suggested that 'you're not considered a real manager in this company until you've had a shouting match with [a certain senior manager]'. I was tempted to ask what it was meant to achieve, but wisely bit my tongue."

Unfortunately, it is not just managers who regard bullying as acceptable; society itself is ambivalent. Until society unequivocally states its abhorrence of bullying as an acceptable management style, and backs its belief by law, the behaviour will remain. It is indeed sad that only a very few enlightened organisations have grasped this nettle; if I was looking to invest long-term, I now know into which companies and organisations I'd put my money.

At this stage in society's evolution, leadership is valued more highly, by remuneration at least, than technical skills. Maturity is not considered, and until it is, abuse will continue. Some people seem to be born with the predominant behaviour pattern of the leader; it is these people who have potential as leaders, and it is they who invariably end up in positions of power. If their behaviour skills are mature, then much will be achieved. Otherwise, they will bully.

The time of bullies is running out.

6   Bully tactics

Individuals with a predisposition to bully will evolve their own methods for achieving their objectives, especially if there is a bullying culture within the organisation. Below are a sample of the tactics employed to achieve those objectives, with some suggestions for how one might handle or counter them. All assume the absence of an anti-bullying policy, or a policy which has been tried but found to be ineffective. Feedback and contributions for future editions of this book are welcome.

The confidence destroyer
This is the underlying strategy of all workplace bullying. The bully has low self-confidence and self-esteem, and in order to feel good about himself, chooses not to bring his own confidence levels up, but to bring other people's down to below the level of his. This is so that, in relative terms, he can feel good about himself. The means of achieving this is criticism, humiliation, ridicule, etc as outlined in chapter 3. However, the victim gradually regains their confidence and the nice warm feeling of relative superiority wears off.

In order to regain that state of comfort and contentment (like craving another fix), the behaviour has to be repeated. This contributes to explaining the addictive and compulsive nature of bullying. However, the victim's inner self sustains damage in the process, and each time this happens, their confidence levels achieve only a 99% recovery. Over a period of time the damage mounts until confidence is destroyed.

Capability procedures
Once an indiscretion has been identified, it is used as the basis for placing the individual on a competence procedure, also called capability procedure, performance procedure, or similar. Effectively, the person is on notice so that one further mistake and disciplinary proceedings are automatically invoked. Sometimes the procedures are implemented in the guise of "helping" the individual with their performance. In reality, it is a means of intimidation and control, as well as a device for facilitating the victim's ultimate demise.

Dual control

One job is split between two people such that neither party ever has a full picture of what is happening. Only the bully has the full picture, and can thus play one person off against the other.

This tactic works best where the two employees work at different locations such as split-site businesses or different branches, or are rarely present at the same time, for example travelling sales representatives.

The diversionary enemy

Bullies have a talent, often perfected through practice, for diverting attention away from themselves and their behaviour. When the victim appears to be close to realising the cause of their problems, an "enemy" is identified and the victim encouraged to enter into battle with this person, group of persons, or organisation. A particularly unpleasant manifestation of this tactic can be seen during or after dismissal proceedings, whereby the bully states "it's not my fault your union/counsellor/GP/solicitor didn't represent you adequately, you should sue them not me."

The nice-guy intermediary

In some situations bullies work through a nice guy to whom no-one will say no. Sometimes the intermediary is aware of the tactic but has little choice, given the abuse of power and threat to job security, and therefore spends much of the time walking a narrow tightrope. In other cases, the person may be unaware that they are being used, with the bully exploiting the person's naivety and instinctive congeniality to obtain information or spread disinformation.

Sickness monitoring procedure

Similar to the capability procedure, this one is instituted when the amount of sick leave reaches a certain level. By this stage, the victim is suffering severe psychiatric injury, but the threat is "take any more sick leave and you'll be subject to disciplinary proceedings and perhaps dismissal on ill-health grounds". The person being bullied is then in the position of coming to work when they are in no fit state to be at work. The downward spiral accelerates towards its inevitable conclusion.

A point to note here is that many victims of bullying, in keeping with their honest industrious nature, actually have some of the lowest sickness absence records in their organisation. "I've never had a day off sick in my life before this blew up" is a familiar phrase.

Legal action following dismissal on the grounds of ill-health where the cause of ill-health was the behaviour of the bully, perhaps sponsored by the employer, is a course of action that victims of bullying may increasingly seek to pursue.

The surprise meeting

The individual is called in for a "chat" in an hour's time (or less), only to find when they get there that this is a disciplinary hearing. Attempts to clarify the purpose of the meeting, obtain representation or have a colleague present are met with denial backed up by threats and intimidation. Variations on this theme all have the same characteristic - the meeting is not what you thought it was, and it's much more serious and formal than you are led to believe. All are designed to catch you off guard and unprepared. In this situation, document the deception in writing and insist on your right to representation.

Denial of representation

The bully claims, often in the form of implied threat, that you are not entitled to representation or have anyone present on your behalf at such-and-such a meeting, hearing, etc. Justifications may include "we don't recognise that union on this site" or "the meeting has been convened according to strict guidelines which do not permit you to be officially represented whilst such serious allegations are discussed" or "I would advise you against bringing anyone along as this could make the situation you are in a lot worse".

Denial of your right to representation could be seen as a form of harassment.

The best friend

This strategy involves pretending to be your best friend, with the bully perhaps divulging a lot of information, especially of a personal nature, about themselves in an effort to build trust quickly. In new relationships, it is the speed, and inappropriateness in terms of the intimacy of detail, which are the clues. To the unwary, the embrace of a new manager and willingness to build rapport may be interpreted as a portent of an impending profitable relationship. In fact, it is more likely to be a set-up, a means of extracting personal information which can later be used for the purpose of control. As such it is a falseness of friendship and a betrayal of trust. This latter aspect - betrayal of trust - is one of the most cruel, callous and hurtful aspects of bullying.

Suggested response: in new situations, particularly in the workplace, become practised at not revealing your intimate details and personal secrets until a respectable interval of time has elapsed. You have a right not to reveal personal details, and it might be wise to make asserting this right a habit. Watch for overfamiliarity in a timescale which is too short for trust and respect to have normally been built. The bully will probably reveal much about themselves - you may sense too much - after knowing each other for only a short time. If you have been caught out, there's little you can do except batten down the hatches, reveal nothing more at all about yourself, and prepare your assertive defences.

A variation of the "I'm your friend, you can trust me, tell me all about yourself" tactic is the "I'm your friend, you can trust me, tell me all about such-and-such a person" approach. Here, the bully plays on a caring person's desire to communicate, especially by talking and sharing, to extract information which with some interpolation and uncharacteristic creativity can be used for less salubrious purposes. The person thus becomes a go-between, trying to maintain loyalty to both parties, perhaps unaware that the information they are divulging puts them in the unwitting position of quisling.

The annual weed

A departmental manager institutes an annual or biannual (twice-yearly) "reorganisation", the stated purpose of which might be "efficiency", "re-engineering", "to better meet the needs of our customers", etc. The real reason for the reorganisation is to facilitate getting rid of anyone whose face doesn't fit. Staff are remarkably adept at seeing through this

deceit, and harmony, unity and team spirit are quickly
replaced by a climate of fear, suspicion and uncertainty.

The snitchers' charter

*"In order to get into her good books, [the department
manager] encouraged everybody to snitch on each other,
a process she facilitated by the introduction of 'peer
assessment'. I do not believe this woman was a fully
paid-up member of the human race."*

A bullying manager is despised by subordinates, and whilst
sensing this, is usually unable to discern why. Because people
are reluctant to communicate the reasons, a method has to be
introduced whereby the manager can find out what people
are really thinking.

One method of gleaning the required information is "peer
assessment", also known as "peer appraisal", or "peer
review". Its introduction is justified as being in line with
modern management techniques. In order to get into the
manager's good books, everyone is invited (compelled) to
assess (snitch on) each other. Those who provide the reports
(tales) closest to what the manager wants to hear attain
favourable status. Those who don't find their lives made
increasingly difficult, and, surprise, surprise, when
restructuring (redundancy) becomes necessary, guess which
members of staff appear at the top of the list?

Suggested response: if the manager's policy is endorsed by
management and backed up by personnel, there's very little
you can do except leave. Publicity through your union will
make everyone aware of the behaviour and subsequent public
outcry might institute change.

The promotion trap

This method of entrapment is designed to impose total
control and domination of an individual and works whether
or not the individual is resisting, either deliberately or
unwittingly.

The member of staff is offered a promotion, either in
grade, allowance, bonus or other remuneration, in return for
accepting "one or two" extra responsibilities. Some specific
tasks may be clearly identified, and the individual gains the
impression that this is all that is required. Sometimes the

additional duties do not appear until after acceptance. Few people can resist accepting promotion, especially if the benefits are glowingly portrayed, and the extra commitment appears small, as in natural progression. The person may already be performing at a level beyond their current grade. There may be an implied threat, such as "if your career is going anywhere, you'd better accept it" or more subtly "it's unlikely there'll be another opportunity like this in the foreseeable future". And, of course, the extra money is always welcome, especially in times of uncertainty.

Once the promotion is accepted, and all the paperwork is signed and sealed, the trap is sprung. The individual is now under the total control of the bully. After a brief honeymoon, the victim feels more and more obliged to "prove" himself; he has to jump when told to, and must dance to any tune the bully plays. He quickly realises that the new position is not all it was cracked up to be, with the aforementioned promises and assurances assuming a distinctly ethereal quality.

Overwork and claims of underperformance backed up by threat and guilt combine to subjugate with breathtaking effectiveness. It is now that the lack of specifics in relation to the content of the new position become evident. Paperwork is scoured but the words which sounded fine at the time now provide little succour. It becomes apparent that those fine-sounding phrases derived their timbre not from integrity but from hollowness.

Suggested response: write down, as clearly, factually and specifically as you can, the duties and responsibilities of the position as you understood them at the time of accepting the promotion. Now ask your manager for a clear statement of the duties, responsibilities and expectations as he sees them. Ensure that everything is specified in measurable terms. Every vagueness is both a let-out clause and a handle which the bully can exert control. Under the provisions of the Employment Protection (Consolidation) Act 1978, an employer is obliged to provide written particulars of employment, including alterations thereto. Section 131 of the Act also covers breach of contract.

It is likely that during this exercise you will realise that the manager himself doesn't know what the new position entails - in so doing, you will have discovered the true purpose (that is, intent) of the promotion.

The one-sided argument

The bully assertively and aggressively highlights all the mistakes, errors and alleged failings of the victim, giving the person little or no chance to reply or respond. A picture is painted for onlookers, witnesses, and, importantly, authorities (for example senior managers, personnel) which is as convincing as it is damning. This person is a liability to themselves, their colleagues, and the employer. Such opportunities as are offered for the victim to explain are engineered such that what is said tends to confirm and add to the picture.

Suggested response: draw attention to the bully's behaviour in the past and pinpoint that as the reason for the present situation. Use repetition; dig your heels in, do not be overruled by the bully's bluster and refusal to let you get a word in edgeways (except when it suits the bully). Reveal this tactic; highlight the behaviour of the bully at this moment and ask why he needs to use this strategy.

The multi-bully scenario

When a report of bullying is laid against a manager there will always be an element of doubt in observers, no matter how convincing the bully's behaviour or the victim's articulation. But what if the bully can prove "conclusively" that it is the other person who is at fault, and not themselves?

The manager, in an apparent act of conciliation and kindness, suggests that the person concerned now report to a different line manager. The words "clash of personality" delicately circumvent apportionment of blame. What the victim may not realise is that their new manager is working in collusion with their present manager, and that they are being passed round like a toy to be played with, teased, tormented, trapped with no room for manoeuvre or escape.

After a respectable interval to allow memories of complaint and grievance to fade, the bullying resumes, this time by the new oppressor. Before long, the victim has to make a fresh complaint. It is at this point that the trap is sprung. "You made a previous complaint when you worked for so-and-so, now you're making the same complaint working

for me. How many managers are you going to accuse before
you accept that the cause of your problems with line
management is within you?"

The effectiveness is increased with the number of bullies
working together. Coming across one bully is unlikely (or
unfortunate, depending on your level of doubt), two in
succession is most unlikely, and three in a row - nobody would
ever believe that! The victim is trapped, completely helpless,
and with no-one to turn to.

Suggested response: in the absence of a company-wide
anti-bullying policy, the best solution is probably to leave. If
you plan to pursue a case of constructive dismissal, make
sure you have as much documentary evidence as possible,
take legal advice, and when you resign, make it absolutely
clear in writing that it is the actions of your line management
which have made your situation intolerable.

The random victim
In most cases of bullying, one victim is selected and then
subjected to the full treatment of control, subjugation, then
elimination; in a few cases, however, the bully has a group of
victims and picks on individuals on a random basis, so that
no-one knows whose turn it is next.

The bully maintains rigorous control through constant
fear and uncertainty; no victim is going to take action which
will immediately precipitate their turn.

Excommunication in absentia
Whilst the victim is off the premises, perhaps on a training
course, annual leave, or most likely sick leave because of
their experience, the bully (or cohorts) clears the victim's
desk and moves their belongings (including personal items)
to a storage area or disadvantageous position such as a
cupboard or poky uncomfortable office some way away,
sometimes in another building.

The rapid demise
In this tactic the victim must be eliminated as quickly as
possible, the speed of dismissal precluding defensive or
retaliatory action.

The rapid demise occurs mainly in cases where the victim
has twigged what is happening and decided to fight back.

Through fear of revelation - which itself can be seen as a tacit admission of wrongdoing - the bully is compelled to end the relationship as swiftly and with as little opportunity for comeback as possible.

Some people have found that from the moment they resolve to stand up for themselves to being unemployed has all come to pass within a fortnight. A state of shock inevitably ensues.

The choice of execution
Throughout the bullying process the bully diligently maintains the upper hand (control) at all times. Sooner or later the person being bullied will begin to realise what is happening to them, and doubt begins to challenge the bully's encouragement to believe that "this is all my own fault". Sensing this rising awareness, the bully now plans how to neutralise and eliminate the offending individual. A meeting is convened and the bully, often having garnered the support of management, personnel or other authority, offers their victim an apparent olive branch to "help effect a resolution". This takes the form of a choice from a number of options.

In some cases, there is no meeting, and the action is effected by telephone, letter, email, or even through a third party. Given the serious nature of what is happening, the words "devious" and "deception" may be appropriate. In avoiding face-to-face contact in this manner, the bully is revealing both fear and reluctance to accept responsibility for the actions they are currently pursuing.

It is made clear, sometimes with implied threat, that the options offered are the only options available. Typically, they include resignation, redundancy, early retirement, ill-health retirement, or dismissal.

The trick here is that the victim is led to believe that these represent the full range of alternatives available, and that they have a free hand in choosing which is "best for them". Having desperately been seeking a resolution to their circumstances, this can seem at first sight like a relief to be savoured, a straw to be clutched, even a much prayed-for godsend. This is the intention. Closer inspection reveals that all the options are in the interests of the bully, but none are in the medium- or long-term interests of the victim.

What is really happening is that the bully is not only covering his own back, but ensuring that if necessary his action can be vigorously and successfully defended later. In granting ostensibly "free" choice from this list of options, the victim is unwittingly selecting for themselves their preferred method of execution. Later, when all is settled, the bully can retort that "you were given a free hand to choose your preferred option and are alone responsible for the consequences of that choice". The bully thereby absolves himself from the consequences of his behaviour, whilst simultaneously dissociating himself from any responsibility in the proceedings. By portraying the victim's choice as solely their own, the bully can then claim the moral high ground if the decision is subsequently questioned or challenged.

Suggested response: although hard to counter, forewarned is forearmed. When this ploy is exercised, the victim needs to add further options to the list and ensure they are discussed. This is your chance to address the cause of the present situation, that is, the bully's behaviour. The bully will resist vigorously, probably claiming that your options are not options at all. Whether you are successful in getting the real issue addressed or not, you will have seized one of a number of opportunities during the bullying process to take control of your situation and turn it to your advantage.

Dig your heels in and ensure *your* options are added to the agenda and discussed openly and fully. It is likely that the bully, and supporters, will refuse to countenance any suggestion of moral impropriety, either in limiting the range of choices available, or in the behaviours you are elucidating. You may wish to have an independent witness present at these proceedings. It is vital that the discussion and outcome, positive or not, are recorded, in writing. A statement of the form "[X] was advised of the [real reasons] for [this situation] but chose to refuse to discuss them" (or words to that effect) may be appropriate. If you go to tribunal later, this could be an important piece of evidence in support of your case.

The diversionary dismissal

In order to justify an employer's action (for example dismissal) against an individual where there are few, inadequate or no grounds for that action, prodigious - and sometimes bizarre - efforts are expended to support and vindicate the decision. This usually takes the form of finding a mistake, or series of mistakes, invariably trivial and insignificant, that the person has made at some time during their career in the company (or in their private life or even before they joined the company) and using this as the basis of substantiation.

This is a diversionary tactic, distracting attention away from the real cause of this situation, which is the bully's behaviour and possibly the fact that management has closed ranks behind the bully. It also has the added advantage of spreading confusion. The victim is put on the spot and feels obliged to justify, explain, excuse or apologise for the indiscretion. The genesis of the urge to explain is guilt. You have a right not to feel guilty, or you have a right not to be made to feel guilty. This is an opportunity to assert that right.

There are other benefits to using this tactic. In a hearing, especially a tribunal, the panel members will become bored with the long, rambling, confusing and largely irrelevant dialogue which degenerates into claim, counter-claim, justification, counter-justification, etc ad nauseum. Panel members quickly tire, confusion stimulates irritation and boredom, and the focus is lost. By default, the panel's decision will go to the employer.

Also, the more explanation, justification, excuse and apology that can be elicited, the more ammunition the aggressor obtains with which to further crucify their victim. When the dialogue is exhausted (it may last several hours or even several days), the aggressor is able to summarise by painting a most uncomplimentary picture of the victim using their own words.

Suggested response: first, if a mistake was made, admit the error succinctly, without justification, elaboration, excuse or apology. Make the admission only once.

"You are correct, a mistake did occur. Thank you for bringing it to everyone's attention".

In so doing, you pull the rug from under the aggressor's feet, denying them the opportunity for in-depth analysis. If the incident was a long time ago, add (replace the words in square brackets as appropriate):

> *"As you know, this took place [xx months / years] ago and in choosing to focus on an incident from so long ago, you reveal a desperation which itself is a tacit admission of the inappropriateness of your action."*

Then, without pausing, draw attention to the obsessive and singular focus that the other side have chosen to adopt, its purpose as a diversionary and confusion-generating tactic, its irrelevance both to the performance of the individual in question and to the circumstances surrounding the action.

If appropriate, you can also take this opportunity to go on the offensive - many bullies have careers littered with mistakes and failings; for example:

> *"In highlighting this trivial and unimportant incident, you are choosing to draw attention to the number of mistakes, errors, omissions, oversights [etc - you can go to town on this] which [the bully] has made over the last [number of] years. These include [a long prepared list - be as specific as possible] which call into question [the bully's] competence to carry out the duties and responsibilities of [position] and further cause everyone present to ask how such performance contributes towards achieving the aims and objectives of [the organisation]."*

Each time you are attacked, remind everyone - publicly - that:

> *""We are here to examine the behaviour of [the bully] and your repeated attempts to divert us from that objective by focusing on a trivial and irrelevant [fact or allegation] only serve to highlight your lack of evidence in support of the course of action you have chosen to take".*

If the other side persists in pressing this angle of attack, repeat the defence again and again - as often as necessary. After each third or fourth time, draw attention to the persistence:

"I have drawn attention [number] times to the fact that you are choosing to focus on an incident which is of no relevance [and whose existence is not in question]. I regret that you choose repeatedly to waste [the tribunal's] time pursuing this line of scrutiny. In so doing, however, you are admitting that you have no real evidence to present, otherwise you would be presenting it. Our reason for being here today is to examine the behaviour of [the bully] and I ask you to remain focused on that objective."

Alternatively, or additionally, the following statement could provide a suitable defence:

"As justification for [action] on the grounds of "[alleged reasons]", the [management] have chosen to focus singularly and obsessively on [mistake] of [how long ago], the relevance of which today cannot be ascertained by any sane intelligent individual and for which a full explanation was provided [on date], accepted by you, [and kept on record].

In bringing [the employer] into disrepute in such a public manner, you have raised serious doubts about the fitness, integrity and competence of [senior management and personnel] of a [status eg prestigious] [company] which is a major player in [market].

By your actions you have demonstrated precisely those behaviours of which you stand accused. One must now ask how such behaviour, and the extraordinary lengths now being pursued to justify such behaviour, contribute to the aims and objectives of [company].

The relentless persecution of a hard-working [and by your own assessment - quote here from employee personnel record] employee who has sought throughout solely to perform their duties in support of the company's objectives warrants investigation at the highest level in the interests of shareholders, taxpayers, [other stakeholders] and ultimately justice."

Vary the wording according to circumstances. You are advised to have representation, either legal, union, professional or other independent person. If you feel your statements could be considered libellous (written) or slanderous (verbal), you _must_ seek legal advice first.

It is important that in all conflicts you focus solely on the _behaviours_ of the person or persons involved (eg "_you have behaved foolishly_"), and not on their _person_ ("_you are foolish_"). The chances of being accused of libel or slander are reduced, and this approach gives the other side little or nothing to turn against you. The style is more assertive and you are likely to be regarded as a person with a high or higher degree of maturity.

In summary
One wonders why people need to resort to the lengths described in this chapter. What is going through their mind when they behave in this way? What are their objectives? What are they trying to achieve with their behaviour? How do these behaviours contribute to the aims and objectives of the company or organisation? How do these tactics bring out the best in staff? How do they contribute to the smooth and effective running of the company? How much income will the company earn as a result of the behaviour of the bullies and their backers and supporters, particularly in the pursuit of victimisation, persecution, and dismissal proceedings?

These are the questions to bear in mind as you learn to perceive the intent behind the content of the bully's behaviour.

7   The victim

"All I want is for it to stop so that I can get on with my job."

As outlined in the introduction, I have chosen to use the word "victim". Whilst some might argue that this confers a humbled status which, by implication, is permanent, my own research indicates it is a transient state resulting from lack of knowledge of how to handle any given situation.

Whilst no-one can change the past, if you have suffered at the hands of a bully you will have been a "victim" for the duration of the encounter. But experience toughens, enlightenment empowers, insight nourishes and learning confers; with the knowledge contained in this and similar books, the experience can be viewed more as an inoculation rather than an invasion. Once bitten, twice immunized - especially when you understand what bit you and why.

Criteria for selection

"I'm too good"

"I sometimes wish I could do a bad job like the others so that I wouldn't be picked on. Unfortunately it's not in my nature to behave like that."

"I thought it was only in my company that enthusiasm was regarded as a negative trait."

There are many reasons why a person is selected for being bullied, but the two principal criteria, which stand out head and shoulders above the rest are:

- **being good at your job, often excelling**: in a decade when greed and self-interest have become the dominant virtues, any flower of excellence has to be lopped so as not to show up others less able; unbelievably, some bullies even quote the tall poppy syndrome as justification for keeping good people down
- **being popular with people**, colleagues, customers, clients, pupils, parents, patients, etc

Other primary reasons include:

- standing up for a colleague who is being or has been bullied

- blowing the whistle on malpractice, illegality, fraud, breaches of codes of conduct, flouting of health and safety regulations, etc
- resistance to subjugation - the bully senses that this person cannot be completely controlled so he must therefore work harder and harder to subjugate the insubordinate individual - if necessary to destruction
- being able to see through any hint of front, falseness, facade, etc

Subsidiary reasons:

- being too expensive - teachers in their 40s and 50s are a favourite target. Because of intolerable budget pressures, many head teachers are reduced to getting rid of older staff who are at the high end of the pay scale and replacing them with fresh-faced graduates who are cheap, easily moulded and unlikely to question authority. Some employees find that at a certain level, usually the lower echelons of senior management, they are unable to take advantage of a redundancy package (eg as part of a downsizing operation) because their age and length of service make them too expensive to get rid of - but too expensive to keep. If an employee can bullied out of their job instead, there are obvious cost savings all round - to the employer at least.
- union duties, especially as representative, shop steward or convener; desire or decision to become a union representative
- being highly qualified, especially when the bully lacks appropriate qualification, or perhaps has none at all
- being highly experienced, especially when the bully has little or no relevant experience
- being successful, talented, gifted, multi-skilled, creative, imaginative, enthusiastic, etc
- winning an award or being recognised in any official, prominent or public manner
- being recognised as a master, expert or guru, especially in the same occupation or profession as the bully
- being perceived as clever or too clever
- being tenacious, resourceful, persistent, determined, etc
- displaying courage, steadfastness, incorruptibility

- exhibiting competence, especially where this highlights, contrasts with, exposes or threatens to expose the bully's incompetence
- having high moral standards which you are unwilling to compromise
- pointing out, however tactfully, a mistake by the bully
- unwillingness to downgrade product quality or levels of service to customers or clients or accept poorer working conditions as part of "rationalisation", especially when such demands are seen as ill-considered and selfish
- daring to disagree with the bully, fighting your corner
- being willing to challenge changes, especially those which are seen as expedient, ill-conceived, short-termist, poorly thought through, or which will have a detrimental effect on staff and staff morale
- standing up for the workforce, especially in the face of restructuring or redundancies
- unwillingness to accept increased workloads imposed for reasons of selfishness, politics, short-term thinking or which are detrimental to customers and clients
- inability to fight back - bullies are cowards at heart and will instinctively pick on those they believe are least able to defend themselves. Reasons for defencelessness include low assertiveness, unwillingness to enter into conflict, naivety, being too trusting or honest, inexperience or dislike of office politics, proneness to feeling guilty, instinctive deference, etc
- convenience - even strong-willed people with good assertiveness skills sometimes find themselves the target of unwelcome attention, although typically they will exhibit the two principal selection criteria above
- any form of vulnerability, eg single parent, living alone, carer, dependency of any kind
- attractiveness, handsomeness etc according to the current yardsticks by which these qualities are defined (this criterion appears more often in cases of female on female, where the bully believes herself to be plain or unattractive, but sees her victim as having the qualities of attractiveness which life has denied her)
- having a different sexual orientation to the bully

- illness, disability or impairment eg epilepsy, deafness, dyslexia, stammer, squint, twitch, etc

- looking different in any way, eg disfigurement, eczema, psoriasis, vitiligo, port-wine stains, etc

- being different in any way - this can be a major difference eg race, creed, colour, culture, religion, etc, or

- a "minor" difference, eg accent, colour of hair, dress, size, weight, left-handedness, etc (these have all been reported as targets for criticism in bullying situations)

Towards the end of this list, the reasons merge with other types of discrimination. This could be significant in that bullying behaviours seem to be present behind most forms of harassment, discrimination, abuse, conflict, prejudice and acts of violence. It's as if when there is a focus for the perceived threat, acts of prejudice and discrimination result; when there is no focus, bullying results.

In the workplace, bullying is often seen as a male preserve, with females the hapless victims. However, this perception is more likely to be based on the spread of gender throughout management; statistics show that currently 88% of managers and 97% or directors are male. Females occupy the larger number of positions where the "real work" is done.

Bullying is not a gender issue. Where women make it to positions of management and power, they too can bully, with equal ruthlessness. Size has nothing to do with performance either, as burly males can be bullied by diminutive superiors just as easily as the other way round. Nor age, as many long-serving loyal and experienced employees find when a fresh-faced graduate less half their age is suddenly and unexpectedly appointed to manage their department. However, whilst young and old alike find themselves the subject of unwanted attention, it is likely that statistics would show a bias towards the mature end of the age scale due to the expensive nature of experienced employees.

Nor is bullying class-dependent - bullies and victims come from all walks of life. Nor is it a cultural phenomenon; it seems that the capacity to bully, and to be bullied, is inherent in all the major races of the planet.

Resistance to subjugation

The unwillingness to be controlled seems to emanate from a rebellious streak which is closely allied to the sense of injustice. Bullying seems to stimulate both of these.

Rather than a rejection of authority and law and order, the instinct stems from an innate distrust and distaste for the use and imposition of authority by persons unfit or unqualified to be in a position to assert that authority. Dissidents have always been despised by tyrannical regimes.

In other words, it is a rejection of authoritarianism rather than authority itself; a good example of this occurs at the end of Steven Spielberg's classic film, where ET, trapped and dying in Elliot's house, is surrounded by an army of representatives of government agencies whose precise affiliation is not defined. The young hero, Elliot, effects an escape such that ET can be reunited with his kin; in the process an army of well-funded and well-armed government agents demonstrate their incompetence by being outwitted at every turn by a group of kids on bikes.

It would seem that dissidents draw on this sense of injustice to sustain their belief in what is intuitively "right", enabling them to endure the appalling hardships and torture of imprisonment often under intolerable circumstances. Names like Solzhenitsyn and Mandela spring to mind, although there are probably millions of lesser known individuals throughout history whose experiences have been equally harrowing, if less well publicised. This defiance of oppression may be one of the ways the human race not only survives but progresses.

What to watch out for

If you're being bullied, keep a journal of everything that happens, no matter how trivial. Over a period of time, the incidents displayed together show a different, but consistent, pattern of behaviour. The bully, when challenged on any individual incident, is likely to play on the trivial nature of an interaction; by itself, it is. The bully can make it appear to the world that you are making a fuss over nothing. When you have a detailed diary showing all the "trivial" incidents side by side, you are on safer ground. This pattern is one of the key defining features of bullying, and which the bully will have difficulty dismissing.

Behaviours exhibited on a regular basis to watch out for include (in addition to those listed in chapter 3):

- any behaviour inconsistent with making you feel valued and worthwhile
- any unwillingness or refusal to substantiate criticism or actions which you believe to be to your detriment
- unwillingness to be specific
- blame, especially when undeserved
- patronising tone or attitude
- use of guilt
- perceived favouritism to colleagues, peers, superiors or subordinates
- any communication by the bully with staff for whom you are responsible, where you are kept in the dark, or only partially informed
- praise which is undeserved or does not relate directly to your achievements
- notes, letters, memos, minutes, copies of slides advocating policies on the importance of staff that which are at odds with behaviours exhibited
- when addressing criticisms or grievance, a need to move the conversation on all the time, ie away from what you want to talk about - a feeling that you end up never having a sensible discussion
- behaviour inconsistent with expressed intent

Thoughts of revenge are strong, but overwhelmingly, victims just want it to stop, they want to be left alone to get on with their job and their life. They also want to feel valued, supported and that their contribution in the workplace is worthwhile. Positive feedback, gratitude and testimonials from clients, customers or charges help, but the bully's insistent pressure induces doubt and the enriching effect of tributes is diminished if the management climate is hostile, threatening or indifferent.

Why and how do people put up with it?

Until recently, awareness of the phenomenon of workplace bullying, as well as the means by which it is carried out, was very low. Even today, many people still know little or nothing of what goes on behind closed office doors. The prevalence of workplace bullying seems to indicate a worsening trend, and it may be that everyone in the workplace is now at risk of having "an experience".

Most bullying is insidious in that it is carried out at the psychological level. If you were physically assaulted, you would be in no doubt that an attack had taken place. But in bullying, it may be months, perhaps a year or more, before you begin to realise that the difficulty you are experiencing with a particular individual, or group of individuals, goes beyond what can be reasonably expected in your place of work.

The main reasons that people put up with bullying for so long include:

- not recognising what is happening to you, and that it is bullying you are experiencing; many people report that it "crept up on them, and when they did realise, it was too late
- being unaware, unprepared through never having had an experience like it
- professionalism - people (especially those who are good at their job) take pride in their work, and strive ceaselessly to "correct" the alleged "criticisms"
- appeals to "professionalism" which in reality is the use of guilt to dominate and control
- ditto claims that "you are not acting professionally" etc
- inability or unwillingness to override and overrule the "assessments" and criticisms of others, especially of a manager in a more senior position who has control over your job and career
- demanding too high standards of oneself
- immersing yourself in your work, keeping your head down, hoping it will go away
- desire to help and care for those in one's charge (eg patients)
- urge to protect and prevent harm coming to those for whom you are responsible (eg pupils)
- belief that survival and prosperity depend on the excellence of service that one delivers to customers
- putting a brave face on it

- rationalism - the bully is just a difficult person, one of many you meet in life
- fear through intimidation, threat, guilt, etc
- fear (with justification) that if the behaviour is reported, the victim will be labelled as a troublemaker
- fear (with justification) that if the behaviour is reported, the victim will be ousted in some way
- fear (with justification) that if reported, the victim will not be believed (disbelief and denial), then the bullying will get worse
- fear (with justification) that if reported, the employer will, when faced with two opposing stories and no witnesses, take the side of the senior employee
- hesitancy and dislike of finding fault in others
- unwillingness to complain about another person, to "get them into trouble", to "grass"
- not wanting to "make a fuss"
- preference for a stable, hassle-free existence
- not wanting the hassle of pursuing formal complaint/ disciplinary proceedings/tribunal/court action
- denial that it is happening
- denial of the symptoms of stress
- being unaware of or unable to identify the cause of stress
- preference for getting on with the job rather than playing and becoming embroiled in office politics
- determination not to let the bully think they have succeeded in getting to them
- belief and hope (and prayer) that the bully will move on soon
- loyalty and commitment to one's employer or place of employment
- unwillingness to work for a competitor
- unwillingness to walk away from a business and project you have played a major part in
- the support of colleagues
- financial dependency, especially if the primary or only wage earner in the family, or if the partner's job (and income) is also under threat
- inability or unwillingness to leave, especially if this requires a move out of the area, which may involve

children changing school, selling house, moving to unfamiliar part of the country, etc
- inability to move house due to financial difficulties, negative equity, debt, etc
- difficulty in getting another job, especially of the same status, remuneration or prospects
- age - the older you are, the harder it is to get any job, especially one in the same line of business and with the same remuneration
- specialism - there may be few, if any, other jobs in your field
- the belief by the person being bullied that it is "their fault", their "problem", and therefore their "fate in life" - shame, embarrassment and guilt are cultivated by the bully to increase control
- believing that you really are "to blame"
- putting other people's needs ahead of one's own
- lack of verbal and quick-thinking skills in face-to-face situations with the bully
- fear that if you do move, it may happen again - or the bully may follow you (this does happen)
- refusal to be "a victim"
- not wishing to appear to be a "failure"
- not wishing to appear cowardly in running away from the situation
- well-intentioned but misguided exhortations from colleagues, family and friends that "you've got to go in there and see it through"
- the "macho male mentality" - if you can't hack it, you're a wimp
- feeling that "I should be able to handle this by myself" or "I can handle this myself" (note - you cannot)
- feeling that "I should stay and fight it"
- naively believing that you are dealing with people who are as honest and trustworthy as yourself
- taboos and ignorance which discourage open discussion about being bullied as an adult
- taboos and ignorance which surround "mental health problems" even though they are a result of the injuries sustained through being bullied

- inability (by everyone, including most of society) to recognise the injuries caused by bullying, plus the often justified fear that this episode will
    - -> be recorded as "mental illness" or "evidence of mental instability" on health and employment records
    - -> affect future applications for life assurance, mortgage, other forms of insurance, credit, etc
- the fear and worry surrounding the right and ability to contribute to pension plans should employment be ended
- loss of confidence and esteem, leading to the belief that you really do lack competence etc
- shattered self-confidence and self-esteem, plus all the other symptoms described in chapter 8
- the mood swings of the bully which include the occasional pleasantness to which the victim warms and sighs with relief
- the forgiving chord - on random occasions, the bully shows apparent concern, the stress lifts and the victim believes positive progress is being made (it isn't - the bully is covering his back)
- the capacity to forgive - every now and again the pressure is relieved (eg bully's extended vacation, assignment, off-site duty, training course or sick leave). The mind pretends it hasn't happened, and attempts a "fresh start". People who are prone to being bullied tend also to be too forgiving and optimistic.

Why me?

Whenever a person suffers a disaster, catastrophe, tragedy or major loss, the inevitable question is "why me?". This question, which can become a quest, is part of the process of coming to terms with the experience. It is essential to gain as full an understanding of the reasons why it happened so that one can move forward and out of the "victim" posture.

The selection criteria above highlight the principal reasons why a person is bullied, and it may be some comfort to know that anybody - rather than you personally - will be selected if they are in that place at that time. This is evidenced by the fact that frequently predecessors have suffered the same fate, as will successors.

People who are bullied are often strongly empathic, and

the need to feel valued and worthwhile is deeply ingrained. Consistency and high standards of behaviour are also exhibited and expected. A lack of awareness of the role of naivety also contributes, as does instinctive deference and an overactive sense of guilt.

Victims of bullying lack the thick skin of the bully; this gives rise to a sensitivity which is often referred to in a critical manner. Without this defence, a person is more easily hurt, and therefore has a greater need to learn defensive strategies, including assertiveness skills. It is unfortunate that this not in the national curriculum.

Profile of the bullied person
By studying the behaviour styles of people who are bullied, a consistent profile emerges. These are shown, with the variations most commonly noted, in the table below.

Summary
Of the many unfortunate and unpleasant after-effects of bullying, one that people report most often is that they find themselves unable to trust others, even those close to them. This is hardly surprising given that bullying is a betrayal of trust. When trust is broken, it takes long time to rebuild; this is a normal reaction.

A further fear surfaces, which is currently often justified. A person who has lost their job through being bullied out of it finds, due to a combination of psychiatric injury, absence from work for perhaps a year or more, lack of suitable reference, etc, that they are now virtually unemployable.

The lack of reference is often crucial in disbarring an individual from future employment, the more so the older the employee. It's hardly surprising the bully acts this way - apart from the satisfaction of denying a testimonial, if the bully provides a deliberately bad reference, this may be detected as being at variance with the employee's record and thus unfortunately betray the bully's hand. However, if the bully provides a good reference, it may be seen as contradicting everything the bully has said as justification for getting rid of their victim.

Attempts to regain employment are often dashed when the prospective employer contacts the previous employer, with or without permission, and whether or not references

The bullied person: general qualities	Variations	
	Introvert type	Extrovert type

kind, caring, sharing
empathic
sensitive
honest, trustworthy
conscientious, reliable
always thinks of others
good with people
people-focused
customer focused
good rapport
helpful, constructive
popular
good organiser
commitment to service
giver
willing to help
willing to please
obliging
long-term thinker
multi-focus (handles
  several tasks at once)
likes to feel valued
likes to do a good job
converses easily
sociable
good-humoured
follower
selfless
tolerant
artistic, creative
innovative, imaginative
full of ideas
intuitive
sense of injustice
strong sense of
  conscience
charitable
conciliatory
modest
forgiving
	quiet, silent
	pensive
	studious
	unobtrusive
	excellent memory
	eye for detail
	meticulous
	strongly analytical
	learned
	shrewd
	prefers arbitration
	  to conflict
	observant
		outgoing
		gregarious
		sociable
		tends to lead the
		  conversation
		very strong
		  sense of
		  injustice
		humorous
		inspirational
		builds group
		  rapport easily

Table 8: Qualities of the bullied person

The bullied person: tendencies	Variations	
	Introvert type	Extrovert type

low assertiveness
indecisive
can't make quick
  decision
often seeks and needs
  approval
needs to feel valued
prone to feeling guilty
naive
over-dependent
deferential
digressive
meek
perceived as wimpish
timid
tearful when hurt
easily persuaded
instinct to self-deprecate
gives long answers to
  short questions
considered
puts others' needs first
  too often
always seeking to
  explain
instinct to share and
  reveal
	needs 100% of
	  facts to make a
	  decision
	shy
	can be perceived
	  as dull, grey
	taciturn
	withdrawn
	perfectionist
		martyr
		exhibits high
		  dependency
		highly prone to
		  feeling guilty
		talkative and
		  digressive
		needs to feel
		  recognised
		tendency to be
		  disorganised
		sometimes
		  perceived as
		  "scatterbrained"

Table 9: Tendencies of the bullied person

are from that employer. The vindictiveness of bullies is such that even having got rid of their victim, they are often unable to resist one last opportunity to behave badly towards that person again.

Occasionally, a prospective employer seems to know of the applicant's alleged failings in advance of a job interview, and in many cases, there is a distinct but unprovable feeling of communication having taken place in the background.

One of the many ironies, given the principal selection criteria and behaviour style, is that victims of bullying actually make excellent employees.

8 Symptoms and effects

"After more than a decade of bullying which subtly but steadily increased in intensity, it got to the point where I didn't care whether I was alive or dead."

The effects of bullying on the psyche of the victim are as yet not well understood. This chapter is a summary of the symptoms most often described. With record numbers of people visiting their GP to report symptoms of stress, further research and study is urgently required.

The individual

Bereft of knowledge or insight into what is happening, and without outside help, the victim becomes trapped in a cycle of constantly trying to do better, doggedly determined to work their way out of their predicament. Performance is continually criticised using a variety of techniques, and every attempt to do better is met with further criticism. Nothing breeds criticism like success, the saying goes, and success and achievement are precisely those attributes which fuel the bully's insecurity. The greater the degree of success perceived or achieved, the more insecure the bully feels. The greater the insecurity, the worse the bully's behaviour becomes. This spiral continues until either the bully or the target leaves. Alternatively, and more likely, the relationship comes to an abrupt and sometimes catastrophic end. Because the bully has such a thick skin, is usually in a position of power or has access to power, and is frequently supported by management, it is invariably the victim who comes off worst.

Whilst the relationship appears normal to the outside world, and with the target often going to enormous lengths to maintain this false air of normality, to the alert observer, the clues become increasingly obvious. Irritability, increasing sense of isolation, impoverished interpersonal skills, frequent minor illnesses, withdrawal, and a growing sense of anger all indicate a seething internal cauldron of fear, confusion and resentment, a human pressure cooker now operating outside its design specification and beyond safe operating limits.

Ultimately the bully's behaviour becomes overtly hostile, whilst the victim struggles to make sense of what is happening. Trapped by a job they love but a position they hate, constantly worried by the threat of job loss, financially dependent on their income and loyal to the needs of customer, clients and family, the stress increases inexorably. The victim becomes more and more introverted, unable to deduce what is wrong with them.

Stress builds, and the symptoms of stress begin to appear. Slowly at first, but increasing in intensity and bizarreness. Unfortunately, as this happens gradually, the sufferer first ignores the symptoms, then rationalises and excuses. Without prior knowledge or experience, by the time realisation dawns that something is seriously wrong, they have been psychologically bludgeoned black and blue by the remorseless onslaught.

"All I ever wanted to do was to go to work, do my job, and come home again."

If people were physically assaulted as often and to the same degree as they are psychologically and emotionally abused, the perpetrator would end up in court charged with a serious offence, with the likelihood of imprisonment for the pain they have inflicted. However one can currently abuse one's position of power to render a subordinate psychologically senseless with the probable expectation of being promoted.

Stress is an inevitable consequence of bullying, and the type of stress that appears is negative. Not the positive stress that adds urgency to life, that can be harnessed to boost performance, but a negative, almost cancerous condition which eats away at self-worth, self-image, self-esteem and self-confidence. Stress-awareness training and stress-management exercises cannot exploit, alleviate or cure the damage being done to the victim's mind and body. Exhortations to turn the stress to positive advantage to enhance performance actually worsen the situation, increasing stress levels still further. An employer's insistence on attending a stress-management course (or its cheaper alternative, stress "awareness") are interpreted as insulting, especially if it is the bully who is insisting. Likewise, stress counselling does little but prolong the agony. Also, relaxation

Physical symptoms of stress from bullying
• aching joints, with no apparent or specific cause
• aching muscles, ditto
• odd pains, joint pains, muscle pains, chest pains, ditto
• backache
• excessive, constant tiredness, listlessness, exhaustion, fatigue
• headaches, migraine, especially if regular, eg at weekends or on specific days
• loss of strength and stamina
• palpitations, breathlessness
• sweating, with or without exercise
• loss of appetite, indigestion, disturbed eating patterns
• disturbed sleeping patterns, inability to sleep or get to sleep, nightmares, constant flashbacks or replays
• waking up more tired than when you went to bed
• frequent, incessant, never-ending coughs, colds, flu and other minor infections, especially regularly, eg weekends
• conjunctivitis, tired and sore eyes
• poor skin quality, skin irritations, eg athlete's foot, eczema, psoriasis, rash, urticaria, shingles
• excessive or compulsive picking, scratching, biting (eg nails), grinding (eg teeth)
• loss of sex drive and libido
• dulled senses, especially touch, taste and smell
• anaesthesia, numbness, pins & needles, eg in hands, feet, lips
• poor circulation, cold extremities eg fingers
• abnormal thirst
• intolerance of certain foodstuffs, eg sugar
• unsettled stomach, from butterflies and trembliness to being sick
• unusual allergies
• irritable bowel syndrome
• thyroid malfunction
• asthma
• anaemia
• flatulence
• unusual hormonal changes
• intense dislike of cold
• vertigo
• sinusitis
• angina, heart attack

Table 10: Frequently reported physical symptoms

techniques and other holistic remedies will make little difference other than bring some short-term relief. There is only one solution to this type of stress, and that is to ***identify and eliminate the cause***. With bullying, this is the ***only*** course of action that will yield results. Once out of the bullying situation, techniques for dealing with stress can then be used successfully.

> *"In the days and weeks prior to my breakdown, I remember a strange feeling which I can only liken to being shrink-wrapped in a restrictive rubber membrane which enveloped my body and steadily got tighter and tighter. With hindsight, I am amazed at how long I survived in that robotic and zombie-like state of non-being; it's little wonder that the subsequent serious symptoms of reactive depression lasted for over a year. The lesser symptoms are still with me three years on."*

Stress produces an almost infinite variety of symptoms and sufferers will recognise many from the tables, in which the effects are differentiated into physical, psychological, behavioural, and those which affect personality.

Symptoms

The complete list of stress-induced symptoms is much longer than revealed here and includes strange effects and disorders which are either not, or only partly, attributable to other causes. This is one of the clues to stress-related illness - the lack of attributability and non-specific nature of ailments and infirmities. Also, anger when bottled up and unresolved exhibits itself in the form of psychosomatic illness, which is difficult to diagnose accurately. Frequently, the severity of the symptoms remains just below the threshold of taking action. This is why it is so important for health professionals and other individuals involved in the management, care and wellbeing of people, especially in the workplace, to be aware of the signs and symptoms of bullying.

> *"When people come to me and relate what they are experiencing, they very often burst into tears and are embarrassed at behaving 'abnormally'. I tell them that if you are hit on the head with a blunt instrument, you'll probably be grovelling on the floor moaning. Now*

grovelling on the floor moaning is not 'normal' behaviour; unless you've been hit on the head with a blunt instrument, in which case it most definitely is 'normal'. Similarly, tearfulness, irritability etc is not 'normal' behaviour unless you're being bullied, in which case it is 'normal' behaviour. It's a normal reaction to an abnormal event. People feel greatly reassured when they realise that they are actually normal after all."

The symptoms which are seen most often include:
- tearfulness - one of the few overt signs of self-confidence and self-esteem having been damaged - there are few reasons why a person should regularly burst into tears in the workplace - or anywhere
- sullenness - another overt sign of psychological hurt
- irritability - especially out of place, out of proportion and out of character
- overwhelming negativism, especially at certain times of day, eg on waking
- obsessiveness - with one's circumstances and with the bully - the situation takes over one's life
- a seemingly irrational inability to touch or handle paperwork or other material associated with the circumstances surrounding bullying or dismissal
- a seemingly irrational inability to go anywhere near the bully, or the bully's or employer's premises
- an overwhelming urge to talk about what's going on, often combined with an inability to define or articulate clearly the gist of the problem
- headaches and other symptoms on certain days, eg weekends and holidays - this may be a result of the fight or flight mechanism standing down after having been on full alert all week
- susceptibility to illness, esp weekends - regular minor infections, eg coughs, colds, flu - one seems to catch everything that's "going round"
- aches and pains, especially with no specific cause, often peaking at unusual times, eg during sleep or on waking
- hypersensitivity to criticism, implied criticism, or any remark or action which might possibly be construed as unfavourable

- hypervigilance linked to the actions or anticipated actions of others, often wrongly termed paranoia
- poor concentration, inability to settle, strong desire to "get on with things" combined with an inability to do so
- intermittent or poorly functioning memory
- mood swings, perhaps several days feeling low, miserable, in despair, punctuated with the occasional high of "I'm going to change the world"
- wavering objectivity which affects decision-making, often to the extent of being grossly under- or over-optimistic
- increased self-deprecation and self-effacement, apologising for everything, almost apologising for existing
- stimulated sense of injustice - an overwhelming and almost uncontrollable urge to "do something about it"

In some cases, there are strong similarities to ME (myalgic encephalomyelitis, now becoming know as Chronic Fatigue Syndrome or CFS), the causes of which are still not well understood. Stress combined with viral infection, possibly in the brain or nervous system, seem to be implicated, and the presence of a virus in that part of the brain which controls energy levels would certainly help to explain the dramatic changes in energy levels experienced by sufferers. Although the mechanisms are not well understood, stress seems to be implicated in a number of syndromes and disorders, including MS and even, some suggest, cancer.

Hypervigilance
Almost all victims of bullying report that at times they "think they are paranoid". However, the term hypervigilant would be more appropriate; there are several important differences:

1) the victim of bullying is aware of their apparent psychosis and can analyse and articulate clearly their fear, as well as describe the irrationality and illogicality of the way they feel; a paranoiac cannot;
2) the person is not suffering from delusions of grandeur - if anything, their sense of self-importance is too low;
3) the paranoiac believes that someone *is* actively pursuing them (ie danger is present), whereas with hypervigilant person is on alert in case danger *might* be present;

4) most importantly, the paranoiac's fear of persecution is usually unfounded, but with bullying, the suspicion of being victimised, persecuted, made a scapegoat, or "being got rid of" *is* well-founded, given the predictability of the bullying process.

The state of hypervigilance, which is a well understood feature of Post-Traumatic Stress Disorder (PTSD) seems to stem from a combination of distrust, obsession, fear, anxiety and alarm - thus "hypervigilance resulting from a constant state of alertness" makes for a more accurate diagnosis.

A further consequence of this state of constant alert is that relationships with one's partner are put under great strain; the person is almost "untouchable", being permanently tense and defensive, and one's sex life becomes difficult, often impossible. This interruption to normal sexual relations may persist for several years and places an almost intolerable burden on the marriage or similar attachments.

In the later stages of bullying, hypervigilance tends to verge on paranoia; this can be a symptom of imminent breakdown, and professional help is essential.

The downward spiral

Once the effects of psychological injury (or rather "psychiatric injury", which now seems to be the preferred term) become apparent, a downward spiral ensues. The person becomes withdrawn, reluctant to communicate for fear of further criticism; this results in accusations of "withdrawal", "sullenness", "not co-operating or communicating", "lack of team spirit", etc. Dependence on alcohol or other substances leads to impoverished performance, poor concentration and failing memory, which brings accusations of "poor performance", etc. At this stage, the risk of accidents increases. Medication, for example anti-depressants or drugs to control epilepsy or other conditions (which may be aggravated by stress of bullying) may produce lethargy and impair performance which elicit a similar response. Lack of sleep combined with frustration, resentment and anger lead to irritability, poor decision-making and a growing sense of inability to cope; these produce further accusations of ... well, you get the picture.

The only way to interrupt this cycle is to identify and take action to address the *cause* of the symptoms.

The ultimate solution

Before long, unusual and often alarming manifestations of the effects of bullying appear. The victim searches harder and harder for a resolution, an escape, a release. Sleep patterns become disturbed, exacerbating tiredness. Such sleep as is obtained is unsatisfying, being fitful and intermittent. Sleep deprivation is a well-known and frequently-used form of torture, usually resulting in rapid capitulation.

The victim's thoughts become increasingly bizarre and start by imagining either the bully or themselves leaving or moving. A pleasurable respite ensues as the mind clings to this hope. As this outcome rarely results, the thoughts move from passive imagining to more proactive deliberations. In order to bring about a resolution, one of the combatants has to go. A sense of injustice rules out the victim moving *("why should I have to move, I'm not the one whose behaviour is at fault")*, so thoughts turn towards engendering a circumstance where the bully moves on. All possibilities are considered, from anticipating promotion to pursuing a grievance procedure. On this latter point, the victim quickly realises that there is so little actual "evidence" that this is not a path to be pursued frivolously - especially when advised that such procedures are generally stacked in favour of management.

And then one day, or more usually, one night, the thought appears. How can I - or how can one - arrange an "accident" for the bully? Reminiscences of Hollywood materialise, with hapless victims being pushed in front of cars, buses and trains, or down the stairs. It doesn't take long for this idea to move from the accidental to the deliberate.

"My boss used various underhand methods to exclude me from departmental management meetings, ultimately merging (ie abolishing) my section and thus depriving me of managerial status. Repeated attempts to clarify my position brought forth plenty of platitudes and linguistic artifice, but no outright confirmation. Then late one afternoon my boss unexpectedly breezed into my office, announced that 'as you are no longer a section manager, there's no need for you to attend

Psychological symptoms of stress from bullying

- anxiety states, permanent or semi-permanent
- panic attacks
- tearfulness
- irritability
- sullenness
- mental breakdown
- inability to cope, especially in situations where you previously were able to cope
- brain fatigue
- poor concentration
- increased forgetfulness
- impaired memory
- loss of humour
- feeling melancholy, gloomy, dispirited, woebegone
- loss of independence of thought and deed
- feeling whingey, blameful
- loss of ability to experience enjoyment (anhedonia)
- clumsiness
- isolation, being "the only one in this situation"
- withdrawal, detachment, impoverished sociableness
- heightened sense of guilt
- feelings of powerlessness
- increasing obsessiveness with everything
- tendency to perfectionism
- constant replays in one's mind, with endings suitably altered to provide a positive outcome (and a negative outcome for the tormentor)
- overwhelming negativism, especially on waking
- depression
- seasonal affective disorder (SAD)
- feelings of fragility, vulnerability, insecurity
- acute self-awareness
- thoughts of suicide
- adoption of "victim mentality"
- being unaware of deteriorating circumstances
- damaged marital relationship
- damaged relationship with one's children
- dramatically heightened sense of injustice
- heightened sense of grievance, bitterness and resentment

Table 11: Frequently reported psychological symptoms

Psychological symptoms of stress from bullying
• low or plummeting morale • wavering, or loss of, objectivity • failure wish, wanting the project/company to fail • loss of interest in job, especially where previously enjoyed • conflict of divided loyalty • work or employment phobia • feeling totally emotionally drained • increasing desperation and sense of futility • confusion • sense of failure • fragility

Table 11: Frequently reported psychological symptoms

*management meetings any more' and breezed out before
I could reply. Half an hour later, when I came down from
the ceiling, I made a further discovery: in Yellow Pages,
there is no section for Contract Killing."*

Counsellors are often surprised by the enormity and
barbarity of such thoughts exhibited by apparently normal,
well-mannered and otherwise often modest people. It comes
as a relief to discover that experiencing this pattern of
thought is normal, and a sign of a sane, healthy personality,
albeit under enormous stress.

They are also evidence of the seriousness of psychological
harm being inflicted, and an indication that help is urgently
required. Such amoral thoughts induce guilt, which further
fuels the stress and feelings of self-doubt. Sufferers become
even more frightened, and fear they are going mad. Without
help and support at this stage, a breakdown moves from
being a possibility to a probability.

The conscious mind is constantly asking the subconscious
mind for solutions to daily problems. The answers can come
immediately, or can take days, weeks, months, or even years
to appear. With bullying, unless the victim has detailed
knowledge of what is going on, for example from a previous
experience, the solutions offered by the subconscious mind
are ineffectual when adopted by the conscious mind.

The two minds become trapped in a loop, with the conscious mind seeking, with increasing desperation, a solution. Unfortunately, it is only possible to break out of this never-ending cycle by (a) the injection of new information or insight, (b) outside intervention or (c) an external or intrusive event of sufficient magnitude.

In the absence of these, the subconscious offers increasingly bizarre solutions to the intractable and apparently insoluble problem. Removing the source of the problem (for example by killing) is the perfect solution. However, the subconscious mind is non-judgemental, so the solutions aren't always acceptable or appropriate - however strong the desire to follow through.

"I saw him [the bully] in a garden centre one day, cowering behind his wife. But for my husband restraining me, I think I would have picked up a spade and hit him with it. I had to go and lock myself in the car for a while for fear I might do something stupid."

The target is now trapped in a vicious downward spiral of plummeting self-confidence and self-esteem, with effects that can impair performance for the rest of that person's life. With the bully often maintaining the impression that he has the backing of his management, indeed intimating that the whole company or organisation is on his side - there's often more than a grain of truth in this - the victim's fear mounts, convinced that the next time they put the slightest foot wrong (or are accused of putting a foot wrong), the wrath of the organisation will be unleashed, and dismissal - or worse - will be automatic. For many people, their worst fears are realised.

The mental health trap

The person being bullied experiences a psychological battering, the effects of which take their toll on mental health just as much as on physical health. If one was bludgeoned day in, day out with a blunt instrument the effect on the body would be broken bones, severe bruising and blood everywhere; the term "grievous bodily harm" (GBH) would be appropriate. Subsequently, the merest caress of any bruise would provoke a sharp pain and an instinctive recoil.

Behavioural symptoms of stress from bullying
• obsession, especially with the bully and with resolving the situation • obsessive behaviour, out of character • tendency to erupt or explode over trivia • poor performance • indecision • impoverished judgement • poor time-keeping • unusual or unexplained absences, often while at work • excessive reliance on coffee, tobacco or alcohol • resorting to drugs, prescribed or otherwise, or use of other "substances" • withdrawal, avoidance of contact with people • unusual mood swings • angry outbursts, intense sudden anger following a trigger • narrow, single focus, especially on the bully • overwhelming urge to talk about your situation • heightened sense of justice and revenge • excessive or unreasonable vigilance, constantly watching one's back • urge to justify every action, including one's existence • very low assertiveness, with occasional aggressive outburst • increased approval-seeking • frequently feeling woebegone, gloomy, whingey, blameful, fault-finding, critical • repeated willingness to secure a "fresh start" • continual resistance and refusal to seek help through counselling or therapy • apathy, passivity, unfeelingness, unconcern, compliance, surrender • unwillingness or inability to trust • avoidance behaviours • suicide - real, attempted or contemplated • excessive or compulsive picking, scratching, biting • inability to touch or handle paperwork or any other material associated with the bully or employer • inability to enter the bully's or employer's premises • unapproachability

Table 12: Frequently reported behavioural symptoms

Behavioural symptoms of stress from bullying
• comfort-buying, uncharacteristic frivolity or spending, perhaps leading to debt
• being hypercritical or oneself and others
• increasingly impoverished decision making
• obsession with double and treble-checking everything
• wanting often to be alone (eg to avoid hurt, stimulation, etc)
• constant self-deprecation and self-effacement
• constantly rehearsing apologies in one's mind
• acute intolerance of partner's failings and foibles

Table 12: Frequently reported behavioural symptoms

"After a long meeting at which I portrayed my boss's behaviour for what it was - that of a bully - and described how I now felt, he then suggested that I was perhaps 'mentally ill'. Unfortunately I didn't have the wit or insight at the time to make it unambiguously and unequivocally clear that the state of my mental health was a direct consequence of his behaviour. In missing this opportunity, I was in danger of falling into the mental health trap. I was fortunate that his amateur diagnosis was treated with the contempt it deserved by the health professionals within the company. Many people are not so fortunate"

If one is bullied day in, day out, the effects are diverse and as described in the tables in this chapter, and the term "grievous psychological harm" or "grievous psychiatric harm" (GPH) would be more appropriate. The mental equivalent of a bruise is hypersensitivity, with the merest hint of criticism evoking an outburst of disproportionate intensity.

Unfortunately, in the case of bullying, there is no blood, no bruising and no obvious injury to substantiate the inner pain. Prejudice is only skin deep and this lack of external evidence, combined with advanced acting skills (pretence, covering, denial, urge to portray air of normality) often cause the victim to be regarded with alarm, suspicion and scepticism. The illogicality of the tendency (which is usually founded on ignorance) to blame the victim for their mental state becomes obvious when compared to the person who has suffered a fractured skull from being hit on the head with the blunt instrument - no-one would think to blame that person for not having a skull strong enough to withstand the blow.

The victim's behaviour becomes increasingly aggravated with a proneness to acting irrationally and emotionally. Despite stubborn resistance to accept and admit to psychiatric injury, ultimately the victim is forced to admit that their mental health is impaired. It is important to realise that the symptoms being experienced are normal in the circumstances, and that you are not going mad. In fact, when you identify or articulate this fear, it is an indication that you are a normal sane person who is definitely not mad. A person who is "mad" cannot see they are "mad". Also, it could be said that if you're being bullied and not experiencing many of the symptoms described in this chapter, then there really is something wrong with you.

The victim is likely to be injured, perhaps seriously, having suffered the inevitable consequences of a sustained and vicious psychological assault. It is vitally important, however, to

(a) differentiate between "mental illness", which people assume, rightly or wrongly, to be inherent, and "psychiatric injury", whose cause is external

(b) understand the important legal distinction in that "mental illness" equates to "not liable", whereas "psychiatric injury" equates to "liable"

(c) recognise that an injury will get better

The victim is now forced to seek remedial help by way of counselling or therapy. At this time the bully may fear that the consequences of their behaviour are becoming visible to other people, and that questions may be asked. In an apparent and very public gesture of concern, he suggests that the person takes sick leave, reports to occupational health, their GP, goes for counselling or therapy, or, more sinisterly, contacts one of the mental health charities.

Herein lies the trap. If the person consents (and their need is dire), they are admitting they have a "mental health problem". If they decline, the battering continues, with the bully pointing out that their victim is resisting accepting professional help. The implication is that the person's judgement is "unsound" and they may be, or are, "mentally ill". Furthermore, the bully is able to imply that the "mental health problem" was pre-existing (that is, "it's always been there"), therefore the victim is responsible for, and has brought upon themselves, the situation now being evidenced. The bully works hard, as always, to maintain this focus with the spotlight firmly on the victim and away from the aggressor.

A further fear surfaces, in many cases with justification, that this episode will be noted on personnel records, and they will henceforth be regarded as "someone with a mental health problem". In many cases, such a note magically and conveniently appears on record, perhaps without the person being aware; the bully's hand is usually not far away.

Another sinister act is often reported at this stage - the bully sometimes telephones their victim's doctor directly, often without the victim's knowledge or consent. In the guise of the "concerned employer", a false picture of the patient's situation is depicted and information may be gleaned from the unsuspecting GP.

Whilst there may seem little chance of avoiding this Catch-22 trap, it is actually a golden opportunity for the victim to take control, catch the bully off guard and turn the spotlight fully on their tormentor. The way to do this is call on as many inner resources of strength as possible, and, preferably in the presence of one or more supportive or independent witnesses (for example union representative), look the bully squarely in the eye, and say:

"the state of my physical and mental wellbeing is a direct consequence of your behaviour towards me over the last xx months/years"

Stick to your guns, dig your heels in and refuse to countenance any alternative reason, suggestion, inference, etc about the state of your mental wellbeing. If appropriate, put it in writing (with the bully's response) and place on record. This may also be the moment to initiate grievance proceedings, depending on your circumstances, company procedures and desired outcome. The bully may bluster, argue, insult, wriggle, squirm, threaten, intimidate - but now, at last, you have the upper hand. Keep it.

In many cases this may be the first time the aggressor has been made aware of the consequences of their behaviour towards others. They may show surprise which appears genuine. Has the bully chosen to ignore the consequences of their behaviour towards others, or has he never been taught or learnt to recognise it? This question opens a large can of worms with important moral implications in relation to criminal responsibility.

In rare cases, the bully may sense his wrong-doing, and genuinely wish to effect reconciliation and reparation. However, given the bully's deftness in pretence and excuse honed by a lifetime of practice and reinforced by the success of this strategy, you will need to remain on red alert; the proof of the pudding is in the eating, and in this case, the bully must demonstrate, through *behaviour* as well as promises, consistency of purpose over a long period of time (several months at least) before trust can begin to be re-established.

The mental health trap is a defining moment in a person's life. After months, perhaps years, of abuse, the bully, in seeking to cover his back, unwittingly has admitted to the consequences of his behaviour, and, in so doing, solicits his own come-uppance.

Awakening

The combination of growing awareness, especially of the causes, with the heightened sense of injustice result in the demeanour of the affected person being regarded, by the bully or the employer, as a time-bomb in their midst, with the countdown in single figures. It is only a matter of time, and maybe very little time, before the inevitable explosion. The person may also be likened to a walking hand-grenade with the pin removed.

In these circumstances, the employer may be apprehensive of taking action, but the desire to be rid of this impending detonation often precipitates a hasty expulsion. Some victims of bullying have reported that from realisation to dismissal has taken only two weeks.

Personality

The effects on personality are harder to define, but no less real to the sufferer. Indeed, the English language lacks appropriate words to describe the feelings of a shattered self-confidence, other than by listing the possible consequences of those sensations. The ultimate conclusion is suicide, although many victims have a behaviour pattern which includes a strong sense of injustice. It is this fighting spirit that thankfully prevents such people from taking that final step.

Effects on personality of stress from bullying
• shattered self-confidence • low self-esteem • impoverished interpersonal skills • diminished behavioural skills • impaired communication skills • low self-worth • loss of self-respect • diminished sense of self-love and self-acceptance • low self-image • loss, or confused sense of, self-determination • occasional over-aggressiveness and over-assertiveness • unusually strong feelings of guilt and shame • humourlessness • increased sensitivity • excessive naivety • wildly alternating optimism and pessimism • sense of unworthiness

Table 13: Frequently reported personality effects

The process of rebuilding a shattered confidence is a long and painful one, and even with professional help, can take years. If the victim has been pushed over the edge, that is, into breakdown, then recovery can take from two to five years - longer if professional help is not sought, or the true cause not recognised. It is likely that some people never fully recover.

Performance
One of the justifications for bullying styles of management is that it increases productivity. Whilst this may appear to be the case in the short term, closer inspection reveals the opposite in the medium and long term.

Positive pressure can encourage employees to achieve hitherto undreamed-of targets for performance and achievement; however, such results depend on superlative interpersonal skills, high behavioural maturity, and superb leadership. Bullies have none of these, but procure their results by threat, domination and various other unsavoury behaviours which are described throughout this book.

> *"It felt as though our company had developed an unwritten policy that achievement of budget targets was paramount, and if there were a few human casualties on the way, that was unfortunate, but an acceptable price to pay. As one of the casualties, I beg to differ."*

For the employer, the consequences of bullying include:
- low productivity
- increase in mistakes due to poor concentration and lack of attention to detail
- unwillingness to follow procedures or guidelines
- reduced quality
- low morale
- absenteeism
- high staff turnover
- unexplained absences during normal working hours
- impoverished interpersonal skills and relations between and with customers, colleagues, peers, subordinates, suppliers, contractors, sub-contractors, authorities, regulatory bodies, professional bodies, etc
- employees spending more and more time covering their backs and less and less time on real work
- employees may exhibit a conscious or unconscious failure wish (the subconscious mind has suggested that such a failure is an effective means of drawing attention to the bullying situation - this is an advanced stage of desperation and action is needed quickly)

Colleagues

Whilst bullying is often seen or reported as occurring between two people, it is just as common for a group of people to suffer, sometimes a whole department. Incredibly, this can number several hundred people.

Sometimes there is a cliquiness between a group of like-minded individuals, whose reticence to admit to the existence of this informal fraternity increases suspicions, especially when bolstered by apparent acts of favouritism. Bullies are cowards, and it is therefore natural for them to gang up - birds of a feather, safety in numbers, the pack mentality, etc. The combined strength of the flock increases, albeit artificially, the sensation of confidence and security felt by each gang member. When the going gets tough (through attention being brought to bear on their activities), they can back each other up. If a gang culture arises, and endures, there is a serious and probably terminal problem with management.

Often, there is a liaison or suspected liaison between two of the principal bullies. A male manager backed up by a female senior manager (or vice-versa) is a surprisingly common scenario, with witnesses reporting the occasional long shared lunch, coincident annual or sick leave, joint attendance at conferences and training courses, off-site business meetings on a Friday afternoon, etc. This apparent pallyness out of the workplace is often in sharp contrast to attempts during working hours to portray no relationship. The power of pillow talk should not be underestimated.

A common tactic, which may have a sexual basis (regardless of gender) is to have an ally at a different level of the hierarchy. A bully in a junior position will often seek the patronage of a senior manager whose power can be exploited when necessary. When the bully is in a senior position, there is often an "agent" in a junior position who can collect information, gossip, etc and who acts as a channel for disinformation. The agent can often be discerned by favoured status, for example being allowed to take charge of the department in the bully's absence, even when there are individuals whose higher grade would make them more appropriate as deputies, or being endowed with the latest equipment whilst everyone else has to make do. The reward might be as trivial as being designated as sole holder of keys to the store cupboard, with all others having to beg permission for access.

Mental illness
For many victims of bullying this is their first encounter with the world of "mental illness" and its taboos. In fact, this lay term is used to cover the whole spectrum of mental health

problems, from the minor and often barely noticeable swings of mood at the anxious or neurotic end of the scale, to the bizarre and occasionally tragic disorders at the psychotic end. Unfortunately, owing to perceptions stimulated by sensationalist media headlines, the term "mental illness" instinctively conjures up images of the latter (rare) rather than the former (common) end of the scale.

Despite statistics which show that at least one in four people will experience "mental health problems" requiring in-patient or out-patient treatment or medication during their life, fear and ignorance sustain taboos and stigma which surround the subject. Depression is so common that one might be forgiven for suggesting that there is something wrong with you if you don't experience it at some time in your life. For most people, the symptoms are mild, transient and often not of sufficient significance to warrant contacting their GP or impair quality of life, and so therefore pass unnoticed.

Although still poorly understood, depression seems to result from an imbalance of the chemical levels in the brain. The reasons for the imbalance may be organic (virus, such as like those implicated in ME), psychological (shock, stress, trauma), cyclic (PMS), seasonal (SAD), hereditary (genetic), accident (injury), birth injury or complications during delivery, or being born with a brain which is not in peak condition (poor health of parents, including drug abuse, poor diet, poor living conditions, lack of attention to self, social and domestic problems, etc). There may be other reasons as well.

For a person to feel not only well, but positive, happy, contented, etc, the brain must be operating with optimum levels of these chemicals, called neurotransmitters. I suspect that a change in levels, which may be so minute as to be measured in terms of a few molecules, is the cause of many of our mental anxieties.

If one assumes the traditional model of a physical brain inhabited by a spiritual consciousness, which in certain circumstances can separate (for example out-of-body or near-death experience), then the spirit requires a fully-working brain with optimum levels of neurotransmitters for the two to work in harmony to produce the well-balanced human being. One could make the further assumption that the spirit is a perfect form, and cannot be damaged, injured or suffer malfunction in any way. It is only when inhabiting a less than perfect brain that the person's psyche seems faulty, unbalanced or insane.

Thus the bizarre, irrational and erratic behaviour often exhibited by people who have suffered severe psychiatric injury, for example through being bullied, can be seen for what it really is - an injury, not an illness. Their subsequent behaviour seems to be fuelled by grievance, anger and frustration, which combine with a dramatically heightened sense of injustice to produce an obsessive and all-consuming desire to "do something about it", such as seek justice, redress, compensation, or work for and bring about change, perhaps on a global scale.

Frequently, such people have previously exhibited a robust and well-balanced mental state, often with little or no history of symptoms of depression, other than perhaps through premenstrual stress (PMS) or following a traumatic event such as bereavement. For many, it is as if the experience has enabled them to discover their purpose in life.

Breakdown

Everyone is at risk of experiencing mental illness, but it is vitally important to distinguish between *endogenous* depression (which is assumed to be inherent), and *reactive* depression (a normal and natural reaction to external events). For the latter, all we need is a trigger of sufficient magnitude to push us over. As already suggested, even the most mentally stable and psychologically robust people will succumb eventually, if pushed far enough. Bullies exert an oscillating pressure, one moment pushing their victim near the edge, and, somehow sensing that they may be going too far, drawing back at the last moment. This alternating nature of being pushed to the limit, then being pulled back (with praise, often inappropriate) sets up a seesaw motion in the victim's psyche. The destabilising effect precipitates the physical, behavioural, psychological and personality disturbances described in this chapter. These oscillatory swings push one back and forth until, like the bridge at Tacoma Narrows (Washington, USA, November 1940), the unremitting frequency, intensity of oscillation and systematic weakening occasion inevitable collapse.

> *"One morning I went into work feeling a bit strange, although by then I'd been emotionally numb for so long I barely noticed. I sat down at my desk and shuffled a few papers, meaninglessly. A colleague came in, remarked how awful I looked, shut the door and sat down. I abruptly burst into tears and sat there for ten minutes, trembling, repeating over and over again, 'I can't cope, I just can't cope'. After more than a year of unremitting psychological pressure, my brain finally collapsed under the strain. That week, several people had spontaneously burst into tears, it was like an infection going round the department. They all felt better after a weep, but I didn't. Such was my mental state that it was several days later that I recognised this as a mental breakdown. Only some weeks after did I begin to realise this was the end of my working life in this career and in this company. It was an unwelcome and unexpected introduction to the world of mental illness, and there followed more than a year of the most bizarre, unpleasant and often painful psychological and physiological symptoms I have ever experienced."*

Mental breakdown can be likened to a computer which becomes so overloaded with applications that eventually the system crashes because the demands the user is making of it exceed the resources available. From the smallest PC to the largest and most powerful supercomputers, all are prone to crashing when demand exceeds capacity. You sit there pressing the keys or clicking the mouse but nothing happens, there's no response. It's died on you. The only solution is to reload and start again.

A mental breakdown, particularly one resulting from bullying, seems to happen for the same reasons. The enormous negative stress caused by bullying exerts demands above and beyond the brain's capacity to operate. Its design specification and safe operating limit is exceeded.

It is important to recognise and understand that in bullying, such demands are unreasonable, unwarranted, unnecessary and unacceptable. Rather than "mental breakdown", the term "psychological close-down" might be more appropriate, which avoids the conventional associations that mental illness has with instability and insanity. In other words, it is a normal reaction to abnormal demands, and in many cases, such people are more "normal" than "average".

Whatever term you use, it is important to refer to the psychological consequences of being bullied as "injury" not "illness", thus correctly attributing the cause to the person who has bullied you. Remain steadfast on this.

The person who has a breakdown through being bullied often does not fit the profile of the "average" person with a "mental illness" and typically, the individual "doesn't fit the normal pattern of breakdown". Victims of bullying are usually hard workers, frequently taking on high workloads and achieving considerable success. After breakdown, that person still expects to maintain a high workload and may have to be forcibly restrained in order to get the rest and recuperation required. Severity of injury and extent to which the individual is traumatised can be seen as a mark of the person's tenacity, resilience, resolve and integrity - precisely those qualities which attracted the bully in the first place - and can also be seen as a measure of character. A further pressure is the need to "prove" that they are not "mentally ill" by trying to carry on as normal. This is an artificial pressure caused by society's current inability to differentiate mental illness from psychiatric injury, combined with the persistence of the bully to have their victim labelled as "mentally ill".

The victim of breakdown also has to face the unpleasant fact that their former faculty for high workload is damaged, and may take many years to repair, although a managed recovery is likely to shorten the time considerably. It may be that following a burnout in these circumstances, some individuals may never be able to sustain such a high workload again, and thus have to face a painful period of adjustment. Events following breakdown, such as loss of job, industrial tribunal, the prospect of further legal action, watching the bully destroy somebody else whilst continuing to draw salary all add insult to injury - literally.

"After working long, full and satisfying days throughout my career, which included a number of voluntary

evening activities, I was horrified to find after my breakdown that I could barely manage to get myself to the supermarket to buy two items. Although my strength is returning slowly, I now expect that it will be several years before I will be able to consider a full-time job. Recovery is long, slow and painful, and I feel so useless at times. I'm assured things will improve, but in the meantime, the frustration of not being able to do what I used to do sometimes overwhelms me."

Suicide

Many people who have experienced the symptoms of severe psychiatric injury (such as those which follow bullying) have admitted that at some time the thought of suicide has crossed their mind. Most people fortunately get no further than contemplating this "solution", and the actual incidence of suicide in these circumstances seems rare. Nevertheless there have been a number of cases where bullying appears to have been a cause, perhaps the principal cause of the decision of the person to end their life; however, no-one knows the true tally.

If the thought of suicide has entered your mind, especially if you are being bullied, it might be wise to report this to your GP as quickly as possible. Remember that the symptoms one experiences from being bullied are an injury, not an illness. Feeling suicidal is also an outward sign of wavering objectivity, and is a common and normal reaction in these circumstances. If thoughts of "ending it all" overwhelm you, contact the Samaritans or similar organisation immediately, then see your GP as soon as possible. You may wish to carry the Samaritans' telephone number with you just in case. There is no shame or embarrassment in doing so; this is a precautionary measure whilst you begin the recovery process.

Shock

Most people think of shock as a natural consequence of a single frightening incident; however, shock can result from a series of small but regular and persistent unpleasant incidents. In bullying, after the victim's inevitable demise, the state of shock is compounded by the realisation:

- that anyone could exhibit such amoral behaviour and get away with it

- that anyone could be gullible or blind enough to believe the bully's specious words
- that anyone, especially the employer, could be taken in by the bully's behaviour
- that the employer could close ranks behind the bully and do the bully's bidding
- that the employer could demonstrate such heartless and unfeeling ingratitude after long loyal service
- that no-one is willing or able to do anything about it

One of the effects of shock is that the victim is unable to find the words to describe what has happened to them. Whilst this state slowly abates, it might be three, six or even twelve months or more before the victim is able to recall and recount a complete and coherent picture of events. With skilled help however, it may take only a couple of weeks.

The state of speechlessness can arise early in the bullying cycle and is particularly acute when the tormentor is present. It is particularly important for those involved in grievance, disciplinary or legal proceedings to understand that the victim's inability to describe what has happened to them is a measure of the severity of psychiatric injury and not an indication of lack of evidence.

Trauma

Trauma is a "physical or emotional shock brought about by force, violence or enduring stress, or the state that such a shock inaugurates". The initiating blow may be sudden, as in accident, disaster, attack, illness, etc, or prolonged, such as through repeated horrifying moments, or regular personal, psychological attacks, as in bullying.

Serious physical injuries such as torn muscles, ligaments, tendons, etc are likely to leave the sufferer vulnerable to recurrent injury, especially if the person repeats the action which caused the damage in the first place - sports activities are a good example. Similarly, but less well recognised, is the fact that a traumatic incident is likely to recall and stimulate painful feelings from a past traumatic event, even if the initiating cause was different.

The debilitating effects of trauma are gaining recognition, as is the requirement for support and a suitable recovery period. Traumas are like puddles in the winding passage of one's life; over a period of time, many puddles collect, each of whose size can only be diminished by appropriate counselling and coming to terms with the initiating event and its consequences. Where traumatic events are not resolved, or not resolved entirely - for instance, the full and proper expression of grief for the loss of a loved one - the puddles remain. As a new puddle swells, it eventually touches others. Like two raindrops running down a window pane, the two droplets suddenly unite to produce one larger drop with no evidence of their former separate existence. Similarly, traumas combine with crippling and confusing consequences. Sometimes a new traumatic event need only be minute, but is sufficient to provide the catalyst to marry several former traumas into a lake of Atlantic immensity.

Bullies will often explicitly link their victim's present psychological symptoms to past traumatic experiences, whether they be the result of shock, grief or illness. This is an attempt to divert attention away from the real cause of the victim's present state of mind, whilst endeavouring to absolve themselves of all responsibility for the consequences of their behaviour. Unless you understand what is going on, you may unwittingly concur with this exoneration.

Post-traumatic stress

The existence and significance of the effects of bullying on victims have yet to be fully acknowledged and accepted, especially where sufferers are seeking redress, for example at tribunal or through the courts.

We know that stress, when initiated by a single, sudden, dramatic incident such as a disaster or other life-threatening event, produces an identifiable and predictable series of continuing and repetitive reactions in some experiencers. These have been termed Post-Traumatic Stress Disorder, or PTSD. The principal symptoms are hypervigilance, exaggerated startle response, flashback, exhaustion, sudden violent outbursts, poor concentration, impaired memory, sleep disturbance, joint pains, emotional numbness, depression, etc.

Where the cause is a protracted series of incidents (such as prolonged active service in a war zone, attending daily accidents as a member of the emergency services, or being bullied regularly) the trauma is cumulative rather than sudden, but the same reactions are experienced, and the term Prolonged Duress Stress Disorder (PDSD) may be employed.

In this state, certain types of event act as triggers (recognised or unrecognised) that initiate a reaction, sometimes violent, sometimes immediate, sometimes delayed, which whilst appropriate to the former situation of danger, is wholly inappropriate to the present circumstances. Examples of triggers include:

- an envelope marked "Private & Confidential" dropping onto the mat (part of the bully's strategy was to bombard the victim with threats of disciplinary and legal action in the form of letters sent in an envelope marked Private & Confidential)
- certain words or phrases (eg "you ought to do such-and-such") which the bully uses frequently
- the sound of a door slamming which formerly heralded the approach of the bully
- an accent or raised voice similar to that of the bully
- the sight or sound of a car identical to that which the bully drives
- any form of criticism or implied criticism where none should be expected and expressed in a manner similar to that used by the bully

Often, the bully seems to recognise the trigger and derives peculiar pleasure from the fear and panic that it provokes. The trigger is then used with increasing regularity and becomes a principal instrument of control. The victim finds that they eventually become paralysed not only by the trigger itself, but even the prospect or thought of the triggering event. Some people find ultimately that they cannot even go near their place of employment, or they cannot open the envelope which may sit on their desk for weeks awaiting attention - with all the others that arrive in the meantime. Inevitably, this state of paralysis means that handling, studying, sorting and collating paperwork for an industrial tribunal becomes virtually impossible within the limit of three-month application limit.

Work on identification and treatment of both conditions is at an early stage, but results so far are encouraging. Space precludes a full discussion of the symptoms and treatment of PTSD, but the work that has been undertaken in the areas of critical incident debriefing and support for those affected (such as in the emergency services and transport industries) promises to have application to those recovering from bullying. See resource section for further reading.

Stress and the body

Also at an early stage is the understanding of the link between mental health and physical wellbeing. Although familiar to holistic-centred healing approaches, the full implications of mind/body harmony have yet to be fully embraced by Western medicine and culture. For instance, informal observations seem to suggest that the type of person most likely to succumb to bullying (caring, empathic, low assertiveness) is also the same as the type of person who tends to suffer from illnesses which affect the immune and nervous system. It might also be that it is not so much the stress itself, but the release from stress which is the triggering factor, particularly if the discharge is sudden.

The bully has an aggressive behaviour oriented around the needs of self, self-protection and survival, if necessary at the expense of others. Friedman and Rosenman, in their original work on assessing proneness to coronary heart disease, term this hostile approach as Type A behaviour. The person who is naturally inclined to this approach seems, if illness strikes, to be more likely to suffer an ailment of a more predominantly physical nature, for example heart attack.

In other words, whilst there is little scientific evidence of a link between bullying and certain types of serious illness, there seems to be a coincidence between preferred behaviour style and the type of illness one is likely to experience, should illness arise. This is a subject and an area in which further research should pay dividends.

If anything, being bullied stimulates the sense of injustice to such a degree that under certain criteria - this may be a moment of enlightenment, or contact for the first time with a previously enlightened individual - or on reaching a certain threshold, such as a traumatic event like a breakdown - a dormant fighting spirit is activated and energised. It would seem that life-threatening or life-changing events are a common precursor to spurring the experiencer into action to bring about change or betterment for the benefit of self, fellow sufferers and society.

Ill-health

A position many victims of bullying find themselves in is being "encouraged" - or rather coerced - into taking ill-health retirement. There have been several cases where examinations by health professionals (including a GP, psychologist, consultant and psychiatrist) have stated unequivocally that there is no indication of mental illness, whilst the employer insists on ill-health retirement. The employee is in the invidious position of being pressurized into accepting a course of action which, to them, is morally unacceptable. A person who has been bullied out of their job by a vicious and vindictive individual has no desire to give up that job, rather they want only to get back to work and carry on their career in the profession of their choice.

A further dilemma is being forced to apply for and accept a pension under false pretences, which might be twenty years or more in advance of the planned retirement date. Whilst the money is certainly useful, especially if employment is now denied, there are strong feelings of guilt and undeservingness, which sit uncomfortably alongside the heightened sense of injustice.

Following termination of employment, the individual may find themselves eligible for unemployment or sickness benefit. The former has many strings attached, which may involve repeated applications for jobs which, for many reasons, may be wholly unsuitable. The psychiatric injuries of bullying may be simultaneously serious enough to impair ability to find and undertake a new job, but not serious enough to be visible or comprehensible. Lack of understanding by society and an inability to articulate the symptoms may exacerbate the situation. Sickness benefit might then be the appropriate course, but the individual may be unaccustomed to regarding themselves as "sick" and "on benefit". Nevertheless, we all pay National Insurance contributions, and now is the time to accept what is rightfully yours whilst you effect a full recovery and rebuild your life.

People who are likely to be bullied are also likely to be sensitive and over-susceptible to experiencing guilt. This may be the moment to turn down one's susceptibility to guilt.

With the obsessive behaviour that victims of bullying characteristically exhibit may go fluctuating objectivity. With drink-driving, the first effect of alcohol is to impair your ability to judge your ability. With the psychiatric injuries of bullying, the baseline of your objectivity starts to seesaw and your objectivity in assessing your objectivity becomes impaired. This unfortunately leads unversed observers to infer "mental instability" and the bully to claim "inherent mental illness".

Fight shy or fight?

In the absence of an employer's willingness to adopt and enforce an anti-bullying policy, an individual either has to accept what has happened, or take action to correct or compensate for the injustice they have experienced. Typically this means going to industrial tribunal. However, the Department of Social Security has recently recognised cases of bullying as industrial injury incidents, and with the effects of stress (bullying is one of the principal causes) being increasingly recognised, bullying may also come to be treated as a health and safety issue. The government's recent acceptance of the unacceptability of stalking is also an encouraging sign, especially the acknowledgement of the psychological harm suffered by the victim. The obsession with eliminating their victim that bullies exhibit in the late stages of the bullying process seem similar to the fanaticism demonstrated by stalkers towards their prey; the proposed prison sentences for such behaviour are also encouraging.

It is important that everyone who has experienced bullying comes forward and alerts society to what has happened to them so that awareness of the problem is raised and a climate of unacceptability is engendered. Society must learn to recognise the serious injuries that bullying causes.

It is sad that the only way many employers (especially the government) can be persuaded to accept that bullying is a reprehensible and unacceptable practice is through their budgets. It seems ludicrous that one incidence of libel or slander (does this really cause injury?) can result in an astronomical award of six figures or more, whilst being bullied out of one's job or career into nervous breakdown or ill-health retirement is frequently regarded as insufficient cause even for going to tribunal. Where cases have proceeded to tribunal, the chances are at best only 50/50 that the case will succeed, and even if it does, the award is likely to be less than legal costs which have typically through circumstantial necessity been kept to an absolute minimum anyway.

So, publicly call somebody a wally and you might find yourself having to shell out half a million in compensation; bully them out of their job, destroy their life, health and career in the name of management, and be promoted. It's a topsy-turvy world.

Grief

After being bullied out of their job, the pain of separation that the victim experiences is similar to that felt following the death of a loved one. This is especially so if (a) it is a position one has occupied for a long time, (b) it is a job one loves and has made a success of, (c) the job involves working with people, (adults or children, especially if disadvantaged) and (d) the termination is through dismissal enacted or contrived through bullying behaviour.

Some might find it offensive to equate loss of life with loss of job, for one is replaceable, the other clearly is not. However, relative merit is not the issue - it is the effect that loss and severance have on the psyche which is the same. Many also find that redundancy, particularly when handled badly, frequently produces a similar traumatic effect - which has also largely gone unrecognised.

Victims of bullying often find that because they are ousted in unacceptable circumstances and through dubious practices, they don't have the opportunity to say goodbye to their friends and colleagues; they are also denied the opportunity to put their affairs in order, tie up loose ends, complete tasks in hand, designate successors and beneficiaries and collect their belongings.

As a society, the need for grieving may be well recognised, but the opportunities for and the methods and process of grieving are less well understood. Mostly, onlookers feel embarrassed, not knowing what to say, lacking the skills or knowledge to help. More often this is unfamiliarity rather than lack of care, although well-meaning attempts can unfortunately take on a demeanour of clumsiness bordering on tactlessness.

Whether or not suitable redress for unfair dismissal is sought or obtained, the symptoms of grief will be present. The loss of job, and usually career as well, is like a bereavement, and the sudden and unexpected severance is the same whether it is a person or a position of employment that has been cruelly denied.

The blow to self-esteem is often heightened by seeing the appointment of a successor. Sometimes this is the bully's favourite, who may have little or no competence; alternatively, or it may simply be the next intended victim, in which case knowledge that someone else is about to endure the same nightmare stirs guilt, aggression and helplessness in equal quantities.

The importance of work is generally not recognised in its contribution to the building and maintaining of self-confidence, self-esteem, and self-worth. Neither is the parental role that the employer enjoys in the fostering and nourishing of its progeny of employees. Nor the responsibilities that such maternal and paternal patronage occasion. Employees savour the security that employment appoints, perhaps unaware of the womb-like contentment of the daily opportunity to learn and grow, sated by the nourishment of regular remuneration.

Further loss

For some, loss of job is only the first of a series of potential privations; loss or reduction in income, particularly when the main or sole breadwinner, can lead to loss of one's house through inability to keep up mortgage repayments or other loans secured upon it. Moving may also entail separation from family, friends, community, and perhaps roots.

In some cases, the enormous strain that bullying and its effects place on relationships may result in separation, divorce and family break-up.

Whatever happens, it is likely that the State will end up footing the bill. Meanwhile, the bully carries on with their next victim.

Relationships

Unless one has enormous self-confidence and maturity, one cannot help but be affected by the behaviours of others.

Behaviour possesses and exhibits a reflective nature in that when a behaviour is exhibited to us, especially on a regular basis and in a place where we expect high (or at least acceptable) standards of etiquette, the human psyche absorbs the behaviour and then repeats it in an appropriate circumstance and at an appropriate time. If a person is bullied at work, the stresses and strains become so intolerable that even the most self-disciplined person cannot contain the pressure of anger at the insensitivity and injustice perpetrated against them.

In fact, the greater the self-discipline, the greater the pressure and the more catastrophic the ultimate outcome. Stress in the human body is like steam in a pressure cooker, but with no proper safety valve. Pressure builds and builds and builds until ultimately leaks occur through the minutest gaps and weak points. In the human body, these leaks are the physical symptoms described earlier. It is a sign that our O-rings are failing. In the author's case, the pressure leaked through the knees, causing painful joints of an almost incapacitating nature. Over two years on, my knees are still the best and most accurate indicator of the amount of stress I'm experiencing.

There are strong similarities between the families of those who have been bullied, and the families of those who have suffered PTSD and it is inevitable that the brunt of the victim's suppressed anger is borne by those closest to them. Spouse, partner, children all feel the wrath of anger and watch bemused, alarmed, exasperated and helpless as events take an unbeknowingly predictable course. Efforts to limit and contain the anger at home make the problem worse by increasing levels of stress. Social life ebbs away and ultimately becomes non-existent. The number of visitors declines and the effort of maintaining contacts outside home and work becomes too great to keep up. Loved ones look on frustrated and frightened as a whirlwind of activity blows domestic life apart. This frantic behaviour drives friends and family to despair; self-protection mechanisms spring into action and unwittingly increase the victim's sense of isolation and helplessness.

As with all forms of psychiatric injury, the person suffering needs the greatest support at a time when their behaviour is most likely to alienate. One is reminded of the parental edict of "children need you most when they are at their least lovable". More often, the effect of the circumstances is likely to leave both partners feeling isolated, rejected and alone.

Without knowledge of what happens in a bullying situation, relationships deteriorate, guilt resulting from angry and uncontrolled outbursts fans the flames of fury. Family members become increasingly confused, bitter and resentful, distancing themselves slowly but surely from this ticking time-bomb. Stable loving family relationships recede into the dim and distant past. "Will Daddy be angry when he gets home tonight?" the children ask. "Will Mummy take us to the park at the weekend or will she be too busy again?" Excuses wear thin as family life steadily disintegrates.

In the case of workplace bullying, the partner and children are the unseen and unrecognised victims. The family experiences at first hand the ferocity of transferred anger and reacts instinctively.

Recovery

If you sustained a broken leg, you'd expect, nay demand to have it set in plaster. If the fracture was severe, you might anticipate being flat on your back in traction. In either case, you'd expect to be out of action for several weeks.

If you're still bursting into tears, or feeling bouts of anger, or still hypersensitive, or exhibiting other symptoms, then you need therapeutic support, for these are signs of severe psychiatric injury. For many, counselling is like a plaster for the psyche, and very severe injury may demand the traction of therapy. Just as you would not be embarrassed or feel uncomfortable accepting hospitalisation or using crutches for a broken leg, there is no shame, embarrassment or guilt in adopting a course of counselling or therapy. Like plaster and traction, they are today's appropriate tools for helping the body heal.

> *"It's an enormous relief to talk to someone who doesn't think I'm crazy, going mad, cracking up, or just a daft whingey female. There's no substitute for someone who has had the experience themselves and can genuinely empathise with your distress."*

Old myths still persist that counselling is only for people who "have something wrong in the head" (the "something" is never actually defined or subsequently referred to), and therapy is for "complete nutters" or "typical Americans" (for readers across the Pond, I'm not suggesting these are analogous). Perhaps the perceived larger-than-average number of psychiatrists with East European surnames or accents might be perpetuating this anarchic prejudice. The fact is, increasing numbers of cerebral casualties are discovering the life-changing and sometimes life-saving benefits of these forms of consultation.

Incidentally, just as drugs are not very helpful for broken bones, so most people find medication unhelpful for psychiatric injury, especially if this is their first encounter with mental malfunction. Paracetamol and its ilk may alleviate the occasional pain just as anti-depressants may bring welcome relief for occasional depression. Whereas the former is widely effective, the latter are much more hit-and-miss. Prozac is new and now widely-prescribed; much has been written about this so-called wonder drug, but controversy surrounds its use. Some report dramatic improvement, others find it has the opposite effect; yet others, including the author, report no effect at all, other than to deplete financial reserves through regular prescription charges following recommendations that "you should take it for several months to see any real effect".

Western-style pharmaceuticals have a largely suppressant rather than curative effect, that is, they tend to attack and mask the *effects* of an illness, rather than address the *cause*. Sounds familiar? This may be an oversimplification, for drugs do play an important role in maintaining health and enabling us to continue our busy lives with minimum disruption. When the answer to a blinding headache is to lounge in a long relaxing hot bath, if you're stuck on the M25 in the rush hour, a couple of hastily-swallowed pain relief tablets is not only expedient but a necessity. The real solution to the cause of that blinding headache is of course to slow the pace of your life down. Perhaps the M25 was built for a purpose after all.

For some people, complementary medicines bring welcome relief, especially when conventional cures have had little, or no effect, or perhaps have produced adverse effects. Some report that the homeopathic preparation of arnica brings relief for trauma. Others find sustenance through alternative therapies such as reflexology, and the rise in the number of clinics and centres offering a range of these services perhaps bears testament to society's need and recognition for a more meaningful and naturally therapeutic lifestyle.

Recognition and validation

Victims of bullying often have an overwhelming and at times almost uncontrollable desire to tell their story. This obsession probably has its origins in the heightened sense of injustice combined with the lack of recognition and want of opportunity to talk to people who understand the unimaginable awfulness of what has happened.

It seems that gaining recognition from a person or persons (including family members, especially a partner) whom the victim deems as worthy of bestowal of approval is an essential step in instituting the healing process. This is a feature common to many who suffer abuse and trauma.

"Language is the key to conceptual development."
attrib. L S Vygotsky, Russian psychologist

Equally important is the need to "give the disease a name". Once the causative agent is identified and named, and the sufferer knows what or who they are fighting, the appropriate defences, weapons, strategies and resources can be engaged and mobilised. Until this milestone, it's like fighting in the dark, surrounded by denial.

Employment phobia

Apart from the severe psychiatric injuries and detriment to general health and wellbeing that bullying occasions, most people who have been through the experience feel that they never want to be employed again. For many, self-employment becomes the only option, regardless of its suitability.

Sometimes this feeling is interpreted as never wanting to work again, and the tag "work phobia" may be attributed with an inference of malingering, skiving etc. However it is more likely that the betrayal of trust which is at the heart of bullying, especially when the employer has backed the bully, leads to the victim feeling they can never trust a manager or an employer ever again. At present, this seems to be an increasingly well-founded fear.

Distinction

Because of society's attitudes towards "mental illness", it is vitally important that the symptoms of psychiatric injury, including breakdown, are recognised for what they are: injury, not illness. The unusual and occasionally bizarre obsessive and hypervigilant behaviour tends to frighten those who do not understand what is happening, especially if they see their formerly stable colleague or partner "cracking up" before their eyes. It might be worth remembering that anyone who has a breakdown is in very good company; Abraham Lincoln had one at age 27. It's also worth remembering the other adage that failure (including trauma, breakdown, etc) is a prerequisite for teaching us the lessons we need to learn for the next step in life. Many highly successful people experience their greatest failure immediately prior to their greatest success.

A characteristic of people who have suffered breakdown as a consequence of stress caused by bullying is their irrepressible desire not only to regain their former strength and carry on with their lives, but to tackle the injustice which is the cause of their injury. This is hardly the profile of the average person with a "mental health problem". It is also important to remember that whereas mental illness may improve with time, psychiatric injury - as with most injuries - does get better.

Even more encouraging is that after a period of recovery (which may take a couple of years or more), many people who have experienced breakdown bounce back to even higher levels of attainment, although their subsequent achievements are less likely to be measured in terms of finance, grade or career progression.

Moving on

With respect to the psychiatric injuries, acknowledgement and comprehension from the medical and legal professions seem particularly important. Once the victim has their experience validated, a weight is lifted, recovery can begin, and the person moves on. In this regard an appropriately experienced counsellor can play a pivotal role.

The Swedish example of a place of recovery or sanctuary where victims of bullying can be helped to overcome their experience and rebuild their self-confidence and self-esteem in a controlled and supportive environment is a model to be emulated. Whilst the short-term cost of such treatment is high, the long-term benefit of an individual who is productive again within a few months rather than a few years (if at all) should be clear for all to see.

9   Cost

"Night and day I'd devise and rehearse my plan of action. Words and phrases to defend myself, approaches to adopt, delaying and defensive tactics, sources of help, location of exits, contingency plans if things went badly wrong, and so on. Survival was the name of the game. If there was any time left, I might do some work."

The costs of maintaining a bully on the payroll have yet to be fully recognised, as has the overall cost to society. The price tag will become clearer as more cases proceed through the courts, although by this time, it could be said that every case has already failed in that for things to have come this far, the employer has lost control - or perhaps never had control in the first place?

Cost to the employer

"I reckon my departure through being bullied out of my job cost the company around £200K. Unfortunately, as the two principal lump sum components came out of restructuring and pension funds, with the rest hidden in various overheads, none was charged to my manager's budget. Had it been, his slim profit for the year would have been a whacking great loss and the true cost of his behaviour would have become apparent. Perhaps also the company wouldn't then have been so hasty in promoting him just before my breakdown."

The main hindrance to calculating the cost of bullying is that rarely, if ever, do the sums appear on paper, and any costs that do appertain are attributed to other headings. How different the accountants' reaction would be if the expenses were clearly labelled "Bullying".

A breakdown of costs might go as follows:

- direct - these are easily measurable costs which already appear in budgets (albeit without the word "bully"), and might include lawyers' and other legal fees, awards made against the employer by tribunals and courts, etc

- staff - the cost in employees' time, including the bully, victim(s), manager(s), personnel, union representative, administrators, etc including communication, investigation, checking and familiarisation with procedures, attending meetings, etc
- overheads - use of meeting rooms, facilities, lighting, heating, storage of records, production of statistics, etc
- resources - use of photocopiers, telephones, faxes, computers, hardware, networks, stationery, consumables, etc
- resource support - ordering and resupply, maintenance, backup, hardware upgrades, installation, network support, storage, retrieval, etc
- performance and productivity - the impoverishing, draining and exhausting effect on all employees in the hierarchy from experiencing, defending or witnessing the bully's repeated behaviour
- sickness - benefit, administration, plus costs associated with ill-health retirement, etc
- medical - including the provision of welfare and counselling, occupational health services, company physician, consultants' reports, etc
- pension - provision, especially in advance of normal or expected retirement age, plus the administration of allocation and payment
- administrative - personnel records, obligatory record keeping, compliance with health and safety and other regulations
- consequential loss from staff leaving, including training investment, knowledge and experience of subject, clients, customers, procedures, etc, knock-on effects from adverse publicity
- unwillingness of investors to invest in an employer who
  -> allows bullies to operate
  -> declines to implement anti-bullying measures
  -> prefers to subsidise the bully's activities either through denial or by backing the bully

- ditto unwillingness of employees, graduates and skilled workers to continue working for such an employer
- ditto recruitment of new employees

These costs are incurred in the pursuit of

- production of paperwork and reports whilst...
- undertaking investigations and...
- pursuing grievance procedures and ultimately...
- defending court actions from industrial tribunals to the European court

Poor productivity and performance

Some of the costs incurred by or to the employee and their department might include:

- regular long tea and lunch breaks
- poor timekeeping
- increased number of mistakes
- poor communication with colleagues, management, customers, clients, suppliers, etc
- ditto poor cooperation
- loss of credibility in management
- unexplained absences during day
- sick leave
- absenteeism
- appointments with GP, occupational health, counselling, therapy, etc
- working at minimum throttle
- diminution of loyalty
- effect on other staff
- impoverished customer service - customers will sense what is happening and gradually go elsewhere

The costs of replacing staff include:

- gaining approval to recruit
- design, production and placement of advertising
- responding to applicants
- selection for initial interview
- interviewing likely candidates
- selection for final interview
- interviewing final candidates
- making selection
- making a job offer and awaiting acceptance
- induction and familiarisation with employer

- up to three months or more training plus
  familiarisation with job, procedures and colleagues

Once a bullying process has been initiated (and it is the bully who is the initiator), then in addition to fulfilling their duties, the victim is likely to spend an increasing amount of time researching and taking part in the grievance and disciplinary procedures; later, they will devote most of their time to preparing for legal proceedings. Work for the employer is relegated to second place - if there's time.

Employers must understand that the cause of the cost is the bully; the bully chooses to behave in this way, and in order to survive coerces or hoodwinks the employer into funding their behaviour. Given the compulsive and addictive nature of bullying, it can be a very expensive habit to subsidise.

Cost to the State

The Health and Safety Executive estimate that the cost of stress to the UK economy is about £4 billion a year. Other estimates range as high as £12 billion, but the actual figure becomes immaterial when the units remain the same. This toll is probably equivalent to at least a couple of pence on the basic rate of income tax. Even with little data, bullying is a clearly millstone round the neck of the economy.

With the pressure on budgets in the public sector probably greater than anyone can remember, and the need for efficiency and value for money through the imposition of "market forces" forming a central tenet of public sector policy, the potential for dramatic savings through tackling bullying is clear.

The cost of nursing each victim of bullying back to health includes the following:

- regular visits to one's GP
- provision and subsidisation of medication
- provision of support and care in long-term illness
- mental health services, including psychologists, psychiatrists, therapists, in-patient care in mental health facilities, etc
- provision and administration of statutory sick pay
- sickness benefit, provision and continuing assessment

- incapacity benefit, provision and continuing
  assessment
- unemployment benefit
- housing provision in cases where the home is lost
- employment services
- the State's share of the cost of marital break-up

Public sector
Here, the full cost of bullying is borne by the taxpayer.
Whether in teaching, nursing or local or national
government, the Audit Commission should have an interest
in the drain on the public purse that bullying imposes,
particularly with regard to employers who support the bully
and choose to defend tribunals and court actions.

Cost to the individual
The cost to the individual is often one of loss of livelihood,
including:

- loss of job
- terminated career
- impaired ability to work lasting for several years
- ability to get new job impaired by lack of reference
- loss of investment in training and qualifications
- loss of opportunity
- prescription charges if medication advised or imposed
- loss of home through lack of job to earn income to pay
  the mortgage, perhaps compounded by negative equity
- diminished credit rating, especially if debts incurred
- inability or difficulty in obtaining insurance due to
  changed financial circumstances
- ditto life assurance
- ditto personal loans, credit, etc
- ditto credit cards or any form of payment card which
  requires personal and financial details to be revealed
- effect on children, perhaps change of school
- potential move out of the area
- marital break-up, separation and divorce

Cost to the family
Often, it is the partner and family who are the unseen
victims in bullying, and in many cases, the partner reaches
the point of leaving. One wonders how many marriages fail

not because couples fall out of love, but because one or other partner is having an unjustly and unnecessarily hard time at work.

Cost of proceeding

The following tables highlight the cost of bullying by identifying the number of departments, people, and amount of time, effort and resources consumed by the investigation and defence of a case of bullying. Most start with the victim lodging a complaint which itself is the subject of investigation; this invariably leads to the initiation of either a grievance procedure by the victim or dismissal proceedings by the bully. Often, it leads to both.

Many grievance procedures consist of two or three stages, each involving more senior employees. The final stage might involve the chief executive or managing director; staff and legal costs mount at each stage. It should also be noted that whilst starting grievance proceedings is normally the recommended route, the grievance procedure is designed such that a line manager (or his manager) is tasked with the responsibility of investigating and resolving the grievance; given the hierarchical nature of bullying, this procedure is inherently unsuited to addressing bullying. Sometimes the employer's insistence on confining inquiry to the grievance procedure could be seen as an attempt to muffle the victim by keeping it in the family. As with cases of child abuse, "there's no need for anyone else to know about it". Few tyrants can resist the opportunity to be defendant, judge and jury. Tribunals may also be inclined to look less favourably on an applicant who has not followed the employer's internal grievance procedures.

The following tables highlight some of the people, activities and resources that are consumed by the grievance procedure for a single instance of bullying, including preparation for the meeting, attendance at the meeting, then reaching and promulgating a verdict. Each stage might absorb as many as five people for half a day.

When matters reach the tribunal stage, then the number of people, preparation, duplication and costs increase proportionately.

Table 14: Grievance procedure: preparation

involves	people	effort	resources
personnel	manager/ officer	investigation preparation liaison	filing writing dictating checking
	secretary	typing photocopying arrange meeting liaison book venue	computer disk space photocopier telephone fax email site network internal post
management	line manager	preparation investigation liaison (rebuttal)	filing writing dictating checking
	secretary	typing photocopying distribution	computer disk space photocopier telephone fax email site network internal post
workforce	employee	preparation typing form filling distribution liaison	computer disk space photocopier telephone fax email site network internal post

Table 14: Grievance procedure: preparation

involves	people	effort	resources
union	steward or representative (employee)	preparation investigation typing distribution liaison	computer disk space photocopier telephone fax email site network internal post

Table 15: Grievance procedure: meeting

involves	people	effort	resources
personnel	manager/ officer	attendance	filing writing dictating checking
	secretary	attendance writing	computer disk space photocopier telephone fax email site network internal post
management	line manager	attendance	filing writing dictating checking
workforce	employee	attendance	computer disk space photocopier telephone fax email site network internal post

Table 15: Grievance procedure: meeting

involves	people	effort	resources
	witness(es)	preparation attendance	
union	representative (employee)	attendance	computer disk space photocopier telephone fax email site network internal post postage

Table 16: Grievance procedure: adjudication

involves	people	effort	resources
personnel	manager/ officer	writing dictating checking follow-up meeting	writing dictating checking filing
	secretary	typing checking photocopying distribution follow-up meeting	computer disk space photocopier telephone fax email site network internal post
management	line manager	follow-up meeting	reading filing
workforce	employee	follow-up meeting	filing
union	representative (employee)	follow-up meeting	filing

Table 17: Industrial tribunal: preparation

involves	people	effort	resources
personnel	manager/ officer	investigating interviewing researching reviewing writing dictating checking liaising	filing
	secretary	typing checking photocopying searching indexing filing distribution	disk space photocopier telephone fax email site network internal post
management	line manager	investigating researching reviewing writing dictating checking liaising	filing
	secretary	typing checking photocopying searching indexing filing distribution	disk space photocopier telephone fax email site network internal post
counsel	employer's solicitor	reading reviewing liaising corresponding	

Table 17: Industrial tribunal: preparation

involves	people	effort	resources
workforce	employee	researching preparation typing form filling photocopying distribution liaison	computer disk space photocopier telephone fax email site network internal post
	witness(es)	preparation	
counsel	employee's solicitor		
union	representative (employee)	researching preparation typing form filling photocopying distribution liaison	computer disk space photocopier telephone fax email site network internal post postage

What does this cost and what does it achieve?

At this stage, employers might like to ask themselves the following questions:

> How much income does the company earn as a result of any single action described in the tables?

> How does any one of the above actions contribute towards achieving the aims and objectives of the employer?

> How much business do the actions described bring in?

> How does any action improve service to customers?

> How does any action increase productivity?

> How does any action benefit shareholders and investors?

> What is the cost of preparation, dissemination, storage and archival?

> What could these all the people be better doing if they didn't have to waste their time becoming embroiled in addressing a bullying situation?
> What are competitors doing whilst the above actions are taking place? In the commercial sector, the company's competitors, especially overseas competitors, must be rubbing their hands with glee at seeing the amount of time and energy committed to in-fighting, internal conflict, disciplinary and legal action between employees.
> Preparation for tribunal requires finding, copying, then collating and distributing several copies of perhaps several hundred documents - these all have to be read by all participants - what could people be doing productively if they weren't preoccupied with this paperwork?
> How does the employer benefit from the adverse publicity surrounding the case?
> What is the effect on other employees who witness grievance and tribunal proceedings?
> Why are you involved in these proceedings?
> Who and what are you defending?
> What will you have achieved at the end of it?

Finally, the following table is offered for employers to fill in for any recent or current case of bullying:

Table 18: The cost of a bully

Activity	Time (including preparation, attendance, review, etc)	Number of people involved	Cost
complaint meetings			
grievance procedure stage 1			
grievance procedure stage 2			

Table 18: The cost of a bully

Activity	Time (including preparation, attendance, review, etc)	Number of people involved	Cost
grievance procedure stage 3			
dismissal hearing			
appeal hearing			
pre-hearing review			
industrial tribunal			
employment appeal tribunal			
county court proceedings			
high court proceedings			
appeal to House of Lords			
European court proceedings			

For an approximation of cost, start with £1000 for a grievance procedure, then add a zero each time the proceedings move to a higher court. On this basis, the bill for proceeding through each stage outlined above will be close to £1.5 million, plus awards. If a bully dispatches one victim every two years, a career of 40 years could theoretically consume £60,000,000 in costs, plus any awards the courts might make.

Perhaps I should become a lawyer.

10   Identifying the causes of bullying

Although bullying has always occurred in the workplace, in the last decade on the twentieth century the incidence seems to have rocketed. Whilst fifty years ago - or even as little as twenty - a person could reasonably expect to complete their working life without encountering a severe bullying experience, today it seems almost everyone is at risk, with the possibility that several such experiences may now be encountered during a normal working life.

It is therefore important that everyone learns to recognise both the reasons why bullying takes place, and the signs that it is happening. One needs to be able to see through the veil of denial by which bullies survive and thrive.

Precipitating and perpetuating circumstances

The following factors seem to stimulate and perpetuate bullying, although they appear to be responsible for the *increase* in bullying cases rather than be the *cause*. However, these influences may also be contributory causes in cases where certain individuals, especially in positions of management who are tasked with implementing changes and attaining tough financial targets, start to take on the characteristics of a bully. The underlying causes of pathological or serial bullying (that is, those who bully repeatedly and for apparent pleasure) are explored later in the chapter.

Finance: probably the principal stimulating factor is money - or rather, lack of it. In the private sector, the longest and deepest recession in living memory has caused most companies to cut costs at every turn; in this context, "costs" is usually a euphemism for "employees". In many cases, especially the privatised utilities, the overriding interests of shareholders mean that customers and employees are now simply the means to achieving the required profit targets. In the public sector, government budgets have been cut year on year and a more business-like approach levied in order to reduce spending and improve services. In the voluntary sector, competition from the lottery has undermined traditional forms of giving, which added to other recessional factors has led to cut-throat competition for funds and friends.

Stress: in the final decade of the century, stress has become a byword for the effect that the workplace has on employees. Many GPs report being overwhelmed by the number of people reporting symptoms of stress, most of which seem to be attributable to patterns of work.

Exhortations by managers to harness the power of stress and turn it into a positive force are increasingly being greeted with derision and contempt. After a number of recent landmark court cases, wise employers are now recognising that stressed-out ears which formerly appeared deaf are undergoing a litigious awakening.

Stress can be defined, albeit rather vaguely, as any form of physical, emotional or psychological pressure, and its endemic presence in the modern workplace probably owes much to insecurity and coercion.

An alternative view of stress is a consequence of the degree to which people feel they lack control of themselves, their situation and their life. If a person feels they cannot influence or control events in their life, they will feel anxious, and hence insecure and afraid.

Insecurity: a recent survey suggested that the average employee now expects their security of employment not to last beyond three months. Whilst the reality may be longer, the current perception has grave implications for loyalty, performance and productivity.

Change: the only thing that is constant in the workplace today is change. As organisations struggle for survival, employees look on resignedly as each reorganisation takes its toll; in some cases, the next reorganisation has already started before the previous one is completed. In some circles, this process has acquired the epithet of "headless chicken syndrome". It could be said that survival has taken precedence over prosperity.

Uncertainty: whereas in former years one could anticipate a climate of stability or gradual evolution over many years, today takeovers, mergers, outsourcing, contracterisation and the like mean that employees have little or no idea of where or who they will be working for in six months, or if indeed they will be working at all.

Understaffing: in an endless bid to cut costs and remain competitive, staff who leave (or who are downsized) are frequently not replaced; each time, however, their work is shared out amongst those who remain.

Long hours culture: the UK has one of the longer working weeks in Europe, and the implicit pressure on employees to work 50, 60 and even 70 hour weeks or more on a regular basis has led to accusations of a "sweatshop economy". In addition, breaks at lunchtime, which are now recognised as essential for maintaining performance, are often regularly curtailed or skipped. Some suggest that scarcity of alternative employment has led to a situation where managers feel it is easier to abuse employees by coercing them into working longer and longer hours rather than face up to and tackle the underlying and fundamental problems of inefficiency and uncompetitiveness. Cynics have suggested that this situation has led to an attitude of "you might as well flog 'em till they drop, 'cos there's plenty more where they came from", a mentality reminiscent of slave labour and prisoner-of-war camps.

Quality of life seems to have been overlooked in the rush to squeeze every last ounce of work out of those fortunate enough to still have a job. An increasing number of people are in no doubt that being coerced into working long hours on a regular basis is bad for health. In Europe, the UK government alone is opposed to the proposed EC Working Time Directive limiting the working week to 48 hours. The alarms bells for employers that the John Walker case rung were clearly not loud enough.

Unfortunately for employers, working longer hours does not equate to greater productivity; as hours increase, there comes a point at which the amount of useful work achieved begins to decline. Where that point is depends on a number of factors, including job satisfaction, degree of coercion, etc. For many people, if hours continue to increase after this threshold, there comes another point where breakdown occurs. This is a well-known and well-documented factor in stress management.

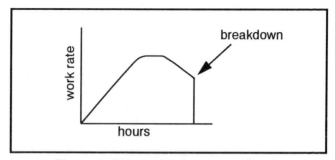

Figure 1: Effect of hours on work rate

The pressure to stay late at work has led to the coining of "presenteeism", whereby employees become convinced they will lose their jobs if they leave on time; they also become fearful of being the first to leave. How much useful work is achieved in these circumstances is open to question.

Contracts: it would be interesting to know how many jobs in the UK these days are permanent and full-time; the workplace has seen an explosion of new types, styles and contracts of employment, including

- short-term contracts
- fixed-term contracts
- flexible contracts
- zero-hours contracts
- daily contracts
- insistence on self-employment status
- part-time work
- casual labour
- temping
- teleworking
- homeworking
- increasing use of labour overseas via communication links, especially countries with low rates of pay

These have numerous advantages for the employer, which may include:

- on average lower rates of pay than with permanent contracts of employment
- subsidised employment for certain categories of trainee

- falling outside criteria (eg 2 years employment) for breaches of employment law, especially unfair or constructive dismissal
- no annual increments
- reduced or no pension contributions and rights
- reduced or no National Insurance contributions
- reduced or eliminated obligations for sickness pay
- reduced or eliminated obligations for maternity pay
- reduced or eliminated obligations for employment, health and safety, and other legislation
- avoidance of issues of equal pay
- weakening or preclusion of union influence or involvement
- avoidance of collective pay bargaining
- avoidance of redundancy costs
- the potential to coerce staff on the basis that "otherwise your contract is unlikely to be renewed"

Whilst the Chancellor may boast about one of the lowest unemployment levels in Europe, it would be interesting to see if this claim is mirrored by the number of permanent full-time positions.

There now exist a number of organisations with large numbers of people but no employees; whilst the "virtual company" is neither inherently good or bad, the potential for abuse is great, especially when the going gets tough.

Artificial expectations: with charters, performance and league tables the "in thing", plus the need to sell privatisations to investors, business has become survival of the fittest. This might sound sensible in theory, but the victims are mostly smaller traders; deserted town centres and boarded-up premises suggest that the wider and long-term effects on the community as a whole may have been overlooked. Pursuit of the cheapest deal at all costs might result in some short-term savings, but when one of the bigger businesses goes out of business, customers find that warranties and assurances are not worth the paper they're written on, and subsequent maintenance, repair and replacement bills may end up costing them dear.

Often, customers are beguiled by PR and advertising departments into believing assurances on service level and availability, only to find that those responsible for providing that service have been denied the investment and resources (usually insufficient staff) to fulfil these promises. With expectations dashed, many customers resort to taking out their disappointment on front-line staff, who consequently feel bullied from both sides.

Accreditation: is very much in vogue at the moment, for example through Investors in People (IiP), or BS5750/ ISO9001. The object of these schemes is to maximise employee wellbeing and performance and to ensure the highest levels of quality and service as a prerequisite for business prosperity. However, care needs to be taken that the laudable intent of these schemes is not usurped by those who exploit them as a window-dressing exercise. If we can make things look OK, they must be OK. What business managers sometimes forget is that there is only one judge - it is the quality of the product or service as delivered to and received by the customer that counts, not how many official looking badges are displayed on the glossy advertising material or the number of pompous letters telling customers how every step is being taken to improve service when in reality every step is being taken to avoid incurring expense through making improvements in the service.

Sometimes particularly in hierarchies where bullying is present and unchecked, it can seem as if the adoption of, and rigid adherence to, prescribed procedure acts as a substitute for quality and care. In some cases, employees may gain the impression that the added bureaucracy of accreditation hampers and detracts from the provision of quality and care, which inevitably induce disenchantment and cynicism. The main beneficiaries of bureaucracy are of course bureaucrats.

Perhaps I'm naive, but I've always believed that quality and care came from the heart, not from a manual. Quality is a culture, not a management technique. If one needs an instruction guide to tell one how to incorporate quality, provide service and value people, then perhaps that person should question their fitness to hold managerial responsibility in the first place. Management by manual is neither management nor delegation - it's abdication.

Psychometric and similar testing: as with accreditation, whilst the intention may be virtuous, there are disturbing doubts about validity, and the aptness of tests is dependent on the integrity and motives of the persons applying them. Even more disturbing is the use of such tests for regrading existing employees, especially for redundancy.

Some research suggests that the tests fail to take full account of cultural and linguistic background, and that issues of dominance and manipulation do not appreciate the difference in male and female approaches to work. Once again, the use of tests could be seen as forming the basis of abdication of responsibility if an employee later turns out to be unsuitable. One might even be forgiven for thinking that with insistence and reliance on such tests, bullying seems to begin the moment you apply for a job.

Imposition of health and safety legislation: there is no doubt that the workplace of today is far safer than it ever has been, although the flip side of the coin is proliferating bureaucracy, administration and restriction of operations.

Employment legislation: another regular beef of employers is the burgeoning red tape of yet more regulation and legislation. The apparent mad cow of imposed European regulation is now red rag to the insular bull of British employers. Unfortunately, more sensible proposals emanating from Brussels (such as limits to working hours) are in danger of being dismissed with the same automatic contempt that greeted the edict to ban the sale of bent cucumbers.

Discrimination and harassment legislation: attitudes in the workplace (and society) towards "foreigners", minorities, disabled people and women have changed dramatically over the last twenty years, with more mature mandatory standards of conduct backed up by law. Beliefs and behaviours ingrained since childhood can be difficult to dislodge, and some people, especially older employees, find themselves having to watch every word they say for fear of precipitating a complaint or disciplinary procedure, even when their intent is complimentary.

Weakening of trade unions: many employees find their opportunity or access to the safeguard of trade union membership denied or hindered. Employers frequently resort to deterring employees from their right of membership, often by distancing trade unions with a dismissive "we don't recognise such-and-such a union here". Legislation to curb former excesses may now have curtailed union influence to below the level required for the needs of today's workplace.

Male/female roles: the changing roles of men and women create additional pressures both in terms of the number and scope of job applicants and the types of job opportunity; some employees, mostly male, still seem to have difficulty with the concept of working for a female manager. Some males adapt to and enjoy the role of parent-at-home, although tolerance by employers and acceptance by peers is not always forthcoming.

Dual incomes: many families rely on two incomes to pay the bills, and when children arrive there are extra pressures and expense of child care. On reaching school age, the disparity of school and office hours becomes a termly nightmare, unrelieved by the hazard of school holidays.

Inflexible hierarchies: many organisations have shed layers of management and become "flatter" - and theoretically less authoritarian - but some disciplines have rigid hierarchies which are less amenable (or is it humanly resistant?) to modernisation. Education is one that springs to mind; the uniformed services is another.

Discipline essential: in the emergency and rescue services, armed forces and other uniformed services etc, discipline is crucial when lives are at stake.

Poor interpersonal skills: surveys suggest that in most jobs, people spend up to 80% or more of their time networking. The importance of interacting with other human beings has yet to be reflected in the average person's upbringing and formal education.

Low behavioural maturity: our behaviour is the principal way others perceive and thus interact with us; as with interpersonal skills, the importance of the way we behave towards others and the way we react to others has largely been overlooked, especially in the context of employment. Current standards of etiquette serve us well in a social context, but are noticeably lacking in the workplace, especially in a manager/subordinate relationship.

Stress has the effect of impoverishing behavioural and interpersonal skills; even the most placid and mature individuals can snap when the pressure exceeds their tolerance level.

Personal problems: divorce, bereavement, accident, illness, tragedy are always with society, but in many cases these seem to pale into insignificance when compared to a bullying experience.

New technology: computers have revolutionised the way we work in the latter half of the 20th century; often it is not the new technology itself which is the problem, but poor implementation and imposition combined with lack or training, support and help with conversion. The vast amount of information that employees are expected to cope with, plus the inability to extract only that information which is needed have now led to a new form of stress termed information fatigue syndrome.

Changes in working practice: tend also not to be well received, especially if the stated motives (improved performance and efficiency, better working conditions for employees, greater security of employment) are distinct from the perceived real reason, that is, saving money (for example by announcing redundancies three months downstream). Examples which have been introduced recently, only to be quietly superseded once the downside (or is that downsize?) has become apparent include the much-hyped business process re-engineering (BPR) vogue. People do not like to be regarded as a "process", and they resent being "re-engineered" (as any people-focused person could have told you before the changes were implemented - or is that just being smug?). Hot-desking seems to be the current fad.

Outdated   management   techniques: some organisations (for example in the public sector) have embraced new commercial freedoms by introducing "modern" management techniques from the 80s, unaware that their time is past.

Poor management: the need for this book speaks for itself.

Culture: resistance to change, for whatever reason (fear of being worse off afterwards, uncertainty of cost and effort required), leads to an attitude of "it's always been like this"; the status quo becomes self-perpetuating.

Acceptance by society: ignorance, unenlightenment, disbelief and denial combine to create a climate of acceptance, acclimatisation and acculturation.

Corporate bullying

Whilst this book concentrates mainly on serious cases of individual bullying, the workplace of the nineties often seems more akin to a battlefield. The pressures of recession on profitability, or reduction in resources for political motives, combined with a never-ending pursuit of profit, performance, perfection, "excellence", quality, etc have brought about an almost panic-like quality to daily life at work.

As with the uncovering of any poorly understood phenomenon, it is not always the individual signs which are significant, but rather the combination and quantity of clues. In the following pages, many of the signs might be considered not only normal, but almost prerequisite of any "standard" working environment. Whether bullying is present or not, most are likely to impair rather than enhance performance and productivity.

> "There was an attitude that 'if you can't stand the heat, get out of the kitchen'. Unfortunately, those who espoused this view could not see sufficiently far ahead to recognise that soon there would be no-one left to do the cooking. There would be no shortage of people to say what needed cooking though."

Some contributory factors which could be loosely termed "corporate bullying" that have been highlighted include:

- when bullying is reported, there is an unwillingness to admit that those responsible for recruitment and promotion could possibly have made a mistake
- ditto if there have been previous complaints or investigations - there are uncomfortable questions of competence, negligence and liability
- ditto for fear of skeletons in the employer's cupboard

- ditto for fear of skeletons in the bully's cupboard, especially if the employer knows this, and it becomes known that the employer knows this
- in departments where bullying is rife, there is an unwillingness to recognise that rate of staff turnover indicates something is wrong
- unwillingness to accept that bullying goes on
- dismissal of evidence, regardless of value or quantity
- an unwillingness to investigate cause of staff turnover
- an unwillingness to recognise cost of staff turnover
- an unwillingness to admit that anything could be wrong
- a cover-up culture
- unwillingness to address bullying
- refusal to define, publish and implement a bullying policy (this could be seen as an overt sign that senior management has no confidence in itself)

One law for them...

- over-rewarding of budgetary skills at the expense of those with people skills
- organisations run by accountants
- fat-cat mentality, with higher than average pay rises for senior employees, often with unacceptable justification, together with minimal or lower than average pay rises for those at the bottom
- chief and senior executives being accorded salary levels which are perceived as inappropriate, especially in a climate of stringency (eg the attitude that "it is important to pay sufficient to attract and retain the right calibre of people", although one might be forgiven for thinking that the "right calibre" is a person who believes this statement)
- sudden and widespread introduction of questionable perks (eg company cars) for senior employees (especially in the public or about-to-be-privatised sectors) which are conspicuously in advance of results
- ditto introduction of corporate hospitality events which become de rigueur for senior employees and which have little or no perceived commercial return

- ditto introduction of apparently frivolous expenditure on branded gifts, especially with limited lifetime (eg the company logo or name changes regularly)
- mismatch of corporate statements (eg "staff are our greatest asset") but the behaviour of senior employees is at variance with such claims
- in the privatised utilities especially, shareholders are now the number one priority
- the natural tendency of like promotes like, like recruits like - who is going to promote or recruit a person who might be a threat to them?
- an employer top heavy with managers and administrators
- shedding of large numbers of "workers", but not equivalent numbers of senior staff
- senior staff getting large pay-offs and handshakes, but employees below a certain level just being made redundant - or bullied out
- ruthless or strictly-imposed limits on capital investments for those doing the work, with apparent profligate spending on corporate matters
- senior staff going on mega-jollies, or attending management courses with impressive titles in attractive locations but with no permanent or ultimate perceived benefit

Inflexibility and imposition
- lack of flexibility, eg when the slightest deviation from budget induces fear and panic and provokes a severe reprimand
- unwillingness to take risks, even small carefully calculated ones
- rigid imposition of management plans, often without consultation or opportunity to participate in the change process
- the use of faits accompli to forestall resistance
- corporate cohesion: senior managers seem divorced from what is happening at the coal face and show blind adhesion to the corporate line, regardless of how foolish or inappropriate such adherence is perceived

- sudden and unusual emphasis on the "latest management techniques" (especially after attendance on the latest management training course)
- ditto the sudden imposition of "mission" and "vision" (if you need to go on a training course to tell you how to have a vision, then...)
- imposition of performance and efficiency monitoring - most employees feel they are better employed doing what they were employed to do rather than spending a significant amount of time recording minute tasks and times; disenchantment and disaffection in this climate are a common stimulus for staff moving on
- ditto other modern management initiatives which are often loudly trumpeted but short-lived

Benefits of regular reorganisation

- regular reorganisation, perhaps as every six, or even three months, which makes it harder, sometimes impossible, to identify culprits, ascribe blame and pin responsibility on those who are guilty (this can happen at every level)
- organisation charts that are out of date almost before employees have time to put them on the wall
- organisation charts where the people stay the same (except perhaps an occasional token sacrifice) but the hierarchy, structure and job titles change regularly
- a climate where job titles keep changing with - from the employees' perspective - little or no reason or benefit
- fancy job titles for everyone, especially at senior levels, with a feeling that perhaps the title is more important than the job (eg the tea lady is a "beverage consultant" and a cleaner becomes "facilities cleansing manager")

Perceived poor management

- extensive use of (expensive) consultants, as if management decision-taking has been abdicated
- lack of imagination
- enthusiasm is regarded as a negative trait
- sudden snap decisions which can't be reversed
- random decision making
- absence of trust at and between all levels

- company policy to fleece customers at every
  opportunity to achieve this year's targets, regardless of
  potential loss of customer loyalty over the long term

Cutting costs by cutting staff

- euphemisms for reducing staff costs
- contracterisation - insistence, sometimes coercion, of
  moving full-time permanent employees on to short-
  term contracts
- facilities management (FM) - certain activities which
  are not "core business" are handed to an outside
  company; permanent employees find themselves
  surplus to requirements or transferred to the FM
  provider on less favourable terms
- outsourcing - as with FM, non-core business activities
  are handed to outside companies to operate, but
  -> can an outside company which is only interested in
     its own profits provide the levels of service and
     commitment that an in-house team provide?
  -> customers and suppliers find it difficult to know who
     they are dealing with - obtaining goods and services
     and paying invoices can mean handling paperwork
     and dealing with three or four apparently unrelated
     companies
  -> when things go wrong, it's harder to identify who is
     responsible - the customer may feel like the ball in a
     ping-pong of denial of responsibility as each
     company alternately blames the other
  -> if there is recourse to law, eg breach of contract,
     liability, negligence, the chances are that the
     companies will have restructured, merged or
     changed service providers so often by the time the
     case is heard that no-one can pinpoint who is
     responsible
- a plethora of euphemisms for redundancy, including
  downsizing, rightsizing, restructuring, rationalisation,
  reorganisation, delayering, corporate aerobics, re-
  engineering, career re-orientation - each avoidance of
  the word "redundancy" drawing attention to the fact
  that the employer is choosing to avoid the word
  "redundancy" in favour of the popular euphemism

- other transparent euphemisms such as amalgamation (closing down), sell-off (closing down), merger (takeover), strategic partnership (takeover), pressure management (panic management, bullying) etc often necessitating or resulting in redundancies
- euphemisms for coercing permanent staff onto contracts, eg casualisation, peripheralisation
- management pep talks which don't match what the employees observe
- a preponderance of job cuts at junior levels without equivalent shedding higher up - perhaps with the feeling that the principal purpose of redundancies is to safeguard the jobs of those further up

Abuse of workforce

- abolition of welfare, counselling and other staff support services, possibly with the statement that all matters should be discussed instead with line management
- an apparent attitude that it's cheaper to bully employees out of their jobs, so that costs don't come out of managers' budgets
- ditto to encourage people to leave through resignation or ill-health retirement when the company or organisation needs to slim down or wants to use cheaper contract or casual staff, thereby saving on redundancy payments
- bullying is used to make peoples' life hell, so they move - this appears to be a substitute for personnel policy
- handling redundancy badly and refusing to recognise the trauma this undertaking causes
- being forced to do the same amount of work (or more) in fewer hours and for less money
- the need for whistleblowing, and the victimisation that follows it
- the grievance procedure stacked in favour of bully
- keeping employees in dark, proffering plenty of platitudes, which are followed by sudden closure or redundancies
- unwillingness to value and reward people skills
- coercion of employees into taking shorter breaks, skipping breaks, or taking lunch whilst continuing to

work (a recent survey indicated that those who don't get away from the workplace at lunch time tend to be irritable and depressed during the afternoon)

- the use of the "mystery shopper" to "snoop" on front-line employees; this practice has the potential for misuse, eg by producing reports that employers want to hear (eg in order to sack staff or close branches), a method by which employees have little or no redress or defence
- employees being coerced into working Saturday mornings, weekends or other unsocial hours, sometimes without being paid overtime
- imposition of "absence management" etc to coerce employees into not taking annual or sick leave entitlement, often backed up with threat of disciplinary action - one might be tempted to think that an employer who introduces absence management has inadvertently omitted the word "of"

Image

- infatuation with charter marks, performance and league tables, accreditation, etc
- obsession with appearance and form over content
- lots of money on refurbishment, signs, corporate logos, insignia, glossies, customer areas, corporate headquarters, decor, latest trends, regular changes of name, image, letter headings, etc, but difficulty in obtaining approval for spending on resources for those at the sharp end
- posters on wall, eg "companies don't succeed, people do", "customer is king", etc, but corporate behaviour at variance with stated claims
- employees ignoring company newsletter or making derogatory or cynical remarks about the contents
- low response to employee surveys, perhaps decreasing with each subsequent questionnaire
- upbeat reports of responses to staff surveys, especially when discussion with colleagues would indicate the reverse

Culture

"Half way through the year, a new manager was unexpectedly appointed which created a new level of hierarchy. She was half my age and although she had degrees coming out of her ears, she had absolutely no idea how to deal with people. Not surprisingly, the former highly-stressed but generally happy atmosphere disintegrated rapidly. Within twelve months, almost all the original team had left."

- devolution - or rather abdication - of responsibility - eg voluntary school governors with legal responsibility and who may have to make staff redundant; patients' charter requiring higher levels of care but with fewer resources
- responsibility for meeting customer expectation is with lower grade employees, but failure to meet targets is met with the appointment or more managers and administrators rather than staff to do the work
- closed minds - this is the way we've always done it (self-preservation)
- fear of change
- fear of being found out
- assurances that all is well, followed shortly by redundancy - either managers must have known about it when assurances were given, or have no ability to manage finances and plan ahead
- trustworthiness declines with grade
- an atmosphere where back-stabbing, politicking etc is not only acceptable, but appears mandatory
- little or no perceived opportunity for career advancement

Clues to look for

In many bullying situations, not only does the victim of bullying not know what is happening, observers often have little or no idea of what is occurring in their midst. Here are some further indicators which might ring warning bells:

- general unhappiness, especially in a group that was happy under its previous leader
- low morale

- irritability and aggression between individuals - because each victim feels isolated and alone, they begin to take out their frustration and anger on others. "He's giving me hell, so why shouldn't I pass some of it on?" "Why is she picking on me and no-one else?"
- touchiness, snappiness, impatience, especially at small and insignificant things
- distrust of colleagues, especially where trust formerly existed
- defensiveness, evasiveness, unhelpfulness, particularly in people who were formerly cooperative and willing
- selfishness, people thinking about themselves, building walls to protect themselves
- staff leaving, for apparently sensible reasons, but it still comes as a surprise
- increasing use of disciplinary procedures based on trivial or specious justifications
- increasing use of scapegoating
- staff taking sideways career moves or moving sections to take shelter behind a kindly individual who absorbs the pressure but doesn't pass it on - watch for people giving up their first love for another job which is too easy for their skills and ambitions, which has limited scope for career progression, and which appears to be a downward step
- hypersensitivity - every incident or apparent word out of place causes a reaction
- an outbreak of hypervigilance which is identified as paranoia - the belief, admittedly irrational, that walls have ears, phones are tapped, office bugged, computers broken into, filestore monitored
- loss of self-confidence in a formerly and otherwise sensible person
- loss of objectivity
- anyone crying for uncertain reasons, especially if this happens more than once, or to more than one person
- anxiety, trembliness or panic attacks whenever the bully is anticipated, present or talked about in any context
- suicide, real, attempted or contemplated

- signs of bullying from anyone - they may be passing on the pressure, or learning by example
- under-resourcing and overwork, people being loaded down, coerced into working long hours, evenings, weekends, even overnight - and not enjoying it; phrases such as "I'm doing the work of five staff", "the number of staff in my section has been halved from four to two", "we're so short-staffed now, we just can't cope"
- people working harder and harder, but with less and less enthusiasm, motivation, efficiency, and effect
- the setting of tasks that everyone sees cannot be achieved
- people leaving home and family to stay nearer to work
- marital disharmony - the partner usually cannot comprehend the mental torment
- illness, especially with vague descriptions, especially those described in chapter 8
- anyone admitting they've been to the doctor, but with nothing specific, perhaps wondering if they are wasting their doctor's time
- unusually high sickness levels, especially with diagnoses containing the word "stress"
- nervous, mental or stress breakdowns, especially if regular, and especially if swept under the carpet
- employees not taking sickness leave when they should
- inability to sleep, or waking up tired, especially after a good night's sleep
- despair or a look of desperation, dejectedness, resignation, folornness
- cries for help, eg "I'm terrified of missing an invoice"
- clues in conjunction with other signs, eg "I'm on leave this afternoon - YIPPEE!"
- people concentrating on the short term at the expense of the long term
- loss of team spirit
- views, activities and actions being dictated; employees feeling unhappy with what they are being asked to do
- workers acting like robots
- people covering their backs - spending more time doing this than working

- high staff turnover, particularly if you are unable to discern the reasons, or detect evasiveness, imprecision, or economy with the truth
- people unwilling or unable to take annual leave entitlement
- petty theft, especially of items of little or no value
- promises made but not kept
- poor or indifferent customer service
- employees acting in a "don't care" manner
- mismatch of service expected/received
- general lack of interest or decline of interest
- unexplained absence during working hours
- people feeling they're in a "no-win" situation
- low morale
- meetings run by minorities
- death wish, wanting the project/department/company to fail
- unwillingness to delegate
- confidential reports of "unpromotable"
- evasiveness
- unwillingness or inability to listen
- people resorting to subterfuge
- inconsistency - one law for him/them, one for us/me
- people putting on a brave face
- disregard of other people's rights
- coteries, cliques, elites
- managers shouting at employees in front of others
- obsession with pointing out other people's mistakes, especially in public
- apparent offers to discuss, but manager's decision goes through anyway
- use of defamatory language (sign of frustration and resentment, including the word "asshole")
- threats of being fired, moved, downgraded, outsourced
- threats to carry out action which technically cannot be carried out, or which would potentially expose the bully
- mismatch of service expected/received, eg employee gives lower or higher service to customer than advertised, but there appears to be no backup
- long or permanent backlog

- people on edge - wondering what their manager or management are going to do next
- cynicism, lack of faith in management

Why do people bully?
With bullying now out in the open, the reasons why some people choose to behave in this manner will keep psychologists and psychiatrists (not to mention employers, solicitors, lawyers, counsellors, academics, parents, writers and employees) busy for some time. The following sections explore some of the potential reasons and causes and are intended to stimulate further discussion and research.

Probable reasons
The causes of bullying seem to involve a combination of factors, primarily:

- immaturity of behaviour skills (bullying can be seen as a form of immature leadership), and...
- low self-confidence and self-esteem, resulting in...
- disproportionate sense of envy, plus a...
- heightened sense of insecurity, culminating in...
- an unnaturally high perception of threat, leading to...
- inappropriate activation of the self-protection mechanism (part of the instinct for survival), implemented using...
- amoral behaviour, including lack of conscience, lack of self-control and self-discipline, etc

Other factors which contribute to bullying include:

- learned behaviours reinforced by acceptance, success and reward
- predominant behaviour style, with some people remaining as bullies (or victims) throughout their lives
- too thick a skin which not only protects the bully from the harsh words and deeds of others, but also prevents him from being able to see the effect his behaviour has on others - this is similar to attitudes (and excuses for) rape, eg "I didn't realise she wasn't enjoying it" (also as with rape, soft sentencing creates precedent and does little to deter offenders)
- compulsion - in the same manner as child abuse, the bully may mean not to do it, may want not to do it, but knows no other way of behaving; with bullying, the

ability to change is further precluded by a steadfast sense of self-reliance

- addiction, as in drug abuse, to the "high" feeling that comes from having made someone else feel bad through destroying their confidence and esteem

- the bully's behaviour seems to be stimulated by their victim's low assertiveness, apparent indecisiveness and approval-seeking through the need to be valued

- often a bully is being bullied by someone else, eg manager or partner, and their way of coping is to pass it on

- the adversarial nature of UK culture (which until recently has been the academic, legal and political basis for stable democracy) tends to teach and encourage one to focus on other peoples' faults and weaknesses rather than their strengths and achievements

One of the most mystifying characteristics of bullying is why bullies choose to perceive threat where none exists. If the above reasoning is correct, one might surmise that the aberrant sense of threat that bullies seem to feel in the presence of a competent and popular person could be a delusion which allays the anxiety that results from insecurity and fear of exposure stemming from low self-confidence, low self-esteem and low self-worth.

Delusions are entrenched beliefs which are adhered to irrationally, often in the face of indisputable evidence to the contrary. Although delusions are sometimes a sign of mental illness, a similar spectacle is occasionally observed in otherwise normal people. For example, scientists, academics and managers will often cling almost obsessionally to their pet theory if they have chosen to make their career dependent on the validity of their proposition even after it has been disproved or superseded by new evidence or research or events.

It appears that the bully feels threatened in response to the anxiety about their own job performance in a climate of general job insecurity. The anxiety is alleviated by inflicting suffering on others, a strategy learnt early in life, probably through mimicry, and reinforced by success, tolerance, encouragement and reward, for example promotion.

If anxiety is indeed the underlying cause of bullying, the relief resulting from reduction in anxiety could explain the apparent pleasure that bullies seem to derive from behaving in the way they do. It could also go a long way in accounting for the recent rapid rise in the incidence of bullying in today's workplace in which stress is endemic and stress levels seem to be increasing inexorably.

Anxiety is often regarded as a conditioned response when the sufferer is reminded of previous experience of pain (either physical and psychological). In bullying, strategies for dealing with perceived threat (which might be likened to avoidance behaviours) quickly become ingrained (reinforced) because of their effectiveness in reducing anxiety. Also, anxiety seems to act as a barrier to learning, and many bullies seem unable to learn from past unpleasant experiences.

The anxious person tends to overreact, which might also explain the bully's perplexing but persistent negative attitude and random mood swings. Road rage seems to be another example of overreaction, sometimes leading to murder. Behaviours instigated by anxiety tend to be disorganised and sometimes destructive, especially when they draw on anger. Followers of Freud might add that the desire to dominate results from sexual frustration, and victims frequently mention the bully's inability to form stable relationships, especially with the opposite sex. Emotional instability plus the dread of being alone may exacerbate the situation. The bully's apparent inner belief in their unworthiness seems to engender envy, as if other people's happiness acts as a magnet for their misery.

Whilst male bullies tend to be physically aggressive and more overtly hostile, the significance of perceived threat might also explain why female bullies are especially manipulative, devious, spiteful and vindictive. Assuming the evolutionary model, females are tasked with the responsibility of ensuring the survival of the human race by raising the next generation and are thus programmed with the instinctive ability to fight tooth and nail to protect themselves and their offspring.

It seems that a person with the predominant behaviour style of the bully reacts instinctively to anxiety by feeling threatened; however, a person with the predominant behaviour style of a victim reacts instinctively to anxiety by feeling guilty. It's as if the bully is born with levels guilt too low (or absent), whilst the victim is born with a level of guilt which is too high

Anxiety is distinct from fear in that the cause of the latter is usually identifiable (and external), whereas the origin of the former is indeterminate. Phase 1 of bullying (control and subjugation) seems to be a compulsive reaction to reduce anxiety in the face of perceived threat. The compulsion arises from the conviction that if no action is taken, the stress may become acute. At the point where the victim shows signs of realising what is happening, and begins to assert their right not to be bullied, the bully's anxiety is transformed into fear, and elimination (phase 2) is the instinctive response. The additional prospect of grievance or legal proceedings further heightens both anxiety and fear, and as the threat progresses from perception to reality, the obsessional nature of the need to reduce anxiety manifests itself through the hastened process of elimination. The pleasurable feeling of habitually gaining relief from anxiety ultimately leads to the behaviours becoming addictive.

The bully is often unaware of the irony of their behaviour; they perceive threat where none exists, then behave in a manner which inexorably transforms their victim into what they originally but erroneously feared. Illogicality and senselessness are frequently a feature of obsession.

Often, the relief from anxiety brought about by elimination of threat is replaced by a new anxiety caused by the fear of exposure, for more often than not the bully lacks competence to fulfil the duties and responsibilities of their job and only survives by virtue of being carried by their victim - the person they have just got rid of. To counter this, a successor of comparable competence is quickly appointed - and the cycle starts again.

Diagnosis

These days, no self-respecting disorder can be properly diagnosed until it has been allotted an appropriate acronym. For the symptoms that bullying occasions in the victim, I suggest Anxiety-Based Uncontrolled Stress Experience, or ABUSE.

Patterns set in childhood

Sometimes it seems as if behind every bully is an unhappy childhood or unsatisfactory upbringing. As an adult, the bully does not seem to have realised, understood, worked through or come to terms with disheartening juvenile experiences, which might be overt and easily recognisable, (for example as in sexual abuse), or more subtle and less easily identifiable (such as conditional praise). Childhood causative factors might comprise:

- being sexually abused
- being physically abused, through violence in the home environment
- being subjected to other forms of violence (including institutionalised violence) such as corporal punishment
- being regularly subjected to conditional love ("we only love you when you behave")
- absence of love ("mummy and daddy didn't love me")
- absence of expressed love, ie their mummy and daddy loved them but were unable to express their love
- not being loved but their sibling(s) was (were)
- being subject to regular destructive criticism ("can't you do better than that?" "that's a stupid idea" "don't be so silly")
- receiving conditional praise or approval, ie always being told how you could have done better ("Well, that's quite good, but if you had done this...")
- never receiving praise or encouragement at all
- neglect of physical needs
- neglect of psychological needs
- lack of example of how to form stable and equal relationships
- lack of example in regard to manners, behaviour, conduct, etc
- not being taught interpersonal skills etc
- learning by example - one or other parents behaving like a bully
- unsuitable role models of other loved, respected or authoritarian figures

- being excluded, eg not being allowed to form relationships with other people (adults and children)
- fear associated with unpleasant childhood experience
- lack of attachment to parents or guardians

Summary

What is often reported is the sense of satisfaction or pleasure that the bully appears to derive from behaving in this manner. One theory suggests that an upbringing which is lacking in or devoid of approval leads in adulthood to a sense or delusion of unworthiness. The need to earn money necessitates gainful employment, and possibly development of career, which in turn incurs the need to be seen as competent. An inborn instinct to lead combined with underdeveloped and immature leadership skills give rise to bullying, which the perpetrator sees as a sign of strength, hence superiority, and hence worthiness. Consequently, in a climate of societal approval and reward, the bully becomes and remains convinced that this style of behaviour is both acceptable and necessary.

Part Two: How to challenge and combat workplace bullying

11 Unmasking the bully

"Nothing in my upbringing prepared me for the experience of working for a psychopath."

Bullies have a Jekyll and Hyde persona which enables them to appear sincere and charming one minute, whilst acting in an aggressive and threatening manner the next. The criteria for selection of these behaviours is usually dependent on who is present.

Another quality is the chameleon-like ability which enables the bully to blend in with the surroundings, to remain innocent and innocuous in the face of danger (of exposure), but to stand out when there is praise, honour or reward in the offing.

So how does one uncover and identify bullying?

Look for clues: as with any mystery or crime, the clues are there if you know what you are looking for, where to look, and what questions to ask. This book is your guide.

Examine track records: in many cases, the victim's career will be characterised by success, achievement and testimonials, whereas the bully's career is more likely to consist of regular involvement in disciplinary proceedings and industrial tribunals, a disparity which can be highlighted and analysed. Sometimes the bully may have a criminal conviction related to fraud, deception or similar.

Exit interviews: these enable staff who are leaving, for whatever reason, to state, without fear of retribution, the precise reasons for their departure. Many people are unwilling to say frank and possibly unkind things about others (the words "snitch" and "grass" come to mind), so the circumstances have to be made as safe as possible. In fact, the type of person who is most likely to be bullied is also the person who is most reluctant to criticise others. Whilst an exit interview might be seen as an attempt to lock the stable door after the horse has bolted, it nevertheless has the advantage of evoking, in most cases, the most honest and forthright answers.

Confidential support line: a service, possibly over the telephone, which employees (or their family) can call (anonymously if necessary) and receive advice on all aspects of personal welfare. Most of the advice will be of a referral nature, but issues (for example bullying) affecting the performance of employees (and hence of the employer) need to be particularly well addressed. Some employers offer this service as part of their employee assistance programme (EAP).

Counselling: a resource available to all employees, and of especial value in times of need. Figures published by the Department of Health indicate that at any one time, around 30% of employees will be experiencing a "mental health problem". This can result in inefficiency, poor decision-making, problems in relationships with colleagues and customers, and higher than necessary staff turnover. Whilst the cause of some people's mental health problems will originate outside the workplace, those that arise within the workplace are - or should be - of primary concern to the employer. Apart from any moral obligation, employers have a legal duty to provide a safe working environment. Whilst the original intention of this legislation may have been a safe physical working environment, the need for a safe mental environment is also paramount. It is likely that employees, increasingly empowered through knowledge, will take action if an employer is negligent in either of these areas. Counselling is one method whereby employees can reveal - or discover - the true cause of any problems they are experiencing.

Upward assessment: allowing an employee to make a confidential report on their boss may be controversial, but it does enable poor managers and difficult people to be identified. Reluctance to implement this type of evaluation is fuelled partly by management or personnel not having the understanding, or procedures, to deal with a person once identified. There is also the embarrassment of having recruited or promoted that person in the first place.

Unfortunately, most people are not going to bite the hand that feeds them, so this good idea may not work in practice.

Staff survey: a device being used increasingly to gain feedback from staff about how they feel things are going. Unfortunately, questions are often limited in scope, poorly thought out, and give little opportunity for explaining or revealing the more intractable people problems. Surveys, especially when used as part of an accreditation programme, are often designed to produce the answers the surveyors want to hear, rather than give the employees the opportunity to say what needs to be said. This suspicion is confirmed when subsequently survey results are published which vary significantly from observations and experience.

> *"In one attempt at a company survey recently, employees had become so sick and tired of receiving meaningless glossy questionnaires that half were immediately binned. Of those that were returned, half (ie a quarter of the total) expressed some satisfaction with the way the company was being run. This was reported in the company newsletter as 'Half the staff are satisfied...' Given that managers account for about a quarter of the total workforce, staff drew their own conclusions."*

Education and awareness: raising awareness amongst the entire workforce enables problem areas to be identified and thus addressed. Unfortunately, many employers see empowerment as threatening and are reluctant to provide too much information to too many people.

The fifteen-step bully identification process
The bully is an individual usually in a position of leadership (for example management, authority, trust), and who has or is required to have the qualities of leadership, but lacks the maturity and ability to develop and display the skills of command. Immaturity of behaviour skills goes hand-in-hand with low confidence and low self-esteem, which result in feelings of insecurity. The bully fears that someone will see through their facade, and find them out for what they really are.

"I thought I was the only one."

Bullies also fear their victims talking to each other and recognising that the cause of their difficulties lies not within themselves, but elsewhere. This is one of the reasons bullies work hard to isolate their victims; divide and rule is a tenet characteristic of bullies and weak managers. The realisation that the cause of their problem is an individual common to all those experiencing difficulties is a powerful enlightenment. Knowledge is power, awareness is empowerment. This is seditious stuff; once people unite, the bully is exposed.

Challenging the bully requires degrees of interpersonal skills, behavioural maturity, confidence and assertiveness well beyond the average. Within the workplace, such an course of action can only be successful if an anti-bullying policy is in place, and endorsed from the top; otherwise, the victory will be partial, with the bully free to turn his attentions elsewhere - or, more sinisterly, deploy covert tactics to indulge his compulsion less visibly. This may include "advising" on the surplus nature of certain employees when the company is restructuring. As everyone knows, once a company has decided to get rid of an individual - or department - it is difficult, and usually impossible - to change, influence or reverse the decision.

Therefore, before challenging a bully, each person must weigh up the pros and cons of their situation. To put up with the abuse? The consequences on health, relationships etc will continue to deteriorate. To challenge the bully? And risk losing one's job, or have further intolerable pressures brought to bear? In a few cases, the bully may back down; the probability at present is that things will get worse. For some, moving on is the only option. But as some people have found, without legislation to outlaw workplace bullying, it can be a case of out of the frying pan and into the fire. Better the devil you know.

When the bully is challenged, whilst they may appear to respond in an unpredictable manner, it is only the *content* of their response which is unpredictable. Their underlying behaviour *pattern* is predictable, showing some - maybe all - of the steps outlined below. By keeping a careful record of the bully's responses, their actions can be shown to conform to the pattern of behaviour characteristic of a bully.

In this way, you let the bully convict himself with his own behaviour. You will need to be firm, resolute and assertive; to improve your chances of success:

- decide exactly what it is you want, or want to achieve (be realistic and truthful)
- use only assertive behaviour
- stick to your guns, employ positive entrenchment (you won't be moved), use repetition (if necessary, act like a record player with its needle stuck)
- ignore provocation, taunts, threats - see these as signs of success, that you are getting through

Your unwillingness to respond to provocation will annoy the bully, encouraging him to exhibit more bully behaviour - which you duly record and compare against the list. In other words, the more impeccable your behaviour, the more corroborating behaviour the bully exhibits. The bully convicts himself with his own behaviour.

Make notes of every interaction, and everything the bully says, does, and threatens. Try hard to see and record the intent behind the content. Where other people are involved or referred to, make a note to check with each person what has or has not been said by the bully. You will need to use tact, diplomacy and subtlety in doing this, as it can be difficult to know who to trust. The bully can be so charming and convincing that third parties may not perceive what is going on. If you are too pushy or nosey, there is a risk that you will be seen as the troublemaker. Be as honest as you can, but remember that you can choose to reveal as many - or as few - facts as is necessary for your purpose. Discrepancies in what the bully says and does, or between what he says to you and others, should all be noted. If there's a confrontation or showdown, such inconsistencies will prove invaluable in the final unmasking.

When challenging a bully, watch for this fifteen-step behaviour exhibition (throughout the process, look out for use of guilt, and record that as well):

Surprise. This may be the first time the bully has been challenged in this manner, and the surprise may be genuine.

1. Surprise
2. Denial
3. Projection
4. Sympathy
5. Alarm
6. Threat
7. Provocation
8. Delay
9. Panic
10. Defence
11. Confusion
12. Diversion
13. Counter-attack
14. Humility
15. Play victim

Table 19: Unmasking the bully

On the other hand, the bully is so accustomed to behaving like this that it is more likely to be an instinctive response. The reasons for their response are not important.

Key words and phrases to watch out for:

What, me?

What have I done?

Are you sure about this?

What have I done to you?

There must be a mistake here.

No, you're mistaken, you're making this up.

The bully will be accustomed to using guilt, and is likely to wield it at every opportunity. Recognise it (through the feeling of discomfort it engenders), understand that guilt is at its most effective when there is a grain of truth (but never enough to justify its use), record it, then ignore it. You have a right not to be encouraged to feel guilty.

I've always acted in your best interests, haven't I?

I thought we were friends?

Note the last proclamation "I thought we were friends" - a statement in the form of a question - or is it a question in the form of a statement? Bullies often confuse questions and statements as a way of projecting their beliefs onto others.

One's instinctive response is to justify or excuse, which increases doubt - whose genesis is guilt. Be mindful, keep mum.

Denial. The first outward sign of an unwillingness to accept responsibility. This is an inborn self-protection mechanism that most people will resort to when alerted to some potential unpleasant consequences as a result of their actions.

I'm not a bully, I never have been.

I've never resorted to bullying, it's not in my nature.

Unfortunately it's part of the human survival instinct and therefore in all our natures.

Projection. The bully now tries to project their own failings on to the other person, who under the pressure of threat and intimidation, possibly backed up with guilt, begins to doubt themselves.

You have an attitude problem.

I can't trust you to do anything right.

You're not capable of doing your job properly.

You're useless.

Sympathy. An instinctive response by which the bully tries to claim sympathy for themselves. It's a form of diversion, and a dry run for the trump card at the end of the process.

Yes, but what about me?

Do you know how much I've suffered?

I'm under so much pressure to achieve...

Alarm. The victim is not going to be fobbed off so easily. The bully may offer to discuss the concerns "openly".

We can sort this out between us.

I'm here to help you.

There's no need for anyone else to be involved.

Trust me.

I'd rather trust a hungry anaconda.

Threat. Put the frighteners on. The victim has always succumbed before; see if they are still susceptible.

This is doing your reputation no good at all.

I'll have to bring this up with the Board of Governors.

You'll lose your licence.

I'll have to consult with our/my/your professional body on this.

I've talked with [a certain person/office] and made them aware of the facts of this case.

If you persist in this ridiculous campaign, I shall have to report you to the Board of Directors/Head of Personnel/ Security/Police.

Note that most of these threats are implied rather than real. In most cases, the bully has no intention of contacting anyone, but the purpose of making threats is to stir up fear and confusion. An enemy confused is an enemy disheartened is an enemy crushed. In a few cases however, the bully may carry out their threat - and follow it up with uncharacteristically meticulous notes copied with equally uncharacteristic rigorousness to all and sundry - or at least all whom the bully regards as allies or potential allies.

A further effect of this approach is to imply that the bully has the full support and backing of the people they name. Again, this may be true. It is also possible that at this moment the bully does not have the support of anyone, but in the event of a showdown these people may side with the bully, thus turning the bully's threat into an eerily self-fulfilling prophecy.

Threats themselves are provocative, anticipating the next step. If you suspect the bully really has consulted a third person, and made them aware of the "facts", pause and consider how to approach the situation. A sudden reaction, which is what the bully wants, may be inappropriate or unnecessary, and may make the situation worse. A considered, discreet enquiry at a suitable time may be more appropriate. If you do decide to double-check, remember that opinions can be challenged, altered, misunderstood and misrepresented - so stick firmly to facts.

Provocation. This is an invitation to act emotionally, irrationally, irresponsibly - an attempt to elicit a knee-jerk and reckless reaction, one which will be regretted afterwards. In provoking you, the bully is gaining ammunition to be used later when portraying you as untrustworthy, immature, unreliable, etc - precisely those characteristics displayed by the bully, and another example of projection. Bite your tongue, focus on recording what the bully says and does, remind yourself that the purpose of this interaction is to allow the bully to give you overwhelming behavioural evidence so that he ends up damning himself.

The beauty of this technique is that the more impeccable your behaviour, the longer the piece of rope the bully chooses with which to hang himself.

If you don't stop pestering / harassing / bullying me, I'm going to the Police.

I know people [in high places] who will put a stop to your game.

I don't see how we can continue to work together if you continue to behave like this.

I'm reporting this to your senior manager this afternoon.

You're behaving in an childish and immature manner.

If you take any action, the company will sue for every penny you've got.

You're embarrassing yourself, me, and the company.

The last provocative remark contains guilt and implied threat. It is a weak, but often effective attempt by the bully to align himself with both high moral standards and the objectives/purpose/standards of the employer. It has a strong isolating effect on the individual.

Delay. Bullies may put off disciplinary meetings, hearings, appeals, tribunals etc as often as they can get away with it. Dates, times and places will be changed, often at short notice, the other party will be informed with the minimum of notice, but justified by seemingly plausible excuses. Important and vital documents will be withheld until just before the meeting; or better still, until just after. Another seemingly plausible excuse and apology is offered. One or two important pieces of evidence may be "lost", "in the post", "wrongly filed", "between departments", in fact anywhere other than where they should be.

Panic. Things are hotting up now. The bully senses a real risk of exposure. It is rare for an opponent to have got this far down the list. Attempts are made to gather support from peers, management, subordinates, the employer, friends, colleagues, anywhere. Time to challenge the victim, and repeat threats heavily laced with guilt. The bully tries to put off meetings, appointments, deadlines, etc, and may unilaterally try to postpone any grievance procedure, meeting, or attempt at arbitration. Confusion, obfuscation are the order of the day. In a show of apparent sincerity, the bully may repeat their offer to discuss openly.

Let's talk.

This isn't a grievance procedure, it's just a meeting to sort out our differences.

I've reviewed your case with [a senior manager / official] and he / she agrees there's nothing in it.

Listen for words like *"misunderstanding"*, *"mistake"*, *"no, you've got it all wrong"*, and repetition of threats.

Defence. Or rather, attack. Time to bring up the heavy guns. There now follow a string of counter-accusations; some will be false, some (usually trivial) will be true, but most will have a grain of truth in them. The bully picks on any faults and mistakes their victim has made, magnifies them, then portrays them as the norm, rather than the exception. Mistakes that the bully has made (usually plenty) are somehow forgotten, overlooked, or "not relevant". The bully's objective is to keep the spotlight and the focus on the victim and what he/she has/hasn't done.

I've reprimanded you often for arriving late.

Tea breaks are a maximum of 15 minutes, I've told you about gossiping before.

You know the procedure, I'm fed up with your mistakes.

Sometimes it's easier to do the job myself.

Look out for unabashed guilt:

After all I've done for you...

Confusion. Leading on from defence, particularly if the tactic does not appear to be having the desired effect, the bully's supporters, or the management and/or personnel, join in with the bully. Consider the following

Employer's position:

I understand from Ms X's last communication to her solicitor, her assessments with occupational health and other health professionals, and her communications with other

members of [this employer] that she has agreed to resign at the end of the current project and that she will not now be pursuing retirement on ill-health grounds which was the option recommended by her GP.

Ms X's position:

I have not resigned.

Ms X has been bullied and is now standing up for her rights; in so doing, she is drawing attention to the unacceptable behaviour of her employer. Sensing this, the representatives on the employer's side are seeking to get rid of her by claiming that she has already agreed to resign when she in fact has not. By putting their claim in writing, validity, legitimacy and authenticity are artificially injected with the objective that it will become a self-fulfilling prophecy. By sowing seeds of confusion and doubt on a regular basis, and involving as many different people as possible, the employer may be able to get rid of Ms X whilst she's not looking.

Diversion. The bully's supporters, or the management or personnel, close ranks behind the bully. The victim's record (perhaps going back over a decade) is scoured for any trivial mistakes, which are now highlighted. This diversionary tactic distracts attention away from the behaviours of the bully, and of the bully's supporters and backers; the giveaway is the triviality and irrelevance to the current situation of the allegation. For example:

Employer's position:

You are being dismissed on the grounds of gross misconduct because you quoted an incorrect grade on your CV ten years ago, and you did not tell us during your interview that you were made redundant prior to joining our company. This constitutes fraud and deception and you are now subject to dismissal on the basis of gross misconduct.

Employee's position:

A letter of explanation was provided for and accepted by the company at the time of my recruitment. This is a matter of record.

The management position, backed by personnel, has now become so entrenched that they are unable to see the foolishness of the stand they are now taking. Typically, the case presented has nothing to do with the employee's performance, which is probably on record as "above average" or maybe "outstanding". It comes as no surprise to find that the triggering event in this type of case is usually the employee filing a complaint against a senior manager who is known to have a history of bullying.

Counter-attack. Start counter-allegations, either related or unrelated. The bully states openly their belief, in the form of a claim or threat, that they are the one being bullied/harassed. In so doing, they are preparing the ground for the final step in their defence.

You must stop harassing/bullying/attacking me.

You're being too hard on me.

The effectiveness of this last tactic can be increased dramatically by engaging a "friend" to say it on the bully's behalf, especially in front of witnesses:

Are you sure you're not going over the top on this?

Oh come on, you're being too hard on him/her.

Cringe.

Humility. This behaviour will only appear if the bully is acting alone, that is, has no peers/superiors/manager to turn to, and particularly if faced with overwhelming odds (for example about to be charged with a disciplinary or criminal offence, has no-one to turn to for support, or has been caught red-handed). The bully's only recourse is to surrender in the hope of winning sympathy, leniency or mitigation. Suddenly and unexpectedly (unless you have this list of course), the bully offers a full, sincere apology and complete cooperation. The surrender strategy is useful if you are fighting a war and are captured by the enemy, who are about to shoot you. In the workplace, the tactic is also highly effective when used on persons not alerted or trained to recognise it. The sudden change of tack touches the forgiving chord in their victim or arresting officer, who through an oversensitised awareness of forgiveness feels a sudden doubt. Have I been too hard on this person? Have I made an awful mistake? This is guilt in action. With bullies, this behaviour is a sham designed to get them out of the hole they've dug for themselves. The bully plays on this sentiment for all its worth. To the alert observer it is also an admission of the bully's unwillingness to accept responsibility for the consequences of their behaviour. Once out of the hole, previous patterns of behaviour quickly reassert themselves. By fooling the person who is about to unmask them, they live to fight another day - and may go on to neutralise or extract retribution on their unveiler.

I had no idea...

Had I had any idea of the effect...

I'm truly sorry...

Sorry, sorry, sorry.

Please forgive me...

I'll do my utmost not to let this happen again...

I'm really sorry, it'll never happen again.

Play victim. Game's almost up, time to play the trump card. As a last resort, feign innocence, swop into martyr mode and play the part of the victim. Ensure witnesses are present. Produce copious tears and a plea from the heart - the performance of a lifetime, worthy of an Oscar. This unabashed use of guilt has a very high probability of success, especially when preceded by the last-but-one warm-up. Who can fail to feel sympathy - and thus yield - to this heart-rending plea of innocence in the face of overwhelming persecution and victimisation. It is indeed a hard-hearted bastard who is not moved ... or is it? Ever wondered how bullies get away with their behaviour for so long?

Why is this happening to me?

Why are you doing this to me?

What have I done to deserve this?

Why me?

Why?

What do you want out of it?

What are you trying to achieve?

What good will it do?

I'm the one who's being bullied.

I'm the victim in all this.

Keep a sick bucket handy.

The bully's need to portray himself as a victim can be seen as an admission of abdication of responsibility for the consequences of one's behaviour.

To counter this behaviour in a disciplinary hearing, or any meeting involving the airing of a grievance, or at tribunal (the performance is highly convincing to observers/onlookers who have not been trained in anti-bullying techniques), draw attention to the behaviours exhibited (intent), rather than what the bully says/acts/does (the content). Refer to this list, make your own list, perhaps with boxes you can tick as each stage is exhibited. At the appropriate moment, summarise what you have observed as evidence. You are then using the bully's own behaviour to identify, prove and convict.

12 Standing up for yourself

Behaving assertively in the face of a bully

"Remember no-one can make you feel inferior without your consent"

Eleanor Roosevelt

It is important to remember that it is exceedingly difficult, and usually impossible, to handle a bully by yourself. To do so requires a high degree of interpersonal skills, unshakeable self-confidence, advanced assertiveness, extremely mature behaviour skills, nerves of steel, plus the financial independence to put your job or career on the line through risking being dismissed, fired, "selected" for redundancy or otherwise ousted from your job. So few people have all these qualities that this approach can be deemed by default a non-starter. Nevertheless, there are many practical steps that you can take to protect yourself whilst establishing a support network.

If you are faced with two or more bullies, or a gang, then your chances of handling the situation are reduced further. Outside help, intervention on your behalf, or escape are likely to be your only recourse.

We are conditioned to believe that asking for help equates to defeat. In fact, knowing how to judge when to face a challenge by yourself, and when to seek help, is a sign of maturity; however, the bully is likely to play on your underlying fear of failure as a means of isolating you further and encouraging you to desist from enlisting independent and professional advice. You can revive flagging spirits by asking yourself why the bully needs to think and behave like this. What does he fear from your seeking counsel? Being unmasked, perhaps, and shown up for what he really is?

Options
Take a step back for a moment, and consider the following approaches (there may be others in addition to those listed here). You can:

- stay where you are and do nothing

Unfortunately, this is the approach most people adopt in the hope things will improve. It's unlikely. Your hell will probably get worse. People who are bullied tend to be optimistic and forgiving, virtues that bullies lack; this tends to provoke further bullying. On the other hand, as bullies are loyal and obedient lap-dogs to their masters, such loyalty is rewarded with promotion, so if their elevation is away from their current management structure, a new boss may be a breath of fresh air. However, given the way that promotions are accorded, and who they are accorded by, it's just as likely that any new broom is a rookie replica of the old.

- stay where you are and put up with it

Ditto. Your circumstances are unlikely to improve, and will probably get worse. If the bullying continues, you will sustain further psychiatric injury.

- take sick leave

In the circumstances, a wise choice, but you need to check your terms and conditions of employment to understand your entitlement to sickness absence. Employers vary enormously in this respect. Many victims of bullying are unaccustomed to taking sick leave, especially for long periods, and feel guilty. Don't - if you are being bullied, you may be suffering severe psychiatric injury and therefore both deserve and qualify for sick leave. It is essential that your GP is involved at this stage - if he or she is unsympathetic, recommend this book. If the employer has allowed the behaviour to continue unchecked, or has encouraged it, they are choosing to be liable for bearing the cost of your injuries.

- stay where you are and be rational with the bully

This may work in the short term, but after a while - usually only a few days - the bully starts again. This approach is a form of appeasement which bullies take as the green light to carry on. They see it as a sign of weakness, frailty in the shadow of their superiority.

- stay where you are and take action to improve your position

Your circumstances may improve, but you are taking a risk. If you've been psychologically battered and bruised for some time, this step will be even more challenging than if you were fresh and strong. Even if you are successful, the bully may change strategy and employ more subtle tactics. Stories starting with racial abuse, moving on to sexual harassment, and culminating in bullying are sadly common. In the absence of a company-wide anti-bullying policy, you are likely to find yourself ostracised, labelled as a "troublemaker", or worse.

• move within the organisation

This can be a successful short-term strategy, but carries the long-term risk you will find yourself in the same situation a few weeks, months, or years later. It's a small world, and it's funny how we seem destined to bump into old adversaries again and again, only for old cycles to restart.

Moving department can also entail demotion, loss of status, loss of pay, remuneration, reward etc, and as you are taking this step because of someone else's behaviour, why should you suffer this punitive measure rather than the perpetrator? And if the company does not have an all-embracing anti-bullying policy, it won't be long before a new bully appears on your scene. Perhaps you'll meet that person on the day you take up your new residency.

• become a total "yes" person

Here, you surrender and become the bully's plaything. The bully plays the tune and you dance. Occasionally, you may play the tune and your subordinates must dance. It may feel good to be in control, however superficially or temporarily. The Devil can seem positively cordial when you wish to sell your soul, but will you ever be able to buy it back?

Capitulation in this manner eases the pressure to a point you feel you can cope with it. You don't like doing what you have to do, but you get rewarded - you are "in". You might even get promoted. The apparent reduction in pressure is welcomed, but unknown to you is a precursor to even greater pressure. The problem remains and you become trapped. You can either absorb the pressure to protect your staff (in which case the pressure becomes intolerable for you and will probably end in a breakdown), or you can make life equally hell for your staff (in which case the pressure becomes intolerable for you and will probably end in a breakdown). If you adopt this approach then it is likely that your subordinates will also read this book to find out how to deal with you. In the same way that violence begets violence, bullying begets bullying.

- take shelter behind a kindly individual - let that person bear the brunt

The pressure eases, but you are still trapped and fearful. You may have to give up a promising and enjoyable line of work to do something less rewarding, less challenging; it may be worth it for the reduced stress. But how long can your protector hold out? Will the bully increase the pressure on this person to get at you indirectly? What happens when your protector moves or leaves?

- take the bully on

Very risky, requires enormous courage, character, maturity and preferably financial independence. The bully increases the pressure, the psychological battle goes up a gear - or two. Your honesty and professionalism are undermined, privately and publicly; your health nose-dives. In many cases, and to the amazement of onlookers, the bully responds by adopting a destructive obsession which appears to have no rational basis. Also, in many cases, the employer stands back, whether from fear, uninterest or ignorance, washing their hands of the whole affair, hoping the victim will take the bully on, win, and solve the problem for them. When you remember that the purpose of employment is for intelligent adults to work together towards achieving the objectives of the company or organisation, the preposterousness of the situation becomes unbelievable - but for many individuals, it is a nightmare come true. What does the employer hope to achieve by adopting this hands-off approach? Answers on a postcard, please...

- put in a formal complaint - stand up for your rights

Risk everything. Your job, your career, your friends, even your marriage. If the management backs the bully, you lose.

"After years of constant bullying by a senior manager, I finally summed up the courage to file a complaint. His reaction was to fire me. I appealed to personnel, who initially blocked the dismissal, but the word was out, and my life became absolute hell from there on. A few weeks later, the combined antics of senior management

*and personnel had made my position so intolerable that
all I could do was do was resign. I was so incensed that I
was determined to go through with an industrial
tribunal, but the managers and company lawyers
threatened me into settling out of court for a paltry sum
with a massive gagging clause. What they were really
frightened of was the fact that my manager had a
history of destroying those who worked for him, the
company knew this, but still continued to back him. In
doing so, they were laying themselves wide open, and
they knew it. As an individual with no job, I couldn't
afford to take the risk that their lawyers would carry out
their threat to sue for hundreds of thousands of pounds
in legal costs should I be unsuccessful in my pursuit of
justice."*

• take action on a wider platform

Human beings are, without exception, capable of great
achievements. Some are born great, others have greatness
thrust upon them and for many, that thrust arrives in the
form of a trauma of sufficient magnitude, an unexpected
bombshell to spur the individual into prosecuting a course of
action which might culminate in bringing about change,
perhaps on a national or even global scale. One of the effects
of bullying is to stimulate the sense of injustice, sometimes to
an overwhelming degree; the individual's desire "to do
something about it" becomes a driving force of unstoppable
proportion. When controlled with appropriate analytical
behaviours, anything becomes possible. All you have to do is
believe that it is possible.

• leave

This is not a failure, but a valid choice, if appropriate for
you, although feelings of failure may haunt you for long after.
It is important to understand that leaving may be the right -
and only - choice, an accurate assessment of overwhelming
odds and a recognition of an unacceptable situation which is
not of your choice, not of your making and over which you do
not have control.

The pressure is lifted but your self-confidence is low, so is
your self-esteem. You have to rebuild your life, which may
take years. And you may not have understood why you were

bullied, or "why I let it happen to me". Not all situations are resolvable, and if the employer is stubbornly resistant to taking positive action, it may be the right time to look for another employer who values rather than destroys employees.

• wait to be fired

In many bullying cases, dismissal is an inevitable conclusion; although it may sound a rather strange stratagem to adopt, there are some advantages. If it is the employer who takes the precipitative action, then at subsequent tribunal, one can claim unfair dismissal rather than having to claim constructive dismissal. You may, with caution, be able to devote more time to collecting evidence.

"When I was finally dismissed, the relief was indescribable. I didn't have to run around every day like an idiot trying to meet deadlines which couldn't be achieved, I didn't have to balance the conflicting and contradictory demands of the departmental managers, I didn't have to put up with people shouting at me regularly, I didn't have to work regular 14-hour days and weekends any more, I didn't have to justify my existence every day - the list was endless. Now I am unemployed and my health is poor, but six months on I'm still savouring that relief. My GP advises me it's probably another year before I'll be able to work part-time, and probably another year or two before I can consider full-time work again. But the relief - you have to experience it to understand it."

• ill-health retirement

An increasingly common option for many people as stress takes its toll. Breakdown, burnout, whatever the reason, the relief is as welcome as rain in the desert. The financial package cannot compensate for loss of career, loss of health, loss of seemingly everything, but many people realise, albeit far too late, that their health and welfare really are more important than their employer.

A point to bear in mind is that acceptance of ill-health retirement means that any future employer (however unlikely this may seem at the moment, it is a possibility and may become a necessity if bills need paying) may be unwilling to consider any prospective employee who has a "record of ill-health", regardless of the cause. Acceptance of life assurance and other types of insurance may also be affected.

• voluntary redundancy

Another common escape route, especially with so many organisations making people redundant (whoops, I mean downsizing). For some people, to take the money and run may be the opportunity to go and do what they've always wanted to do. Beware that the severe psychiatric injuries of bullying can cause poor decision-making, so this step needs to be taken with the utmost caution.

• severance package

Similar to the voluntary redundancy package, but the employer is persuaded to enhance the package in return for your not making a fuss. Your integrity may cause you to baulk at this suggestion, but the legal process is unfriendly, unsympathetic and very expensive, especially when you consider the average tribunal award is only about £3000.

• settlement

Similar to severance package - the wording varies, so if the employer wants to use their own jargon to save face, this is a rare opportunity to be conciliatory, but don't make it a habit - with bullies, you are dealing with people who often have no conscience.

• legal action

Workplace bullying potentially breaches several areas of law; this is discussed in chapter 14.

Making a choice

Which option you adopt will depend on your circumstances, your feelings, your confidence, the degree and quality of support you can depend upon, your longer-term plans, your employer and their staff policies, your personal, domestic and family obligations, and much more. Only you can decide, and this is where counselling can help by encouraging you to find for yourself the most appropriate approach.

From this, you can develop an action plan, which should have short, medium, and long-term goals; precisely what those goals are will be for each individual to determine. More than anything else, this will instil a sense of purpose and direction, and give your life meaning once again.

Learning assertive behaviours can be both a short- and medium-term goal, although it should be remembered that assertiveness is a life skill which takes years of practice to perfect, especially if you were not taught to behave like this during your upbringing.

Assertiveness will not only help you deal with bullies and other autocratic types, it will help you in your everyday existence, whether with partners, children, parents, in-laws, family, friends, colleagues, committees, salespeople, shop assistants, anyone we come into contact within the business of normal daily life. The benefits to self-esteem, self-confidence and feelings of self-worth will be noticeable almost straightaway, as you learn - or relearn - to play the game of interacting with human beings.

Being assertive with a bully takes a *lot* of practice, so it may not bring immediate success; it will however, stop the rot, and at least enable you to stabilise your self-confidence. In short, you will be breaking the hold the bully has had over you. Once empowered, you can begin to make positive, informed choices once again.

Contrary to some peoples' opinions, learning to behave assertively does not change one's personality. The advantages are that you stand up for your rights (which are yours, belong to you and cannot be taken away), whilst giving the bully nothing to hold on to or criticise. On the first occasion that you adopt an assertive stance, you may feel nervous, perhaps terrified; this may be especially so if you are acutely sensitive to the reaction of others, and if you've been bullied, you're likely to be already hypersensitised. This is the advantage of assertiveness - you can claim your rights without hurting other peoples' feelings or trampling on their rights. The bully is more likely to be confused than angry. By the time they've worked out that their former behaviours of dominance, manipulation and threat haven't worked, the conversation will be over and, perhaps for the first time, you will have stood up for yourself in a way which the bully will find difficult to criticise.

Bullies are adept at encouraging their victims to reveal all about themselves, and about others as well. This "confession box" mentality is common, being a manifestation of guilt to which empathic people are prone. However, you have a right not to reveal any more than you wish. Bullies are nosey and inquisitive, an overt sign of insecurity, and consequently skilled at wheedling information out of you which may later be used for the purpose of control. Tell yourself that you do not have to reply, and if you can't think of an assertive response on the spot, use the power of silence - it is your right to refrain from answering, you are not obliged to say anything, but if you do, it will be noted in the bully's memory and may be used against you.

A favourite tactic of the bully is to highlight a small mistake you have made. The sense of irritation that this tactic provokes is usually due to the contrast between the insignificance, irrelevance and triviality of the error, omission, oversight, indiscretion, etc, and the importance now being ascribed to it; the contrast is brought into sharper focus when compared against the scale, quantity and frequency of the bully's imperfections.

Your instinct may be to explain, clarify, elaborate, which leads you to justify, substantiate, excuse, and culminating in an urge to apologise; empathic people have a strong sense of justice, rightness, a feeling of openness which manifests itself through a yearning to share, usually through verbal exposition. These impulses are the spur for - and by - an assumption of guilt which can only be assuaged by lengthy explanation followed by "appropriate" apology for "your share of the blame".

In this situation it is important not to start down this path - for in so doing, you are implicitly accepting blame, and in accepting blame, you are also accepting responsibility. By the time you've finished your monologue - during which the bully may have sat stony-faced and silent - you will have convicted yourself, and in so doing, absolved the bully of responsibility for your situation. The bully's skill is to encourage you to deflect your instinctive empathic behaviours back on yourself, a tactic accomplished largely through a small stimulus and a period of silence.

It is unwise and unsafe to build a relationship with the bully, as your faith and trust may be seriously misplaced. Promises of "things will be different from now on", or "I'm sure we can work well together", although well meant at the time, will be short-lived. The bully, with a selective, short-term memory, conveniently forgets these fine words as soon as the pressure rises. If it is possible to trust the bully, then he is unlikely to be bullying you in the first place. Bullies are insecure, frightened individuals, and are likely always to perceive you as a threat.

In the same way a child cannot fully care for an elderly or infirm adult, a victim can never satisfactorily "help" or "cure" a bully. The dependent and destructive relationship is likely to continue, albeit in modified form, possibly with more than a hint of co-dependency; in this type of liaison, one partner gives up all their rights to become a "supercarer" attending to the other's every need. Such unhealthy and unhappy alliances almost always end in tears.

The only way for a bully to improve their behaviour is through a programme of training, counselling, support (perhaps through mentoring) and supervision in an anti-bullying environment. Given that bullies are often born with instinctive leadership behaviours, and that bullying is an expression of those behaviours at their least mature, the long-term benefits of "re-education" could be very worthwhile indeed. Unfortunately the bully's steadfast self-reliance often precludes choice or acceptance of such a course of action.

Bullies find it difficult to engender loyalty in their staff, which aggravates their behaviour. Loyalty is based on trust, and trustworthiness is a sign of maturity; a mature leader doesn't bully, for he has no need to.

For the person being bullied, it is of the utmost importance to secure support immediately. This prevents self-confidence, self-esteem and self-worth from falling further, and is an essential first step to recovering confidence levels to where they were and should be now.

The recovery approach for each individual depends on their own situation, but it is unusual for people to be able to heal themselves, despite dogged determination. Seeking help at appropriate moments is not a sign of failure, but one of strength and maturity.

Behaving assertively

Most of us have had the experience of coming away from an interaction and thinking later "I wish I'd said so-and-so", or "I wish I'd thought of that earlier". For empathic people, assertiveness skills are not instinctive, but have to be learned. This takes time and practice. Spontaneity is onerous to acquire at first, but with patience and persistence, using the words, phrases and sentences suggested in this chapter, as well as from other sources, you'll develop an array of responses, and response types, that will eventually come to you easily, even under the most ferocious attack.

Assertiveness and behavioural maturity go hand-in-hand, and when used successfully, they increase our confidence. As confidence rises, we become more assertive - and so on. Many training courses teach the principles of assertiveness, but what matters most are the words and phrases that you need and use on the spot. You need to be able to respond there and then, not have to think about it for a few minutes or hours, or refer to a book or manual.

The traditional definition of "assertive" means

- understanding your rights, and other peoples' rights
- being able to stand up for your rights, but without violating anyone else's rights
- being able to express your needs and beliefs in an open, honest manner, without imposing them on others, and without allowing those needs and wants to be diminished by others
- having rights in what to expect of others, and what others are entitled to expect of us

There is a further definition, which in the context of confidence, helps us in

- understanding the difference between "I" and "others", and therefore the *rights* and *needs* of "I" and "others"

It means knowing where to draw the line. When someone asks you to undertake some task for them, it means being able to decide spontaneously whether the request is reasonable and whether it should take precedence over your needs - and if necessary being able to say no politely, firmly, and, most importantly, without feeling guilty either at that moment, or subsequently. You can walk away feeling good, without remorse, or doubt, or irritation, even if the other person's response has been to use guilt to increase artificially the probability of persuading you.

This balance between the rights and needs of self, and the rights and needs of others, is at the heart of understanding a bullying relationship. The typical bully is a person who cannot assess their own failings and who cannot understand the effect their behaviour has on other people. On the other hand, the typical "victim" is a person who, especially under the stress of a bullying situation, finds themselves unable to assess and measure their own strengths and performance, deferring instead to the apparent validity of criticisms of the bully.

From an early age, most children are taught by their elders to think of others, but are not taught how to think of and value themselves. This is regarded as "selfish", and such ungenerous behaviour is often disciplined accordingly. Children are also taught to be "modest", and not to "show off". One is directed to be deferential at all times, and to obey without question. Transgressions solicit punishment and the lesson is learnt, sometimes painfully. On the other hand, some children grow up never having been taught how to value and respect others (nor, incidentally, themselves).

For a child, the attitudes that adults exhibit can be very confusing. For instance, taking pride in one's work is OK, but feeling proud is often not. Sharing the joy of achievement is OK (usually), but trumpeting our successes is viewed as immodest, even arrogant.

Whilst obedience and humility are a necessary (perhaps divine) frame of mind, without underlying confidence and assertiveness, the balance often swings too far. This is especially the case for those who are empathic by nature. As a result, many people reach adulthood with an imbalance of attitude towards the needs of others, often putting other people's needs before their own. The urge not to be seen as selfish is so deeply ingrained that often, even under pain of death (or so it may seem), we are unable to say no. However, for some people, the opposite may be the case.

Extreme examples of the inability to differentiate appropriately between self and others are the huge salaries, executive share options and other perks etc enjoyed by the few most senior individuals in businesses, and especially in recently privatised industries and government sectors such as health. Incomes which are ten times or more the level needed to provide a modest standard of living for the average family are earned primarily at the expense of jobs and livelihoods, and are merited not so much by the self-proclaimed efforts of the executive as by politically determined cost-cutting targets. At the other end of the scale is the co-dependency exhibited in abusive, alcoholic and drug-dependent relationships when a partner gives up all rights in order to support and serve (that is, live their lives through) others. Paradoxically, this "super-caring" mode often nourishes and perpetuates the abusive behaviour.

The desire to say "no", combined with the inability to articulate the word, breeds resentment, with the result that we become increasingly embittered. Only when catastrophe looms does that little word make its entrance, often with an inappropriate display of emotion, followed by a deep trough of guilt in which we wallow for days, or even weeks. Even after escaping the ensuing depression, the experience becomes part of our daily baggage.

Sometimes the pressure builds to such a peak that a person "flips" and displays aggressive bully behaviour, sometimes inflicting physical harm (or in extreme cases even death) on those whom the person sees as responsible for their predicament, regardless of the consequences or sense of their actions.

If the person to whom you finally said "no" lacks confidence and maturity of behaviour skills, and particularly if they're a bully as well, there may be overt use of guilt which makes matters much worse. Funny how your explosion always seems to happen with the least appropriate person. That final straw may have been the least consequential, but that's little comfort to the person who has been pushed over the edge, or to the placer of that terminal triviality.

Saying "no" is acceptable, indeed often mandatory. Provided you respond assertively, you should feel no guilt

whatsoever, and any attempt by the other person to use guilt
must be rebuffed. Good phrases to use are:

> "I would be pleased to help, but I regret I am unable to
> on this occasion"

You have asserted your willingness to help, but owing to
other commitments are unwilling and unable to compromise
them at this moment. Nothing to argue with there. If guilt
raises its ugly head, and this is the moment when it is most
likely to, resist the urge to make a long and detailed excuse.
If you are stuck for words, simply repeat the phrase. You do
not have to make excuses or justify yourself (confession time
again), for the more you say, the less credible your excuses
become. The other person immediately senses that either you
are being economical with the truth, or with a little extra
push, you can be persuaded to give in. Even when you do tell
the truth, you will be doubted. Using the phrase above states
your position honestly and openly, which is your right. You
also have a right not to feel under any obligation to state your
reasons.

If you are unable to decline completely (you may find this
impossibly difficult at first), you can adopt the deferred
technique. For example:

> "I'm sorry I am unable to help you at this moment, but
> I'll be pleased to assist you tomorrow afternoon once
> this task is completed"

This lets the other person know that whilst you are willing to
help them, they are not entitled to distract you before you've
finished the current task. They are not permitted to jump the
queue in your list of priorities, and override your rights by
superimposing theirs. These are your rights, and you are
entitled not to have anyone else violate what is yours.

Occasionally, another person's needs will be great, and you
need to be able to sense this. This requires practice, but in
some cases you will already be doing it. For instance, if you
are using a public telephone and someone bursts in needing
to call an ambulance urgently, you'd agree without question.
If their reason is more mundane, you have the right to
decline with a response of the form

"I shall be pleased to leave this telephone as soon as I've finished my call"

Replying in the positive ("I shall be...") whilst including a reasonable and acceptable condition ("as soon as...") increases considerably the probability of a successful interaction. One word which riles the bully is "no", and lacking anything else to focus on, will grasp this negative as an affront to his needs, inducing aggression and arousing the urge to dominate and overrule.

You will learn to use tact and discretion, and in the early days if you're unsure, it's better to give people the benefit of the doubt. Use each interaction as a learning exercise. Be comforted by the fact that you learn most from the biggest mistakes.

Persistent offenders soon reveal themselves, as a quick analysis of their needs will show. Does that photocopying, which "has to be done for a meeting in five minutes" really require you to unload your work and then stand there waiting for the next ten minutes? We all experience last-minute panics, but persistent offenders betray themselves by that fact - they are persistent. More often than not, this is the result of poor organisation and poor planning, whereby the person habitually leaves everything to the last minute. To handle this situation, especially after you've identified the persistence, assert yourself with a response of the kind

"I'm sorry but I'm in the middle of a job at the moment. I shall be finished in about ten minutes, but there's another copier on the third floor which you can use if you're desperate"

If the person's need is not really urgent, you have let them know that to interrupt you is a violation of your rights which is not acceptable. If their need really is urgent, they have an alternative. You'll be surprised how often the professed "urgency" diminishes.

This approach is especially effective with a person who becomes a nuisance by persistently asking you to do things for them. A moment's thought will tell you that more often than not they could easily do the job themselves if they didn't waste their time trying to persuade others to do it for them.

This reveals another element in the assertiveness game: intent.

A point to note about the type of response suggested so far is that it uses an apparent apology. Apparent, because it's one of the few examples where the word "sorry" is not used for the purpose of an apology. You're not sorry at all, of course, and you don't have to be. It's your right not to have to feel sorry, as it is also your right not to be made to feel sorry - and guilty - by the other person transferring their irritation (because of low confidence in themselves) on you. "Sorry" in this context is an expression of regret; it also softens the assertiveness, reducing aggressiveness, and helping empathic people feel comfortable with standing up for themselves. Simply saying "I see you choose to think like that" sounds blunt and is too aggressive for apprentices of assertiveness.

When behaving assertively, it's important to avoid using self-deprecating language, through which you are intimating that you believe yourself to be inferior in some way. Only highly successful professional speakers can successfully employ self-deprecation, and unless you are in that fortunate position, you only demean and belittle yourself. If you are trying to prevent someone else from belittling you, you will shoot yourself in the foot if you exhibit the same behaviour. Learn to recognise phrases such as

"I'm know I'm not very good at this, but..."

"I know I'm being a bit thick here, but..."

Rather than rephrase these put-downs, omit them altogether. If you're dealing with a bully, the chances are that you are already more skilled, talented etc than your aggressor, and brighter as well. Nothing attracts a bully faster than other peoples' success, popularity, etc.

Also, avoid apologies unless genuinely necessary. The key word here is "genuinely". If you've spilt coffee over someone, or been unable to keep a commitment, then apologise as etiquette demands; having apologised, succinctly, move on to a positive note and don't hark back to the apology again and again.

A person who is sensitive to the needs of others often introduces an interaction with an apology, as a gentle way of starting a conversation. Listen for yourself saying

"I'm sorry if I'm taking up your valuable time, but..."

"I'm so sorry to have to say this right now, but..."

Once again, don't rephrase, just omit - by doing so, you've already begun to assume a more assertive air. If this is too big a step for you at first, use the universally accepted intervention "Excuse me...".

Another form of self put-down is the approval-seeking behaviour indicated by the regular use of "Can I...", "May I...", "If I can just...", etc. Here, the enquirer is automatically judging themselves to be of lower importance, priority, etc by assuming that permission is required for them to make a contribution. Whilst the necessities of etiquette may occasionally demand that such permission be sought, if you find yourself asking for it at every opportunity, a review of your rights might encourage a more assertive approach to redress the balance.

Being bullied generates feelings of an intensely personal nature, and when backed up with threat (real or implied) and guilt, the effects are deep and long-lived. You have a right not to be treated in this manner, and you have a right to be respected regardless of who or what you are, the nature of your job, your background, race, creed, colour etc, etc. A mark of the maturity of today's society is that these rights are now enshrined in law. Discrimination is still practised, but society now unequivocally deems behaviour of this type unacceptable. You also have a right not to be discriminated against or harassed because you are a victim of bullying; society is in the process of recognising this.

Assertive responses

An assertive response means that you

1. state your beliefs (it's your right to have beliefs); this is indicated by an "I" statement

2. label the opinion expressed as belong to the other person; you do this using a "you" statement

3. if appropriate, draw attention to the other person's freedom to choose the way they think/act/feel/behave etc

For example:

"I'm sorry you choose to think like that"

If the abuse is behavioural (for example physically unpleasant or threatening) rather than just verbal, then say:

"I'm sorry you choose to behave like that"

You are stating, honestly, openly and without prejudice, that this is your belief ("I'm"), and that the behaviour exhibited belongs to the other person ("you ... behave like that"), and that the other person has chosen ("you choose") to behave in that manner You are also expressing regret ("I'm sorry") that in your opinion the other person has chosen not to behave in a more positive and constructive manner. You are also stating your right not to take on board anyone else's behaviour, opinion, etc, unless you choose to do so. You are refusing to allow your own beliefs to be belittled or diminished, which is also your right. Most important of all, you give the bully nothing to latch on to, no points to be picked up on, no opinions to be argued with, no judgemental remarks to be disputed, no stick with which to beat you. You are asserting your rights and expressing your beliefs in an honest and open manner. That is your right, as it is your right not to have your rights violated. All this in only nine words.

Practice saying this phrase, out loud, several times a day. Learning a new behaviour takes at least three weeks (or more) of daily repetition before it becomes part of your normal (instinctive) thinking. You'll need to reinforce this learnt response by further regular practice, perhaps modifying or adding non-verbal gestures such as a smile or a shrug. After a while, other similar phrases will come to you, so add these to your repertoire of daily drill.

Rehearsal

You may find it helpful to practise with a supportive friend, to rehearse standard assertive replies to different types of aggressive question or request. On the first session, a little Dutch courage may relax you sufficiently, enabling you to draw on plenty of entertainment behaviours, but don't let it become a habit! In real life, you need a clear head and your wits about you.

Draw up a sheet of twenty or so statements which the bully has used, or might use, then ask your friend to fire them at you. Remain poker-faced whilst echoing a standard reply. At this stage, the objective is to program the words and phrases into your brain so that they are there for instant (instinctive) use when the occasion demands. As confidence rises, you may find yourself automatically exhibiting other forms of body language such as the open, palms-up gesture. Savour the feeling of what it is like to stand up for yourself assertively. Perhaps this is the first time in your life you have had the opportunity to do so.

Remember that the bully has a thick skin, and what to you may seem on the aggressive side will be unnoticeable to the bully. In the early days, laughter aids the exercise, although in a live situation avoid any hint of the type of smile which may suggest gloating. With practice, you may be able to inject some lightness using a combination of smile and shrug, but only if you can impart a genuineness derived from confidence.

Once you have gained experience, you'll feel confident enough to increase the level of assertiveness, for example:

"I understand your need to behave in that manner"

This is strongly assertive, but hold fire until you have gained confidence in your ability to answer assertively. You are saying that you have twigged what is going on and that you are no longer prepared to accept that type of behaviour. This will probably frighten the bully, although he may not understand why. If you are fortunate, he may back off and choose not to bully you as much, or at all. It may depend on whether he can shift his attentions to someone else. At the moment, this should not worry you, for as your confidence grows, you may be able to tackle the bully by additional means, perhaps also helping others in the same position.

The bully's choice of reaction will also depend on the reasons why he is bullying in the first place. If it is because of stress rather than an underlying immaturity, the reaction is more likely to be a positive, or at least non-aggressive one.

Alternatively, where the bully is immature and lacks interpersonal and behavioural skills, the response to this statement is more likely to be aggressive, and you need to

have several more of these defences lined up to fend off a
sustained attack. In rare cases, the bully may become
physically violent; if you think this is a possibility, ensure
there are witnesses in the vicinity. Better still, leave this
approach until you have official backing, for example either
from personnel, or your union. If the bully flips, you've got
support when you need it. You will have greater credibility
and are more likely to be taken seriously, and therefore be
believed, if you have taken the first official (mature) step.

Whatever you do, avoid the temptation, however great, to
add criticism, especially guilt and sarcasm. This immature
response to provocation negates the assertive value and gives
the bully a stick with which to intimidate you. For example

"I'm sorry you choose to behave like a Neanderthal."

introduces an opinion which can be challenged. The bully can
then label you as childish, immature, emotional, a person not
in control of themselves. If you are female and the bully is
male, you also leave yourself open to stereotypical
accusations such as "typical female behaviour", "emotional",
"having trouble with her hormones again", etc. These can be
hard to counter, especially in a predominantly male
hierarchy.

When you respond inappropriately, the bully can counter-
attack your confidence in its most vulnerable point, which
makes you feel dreadful. You can, of course, learn to recognise
that feeling, and interpret it as an assault on your confidence.
This takes the sting out of the attack, and although at first
you'll continue to feel dreadful, with practice your confidence
in this area will rise such that it cannot be attacked so easily.

If you are provoked into saying or doing something stupid,
and are consequently threatened (for example with
disciplinary action), make it clear, in writing if necessary,
that your behaviour was the result of provocation - this is
also an opportunity to draw attention to the bully's behaviour
over the entire period of time that you've been on the
receiving end. By stating you were provoked, you are drawing
attention to the *cause* of the provocation, and turning the
attention back on the bully to justify his behaviour.

Sarcasm can appear unintentionally, and you need to
guard against this. For example, in

"Thank you for taking the trouble to share your thoughts with me"

the phrase "taking the trouble" can be a disguised criticism, which becomes more evident if you accompany it with appropriate non-verbal gestures such as looking disdainfully down a nose held high in the air, or if your tone of voice is dismissive or patronising. This can happen inadvertently when you are nervous. If you are unsure as to whether your response contains criticism, say it aloud (when you are alone), and exaggerate wildly the tone of voice and non-verbal gestures.

Sarcasm is one of the many guises of criticism. From the overt "I suppose you'll get it right some time", to the covert "Never mind, I'm sure we can get someone else to do that another day", the purpose of criticism is to hurt. In this respect, sarcasm is the unkindest form of criticism. The person who criticises has convinced themselves, or allowed themselves to be convinced, that they can never be as good as the other person. Rather than face up to this belief, and overcome it, the bully instead chooses to project his own failings on to other people by claiming they have the inabilities he fears he has.

An alternative form of sarcasm which appears regularly is the patronising attitude. The "I'm better than you, you're just a snivelling little nobody" posture is an effective put-down, belittling and demeaning the actions of others, designed to make people look foolish in the presence of a supposedly superior intellect. "What do you know about..." is another giveaway. One way of handling this is to draw attention to the behaviour, eg:

"I'm sorry you choose to try to patronise me"

If you feel emboldened, you might choose to add

"...but in so doing, you reveal a lot about yourself"

Don't go overboard and let your new-found confidence run away with you though - this rider could itself be seen to be provocative and threatening. It is wise from the outset to choose not to mimic the behaviours you are resisting.

The habit of criticism is learnt in childhood, usually from parents and other authority figures who are unaware of the causes or effects. Parents learn it from grandparents, and so on, and unless the cycle is broken, it perpetuates. For someone with low confidence, reducing another's confidence produces a satisfying feeling of superiority and supremacy, of "success", which reinforces the behaviour.

Criticism is endemic in an adversarial society, an activity encountered on a regular, daily basis. One of the biggest steps towards behavioural maturity is to eliminate criticism from your own vocabulary of behaviours. Express a difference of opinion - yes, agree to differ - yes, hold alternative or opposite views - yes; but simply criticise? No, for all you achieve is to reveal something about yourself.

Sarcasm is the most hurtful form of criticism because it attacks confidence subtly but directly. It also employs guilt. The other person feels bad, but may be unaware of how or why the attack took place.

Having become alerted to sarcasm, you can begin to eradicate it from your own vocabulary. Remember that when you are sarcastic, you are revealing your own lack of confidence. Whilst most of us would not dream of using overt sarcasm, it's surprising how frequently the occasional word slips in. Consider the following two responses:

"I'm getting this job done before..."

"I'm trying to get this job done before..."

The first is a positive, honest and assertive statement, one person's opinion ("I'm"). The second is altogether different, and the clue is the word "trying". Say it out loud with exaggerated emphasis on the word "trying". Completing the sentence reveals an intent, probably unwitting, behind the innocuous words: "...and if you weren't so stupid as to interrupt me, I would have finished it by now". This would probably not be the case, but it reveals that the person is using blame to displace their own feeling of lack of self-worth and ability.

There are several sarcasm words to look out for:

"Perhaps you'll finish that task today"

"Do you think you could manage to get here earlier?"

"Maybe we'll get through one day without an argument..."

"I suppose it's all right"

Without sarcasm, these can be rephrased:

"I shall be pleased if you finish that task today"

"Please could you get here earlier?"

"We'll get through one day without argument"

"It's all right"

Often, behaving assertively requires only that you omit an offending word or words. Observe your interactions with others, and look out especially for the words "trying", "perhaps", "manage", "suppose" and "bother". Once you become alerted, practise eliminating them.

When you detect sarcasm by others, don't respond aggressively, which is often the instinctive reaction. As calmly and assertively as you can manage, draw attention to the sarcasm. Often, sarcasm is based on a grievance, which may be real or imagined; use of this device then becomes an opportunity for you to tease it out firmly but politely. The grievance may be with you, or it may be with others. There is no obligation on you to aid resolution, but if it involves you, here's a welcome moment to address it.

"That's the second time you used sarcasm. What's going on here?"

"Excuse me, I notice you used sarcasm. Shall we look at your grievance together?"

By remaining calm and focusing on the intent, you are exhibiting mature behaviour, and the first time you handle this successfully, give yourself a reward - you've earned it. Few people are able to deal with sarcasm maturely.

There is one acceptable form of negative criticism; satire is the safety valve of democracy, and its use requires great skill. Its most effective application is on prominent figures or institutions such as government and bureaucracies, or on people or organisations abusing their position of trust or power. It is a device hated by tyrants, dictators and the like, for whilst seeming innocuous, it has the power to persuade on a national, even international, scale. Seditious stuff.

The first time you respond assertively will surprise the bully. He won't be expecting it, and you'll likely catch him off guard. This is not the "you" he knows, the person he controls and dominates, the subordinate he subjugates daily. You have cast off the yoke of subordination to become equal, in personal if not in managerial terms. You need to think how the bully may respond, and how you're going to respond in turn. The approach you take depends on the situation, the personality of the bully, and the degree of support you have at your disposal.

At first, try out your new-found behaviours in a small-scale situation. Choose an issue of little consequence, so that if it does go badly, your world won't collapse. Observe the bully's behaviour closely, and write down the dialogue, as soon as possible after the interaction. Treat it as if you are editing a film script; the next shot will be perfect. If it isn't, repeat the process, perhaps modifying your words slightly, until it does go well.

The bully's instinctive response may be to increase the aggression. Stick to your guns. Call on all your acting skills to behave assertively, making sure you use no criticism whatsoever. If you have a role model, such as a film star, or politician, or leading business figure, visualise what they would say in this situation, and how they would say it. Take a deep breath and go for it. Remember that bullies are insensitive, and their thick skin works both ways; it prevents them from being hurt through verbal attack, as well as inhibiting them from seeing the effect of their behaviour on others. The first time you stand up to a bully may seem like the start or World War III to you, but to the bully it's just another skirmish, one of many he anticipates - perhaps even enjoys - each day.

Keep judgemental, comparative and relative expressions out of your conversation; replace words like "unjust" and "unfair" (echoes of the whingeing child) with words and phrases such as "unacceptable" and "not acceptable". It is much harder to argue with assertiveness.

Handling criticism

Handling negative criticism successfully is a skill which most people need to be taught how to acquire - it is not a faculty we are automatically born with. What we are born with is the ability to learn that faculty - an ability which no-one can deny.

One technique is to remain focused on *intent* rather than *content*. When a person makes a criticism, rather than responding defensively or aggressively, as is our instinct, train yourself to pause and ask "I hear the content of what this person is saying, but what is the intent behind it?"

In bullying, the intent is usually "to attack my levels of self-confidence and self-esteem, therefore to make me feel worse inside than they do". If stuck for a suitable response, call on the assertive phrase "I'm sorry you choose to think/ act/feel/behave like that".

Other intents include diverting attention away from the person's behaviour (you're getting too close, the bully fears unmasking), provocation (with intent to elicit a knee-jerk reaction), threat (to make one feel frightened), and invitation to convict oneself through explanation, elaboration, apology etc.

When you are practised in the art of standing up to criticism, especially of an unwarranted and unjustified nature, you can move on to ask another question: "In choosing to behave like this, what is this person revealing about themselves?" On many occasions, the bully will be telling you their thoughts, feelings, attitudes, beliefs, especially about themselves, the weakness they perceive in their personality and make-up. Because bullies choose not to face up to their own weaknesses and failings, they project them on to other people. Using assertive defence, you decline to take these failings on board, but reflect them back on the other person.

The techniques of assertive defence require practice and patience, and you must overcome the urge to hit back, which is exactly what the bully wants you to do. Resist it at all costs - the mature individual has no need to retaliate. By pausing, reflecting, and asking yourself these questions, you are asserting your right not to be psychologically violated. With practice, you will be able to see intent more clearly and quickly as your response becomes instinctive. You will also learn to decode the bully's words and behaviour to perceive how they feel about themselves. The information you glean will, if necessary, help you contest any subsequent disciplinary, grievance or tribunal procedure.

Bullies are unable to focus on issues which trespass on their insecurity. The greater their insecurity, the more likely you are to encroach on areas which threaten to reveal that insecurity. With a short-term focus and memory, conversations meander and weave, leaving the injured party confused and wondering why they "never seem to have a proper conversation" with this person. The way to handle this type of evasive and elusive interaction is to be specific and stay specific. Prepare in advance the points you wish to discuss and let nothing divert your attention. If the bully refuses point blank to discuss your grievances, draw attention to the bully's disinclination to answer the question, and add that to your journal. In so doing, you will have taken your first steps towards addressing the intent of what the bully has said, rather than the content.

A little research on the line management hierarchy in your department or organisation can strengthen your negotiating position, as you may be able to determine the bully's allies, allegiances and loyalties. Be prepared for surprises; people are not always what they are cracked up to be, and bullies are masters of disguise. Trust no-one. Whilst there may not be a conspiracy of X-files proportions, it is unwise to place too much trust on anyone in your management hierarchy. Bullying is a cowardly behaviour, and few bullies operate alone, or in a vacuum. Help and support for victims of bullying need to come from independent sources such as personnel, equal opportunities departments, occupational health, welfare and counselling, and so on; such people are - or should be - skilled in spotting deception and insincerity.

Bullies often have a history of exhibiting the behaviour; unfortunately, in may cases, the employer chooses to cover this up, but having done so once, makes themselves liable the next time, which invokes even greater attempts at cover-up, and so on. More advice on this aspect follows in chapter 14.

It is important at this point to understand the role of the personnel department. Whilst most employees believe that personnel exists to protect and act on behalf of employees, many victims of bullying are horrified to find - too late, and often to their cost - that their personnel department exists to implement the policies and procedures of the employer on behalf of senior management. Whilst individual people in personnel may be sympathetic and supportive, if there are no policies and procedures covering bullying at work in the company, you may not receive the practical support you expect and need. An additional function of the personnel department can be to minimise staff costs throughout the organisation, although in many reported cases, the personnel department itself seems to be an exception to this rule.

Nevertheless, check out your boss's relationship with his boss, but be prepared to discover more bullying. In any case, your second line manager is not doing his job if his subordinate is bullying and getting away with it. Tread carefully; cases where a second line manager has successfully intervened and taken direct supportive action are rare, although not unknown.

Guilt

One of the hardest forms of control to overcome is guilt. Guilt acts as much on the subconscious as on the conscious mind, and on most people, success is virtually guaranteed when used by skilled practitioners. One become skilled by learning it from parents or other authority figures. Children master it by the age of two, although to them it's just an instinctive behaviour which almost always brings the desired result.

Until guilt is pointed out, you may be completely unaware of the forces at work. Once alerted, you'll have taken another step forward towards full behavioural maturity. Note that certain types of people, especially those inclined to bully, may not be able to recognise guilt even when explained to them.

Empathic individuals are especially prone to feeling guilty, and this is seen during the process of explaining trivial mistakes, as described earlier. The urge to explain, elaborate, apologise etc stems from an assumption of guilt, that "I am somehow responsible for the situation I am in and must explain what happened, why I did what I did, my role, etc".

Another effective form of control through guilt is with statements such as

"By taking this action, you will be harming the children's education"

"In behaving like this, you will be putting patients' lives at risk"

In both these examples, guilt is used both for controlling people's behaviour, and to divert attention away from the bully.

The way to handle guilt is to draw attention to it, which puts the onus on the guilt user to justify their use of it. This needs practice, not only to come out with an appropriate response, but to spot the guilt in the first place. At first, you may only recognise the guilt perhaps several hours later, but once alerted, the time period becomes shorter. Once you have mastered the basics of assertiveness, handling guilt becomes much easier. The next time it happens, try stopping the conversation by saying, perhaps with a wry smile to lighten the moment:

"You're not trying to make me feel guilty, are you?"

or, when emboldened:

"Excuse me, that's the second *(or third or fourth etc)* time you've used guilt - what's going on here?"

"Why do you choose to use guilt?"

These are defensive responses to help you assert your right not to have your course of action determined by guilt. Decisions (unless involving criminality) taken solely on the basis of guilt are unlikely to be good decisions.

"I prefer not to use guilt when making decisions"

"You know, I'm much more likely to agree when you don't use guilt"

These rejoinders have a higher chance of success, especially if accompanied with a smile and a hint of humour to relieve the unpleasantness. Like your first attempts at assertiveness, the first few occasions may require you to smile through gritted teeth.

It is likely that this is the first time your adversary may have had their use of guilt challenged, so tread assertively but tactfully and diplomatically. The use, and effect, of guilt is largely unrecognised, being an instinctive behaviour learnt from others, reinforced by frequent successful use. The user may not even be aware they are using guilt. Only institutions of power and control, such as government, Church, etc understand fully the potency of guilt as an instrument of control.

As a precursor to tackling guilt positively, use your imagination to enact a successful outcome. As a human being, if you can visualise yourself doing it, your brain is capable - you already have it within you, and no-one - but no-one - can take that away from you. Others may encourage you to believe you can't do it, but they are only revealing their own inadequacy by trying to project it onto you. With practice, new behaviours become instinctive; you will amaze yourself once enlightened.

The bully is not immune to praise, and if you give him a choice, and he responds with an appropriate behaviour, a statement such as "I'm pleased you feel able to make a positive choice" might just stroke his ego. Be very careful to resist the temptation to inject sarcasm - this will have the opposite effect, and you'll be back to square one. Also resist the temptation to bully back - whilst the feeling of controlling others may surpass almost every other satisfying feeling you've ever experienced, don't fall into the trap of falling in love with the sense of power that accompanies it. This will make your behaviour as bad as - or worse than - the bully. Two wrongs don't make a right.

If the bully persists in attacking, you can take the initiative by using an assertive response (in increasing order of boldness and confidence):

"I'm sorry you feel the need to criticise me like that"

"I'd appreciate it if you didn't criticise me like that"

"We're here to [state objectives] and I don't see how your criticism helps us achieve those objectives"

Other defensive tactics include:

"I'm sorry you choose to adopt that approach"

or, more boldly:

"I'm sorry that you need to convince yourself that..."

"I'm sorry you choose not to see the effect your behaviour has on other people..."

In the face of unpleasantness, you may find the following response easier to produce:

"Thank you for sharing your views with me"

Once again, you are labelling the opinions expressed as belonging to, and the choice of, the other person. You are asserting your right not to take those views on board.

It is also important to understand the use, and power, of silence. Just as nature abhors a vacuum, so conversation abhors a silence. One's instinct, especially if you're victim of bullying, is to fill the silences by explaining, excusing, elaborating, etc. Don't. Use the assertive response then stay silent. You have a right not to have to say anything, especially if it may be taken down and used against you. Imagine your lips superglued, except for repeating the assertive response. If necessary, after defending yourself assertively, just walk away.

With practice, behaving assertively becomes instinctive and natural. Whilst assertiveness alone may not solve a bullying situation, you will be able to defend yourself against regular attack and come away each time with your dignity and self-respect intact.

Over time, you'll be pleasantly surprised at how much better you relate to and with other people. You'll also feel better about yourself - an indication that your confidence is rising.

13   What to do if you are being bullied

This chapter lists practical steps you can take if you are being bullied. For some, all the suggestions may be applicable; for others, only a few. The list is by no means exhaustive and there may be alternatives not explored here.

Be aware that bullies can be spiteful and vindictive, and that taking positive action can make their behaviour worse. Frequently, other senior managers, the employer and personnel departments choose to back the bully, thus making the position of the person being bullied much more difficult. With the continued raising of awareness throughout society, the gradual introduction of anti-bullying policies, and perhaps ultimately a change in the law, prospects for those being bullied are gradually improving.

Even if you are unable to resolve your situation satisfactorily, the knowledge and insight imparted in this book, with the practical steps outlined below, will enable you to emerge from a bullying situation with your dignity and self-respect intact; you will also have begun to rebuild your self-confidence, self-worth and self-esteem, which are the principal casualties of bullying.

The advice below becomes increasingly adversarial and the stakes rise with the personal and financial costs. Interaction with the bully, or the bully's backers and representatives, is almost always adversarial through the bully's choice of intransigence in the face of reprehensible behaviour for which the bully has chosen to abdicate responsibility. Often, as in the face of other behaviours which society has deemed unacceptable and consequently criminalised, one's final recourse will be to law. In the case of injustice where the law does not specifically apply, one's efforts may need to be directed to changing and updating the law. This is how society progresses and how we make the world a better place in which to live and work.

• Identify it as bullying

This will be a turning point as you understand there is actually nothing wrong with you, and that the behaviours exhibited towards you are not your fault; most people who are bullied are kind, conscientious, caring people, good at their job, popular with people, and successful - qualities which the bully lacks. Our society encourages us to look up to leaders, managers, authority figures etc - it comes as a surprise to find that someone you have trusted - or should have been able to trust - is unfit for the position they hold.

• You are not alone

Being bullied makes the victim feel isolated. You are unlikely to know who else is in the same boat, if anyone, and you fear that making any enquiry might reveal that you are the only victim. You need to establish whether others have "ganged up" in a bullying cartel, or whether the bully is on his own. In fact, bullies rarely act on their own - they are too cowardly - but frequently operate in a climate where bullying is "acceptable". Their Jekyll and Hyde nature also enables them to present a picture of perfection to colleagues and superiors when the need arises. You cannot handle this by yourself; you must seek help, then act with courage, resourcefulness, determination and tenacity. These are qualities that you almost certainly have already, being the subject of the bully's envy and often the reason for picking on you in the first place.

Up and down the country, there are thousands of other people like yourself who are being bullied. The true figure may run into hundreds of thousands. Those cases which have come into the open are probably the tip of an iceberg of Titanic proportion.

It is highly likely that others in your section, area or department are being bullied too, but may not show the same symptoms. They may be frightened, perhaps terrified, and thus unwilling to admit to being bullied for fear of being picked on next. They fear for their jobs, their security, their livelihoods. They may have sufficient assertiveness to be able to defend themselves, or at least cause the bully to look elsewhere. Or they may just be keeping their heads down in a daily battle to remain inconspicuous.

• Seek help - you cannot handle it alone

To handle a bullying situation successfully requires high maturity, confidence, steadfastness, etc. If you have these, the bully probably won't pick on you in the first place.

In a bullying situation, it's likely that your confidence will be low; it may already have hit rock-bottom. Your self-esteem has taken a battering, and your feelings of self-worth have been severely diminished. Seeking help is a strength, not a weakness. You are recognising, sensibly and maturely, that you do not have the resources/knowledge/experience/training/etc to cope successfully with circumstances which are not under your control and in which there is an abuse of power. Standing up to a workplace bully is not an even contest, as the bully, at this moment, has control of your career. Bullies also cheat, the more so as they sense exposure. By seeking help, you are creating a level playing field.

• Contact a bully helpline or support line

At the time of writing, there are at least three support lines that people who are suffering in a bullying situation can call for advice. See the resource section for details.

• Contact an appropriate organisation

There are also a number of organisations and charities that offer advice and support. These include the Commission for Racial Equality, Equal Opportunities Commission, Public Concern at Work, etc (see resource section).

• Seek support from a friend

If you have someone you can turn to, a shoulder to cry on, this person can provide some much-needed moral support as you piece yourself together and plan a course of action to extract yourself from your circumstances. It is important that your friend has an appreciation of bullying and its effects, otherwise well-meant advice may be inappropriate. Support of this nature and in this context may not come from your partner, who may be alternately perplexed and weary of the whole business. A person with whom you have no emotional involvement may also be able to provide greater objectivity, as well as be able to remain aloof and unaffected by your unavoidable mood swings.

- There is nothing wrong with you, it is not your fault

Read this aloud, and even if you cannot bring yourself to believe at the moment, use your logical, analytical behaviours to instruct your subconscious mind to adopt this view. Remember that it is the virtues that victims possess that attract the bully in the first place.

- Read this book from cover to cover

Preferably twice. Use it as your crutch. Standing up to a bully requires knowledge, insight and guidance. If you have not been through this experience before - and come out successfully - it is unlikely you will have the knowledge or training to be able to deal with it. It is only recently that society as a whole has acknowledged bullying, and more importantly, its effects and consequences. This book gives you authority and legitimacy.

- Refresh your memory as to behaviour styles and the effect of assertiveness

Observe the bully and compare behaviours with those outlined in chapters 3-6. Remember that self, short-term and insensitivity are to the fore. Don't expect the bully to behave otherwise - immaturity precludes this.

Plan and practise assertive responses such as those suggested in chapter 12, then put them into action. Don't be despondent if they don't work first time - you are changing behaviour patterns ingrained over several decades, and it is difficult to dislodge or replace these overnight.

A person being bullied has, by virtue of this position, low confidence, so a failure at this stage may have an unnecessarily large effect. If you are prepared for this, you will be able to cope better, and support from counselling, coaching, or a sympathetic friend are invaluable.

- Read Andrea Adams' book "Bullying at work - how to confront and overcome it" (see resource section)

Ask you local librarian or bookseller to search their databases for any other books on the subject of bullying. Even books written for children are useful, as they speak in simple, straightforward terms (which may be appropriate in your current psychological state!). Such books also help us relate to our own childhood and where we could have picked up defensive strategies during our formative years. You may also gain advice on pinpointing ways of helping you feel good about yourself, a prerequisite for resolving any unpleasant situation. Being bullied gives you an opportunity to find areas of personality and character which you can strengthen, and re-examining the child within can be an enlightening experience. The knowledge that our parents can only give us approximately the same degree of behavioural maturity and interpersonal skills that they themselves had, and that their levels of these were determined by their parents, and so on, can also aid enlightenment, forgiveness, acceptance, and act as both a basis and spur for our own programme of self-improvement in these areas.

• Keep a journal

Write a journal or diary of everything that has happened and is happening to you. Include dates, times places, etc where known, what the bully said or did, how you felt, how the bully responded if tackled - everything, no matter how trivial. Don't worry if there were no witnesses. Try also to ascertain the intent of the bully's action, as well as the content; what was the person trying to achieve by choosing to exhibit this behaviour? Very soon, the sheer size of the journal will speak louder than the contents. Keeping a record is VERY important - as well as a cathartic exercise, it will help clarify and clear your thoughts, and also form the basis of your case if you go to tribunal or court.

• Keep your journal secure

Once you have started your journal, it is wise not to reveal you have done so, otherwise the bully will be on his guard, and your challenge will become harder. The bully is likely to be even more secretive, obtuse, and furtive.

In some cases, people have reported that the bully has broken into their desk, filing cabinet, handbag etc in order to read the diary. If you keep your diary on a computer, beware that it is an easy job to break into your filing system. A standalone computer can be powered on or rebooted whilst you are not at work (for example in the evening, over a weekend, or whilst you are on leave or out on "assignment"), and a computer on a network can easily be broken into from anther machine on that network. The bully may use his position of power to gain access directly, or force another individual (for example the system or network manager) to do it for him. Bullies are not trustworthy, and are happy to operate outside the law if they feel the need to do so. Even if you catch the bully out and report the trespass, their capacities for excuse are such that they will more than likely be able to justify their actions.

• Policy documents

The MSF (Manufacturing, Science and Finance union) has produced "Bullying at work: a guide for representatives and members", and the teachers' union NASUWT has produced "No place to hide: confronting workplace bullies". Both booklets are available to non-members. See resource section for details. If you are in a union, ask for a copy of the union's policy document and guide to workplace bullying.

• Line management

Consider taking the matter up with your line management - beware though, most bullies *are* line managers. If your manager is a bully, there's a more than reasonable probability that he's being bullied by his manager, and so on to the top. Few bullies exist in isolation, and most operate in a climate of acceptability of their behaviour. It may still be worth working your way up the chain of command, if only to establish the attitudes and integrity of your employer in relation to handling this reprehensible form of behaviour. It can also help to raise awareness of bullying within your organisation, and whilst no-one wants to be the guinea pig, the pioneering and altruistic feelings can do wonders for your self-confidence and self-esteem.

• Get everything in writing

Keep writing asking for justification, clarification, etc; everything the bully writes - or declines to write - can later be used to identify intent and may be used in evidence. The action of writing also helps to maintain a feeling of usefulness and purpose - which feed back into self-worth and self-esteem.

If criticised, insist that the bully be specific, then ask for it in writing - if what was said doesn't match what is written, record this discrepancy in your journal. Make a note if the bully refuses to put anything in writing. It is unfortunate to have to go to these lengths, but it is the bully who has chosen to behave in a manner which necessitates your taking this action now.

• Check accuracy of notes, minutes, etc

It is essential in meetings to make notes of what is said and agreed. Expand them immediately after the meeting whilst your memory is fresh. Get a colleague to take notes as well if appropriate. If official minutes are produced (by the bully or a cohort), their version of events and what was agreed may differ markedly from yours. Record this difference in writing.

• Check phraseology

In minutes of disciplinary, grievance and appeal hearings etc, look for overemphasis on the victim. Phrases like "when you're upset", "you have an attitude problem", "you did this or that", "you must", "you will" etc all indicate an unwillingness to examine the *cause* of your problems - the behaviour of the bully - as well as an attempt to portray you as the guilty party.

• Get the facts

Every time a criticism is made, first establish the facts. Vague statements such as "you've been criticised for..." have no validity unless the bully can identify who said it, to whom, when, where, for what purpose. Challenge the bully to substantiate every claim, and note any reluctance to comply. If the bully is subsequently unable to be specific, record and draw attention to the fact. In this instance, you will have perceived the intent - the bully's statement is not a valid criticism, but intimidation and threat, designed to make you feel small and frightened. It is a violation of your rights. Note the discrepancy between content (an apparent criticism by a third party) and intent (disguised threat and intimidation), and the violation of your rights. If appropriate, confront the bully with this, preferably with an independent witness present. You have a right not to be treated in this manner by a person who is in a supervisory position and who may be abusing their power in this way.

• Refusal to substantiate

If the bully makes critical remarks, but refuses to substantiate, note this refusal in your journal. Challenge the bully on why he chooses to refuse to substantiate his criticisms, then record his response to this as well. Insist that the criticism is specified in writing. Claims of complaint and criticism which are not backed up in writing could be seen as a form of harassment.

A frequent ploy is to claim that "someone has made a complaint about you...", "someone has reported that you have...", etc. Mostly, no-one will have made any complaint. Occasionally, however, an innocent individual will have been goaded or harassed into initiating a "complaint"; sometimes the bully will have deliberately misinterpreted another person's remarks so that he can make the claim. These approaches have the added advantage that when the victim hears a whisper (originated by the bully) as to who might have made the allegation, suspicion and mistrust spread like wildfire. Setting people on to each other in this manner is a tactic popular with those of the "divide and rule" school.

Alternatively, and often, the complaint will be a figment of the bully's imagination. Given that bullies can only think short-term, perhaps as little as a day or less, and that this applies to memory as well, it is possible that the bully is genuinely unable to distinguish between fact and imagination. The implications are worrying.

It's not so much the individual incidents that count, (although the more serious ones may be enough on their own) - it's the overall picture painted by the volume, frequency and combination of all incidents (including the bully's unwillingness to substantiate) that are convincing.

• Witnesses

As bullies are completely untrustworthy, have a habit of not recording or putting things in writing, lie with impunity, plus a host of other endowments, it is essential for interactions with the bully to be witnessed. As an individual you have assertive and democratic rights to be accompanied at all meetings etc by your chosen representative. If the bully, or his cohorts, supporters or benefactors try to deny you these rights, affirm them assertively and aggressively. Anyone denying or attempting to deny you these rights has something to fear; bear in mind that fear can be seen as a tacit admission of guilt. Denial of the right to be accompanied or represented could be seen as a form of harassment.

• Refusal to cooperate

Record the effect of the bully's unwillingness to cooperate and communicate on your work rate and ability to do your job, also the effect on the performance of your department, your company or organisation, the ways which the bully's behaviour inhibits, prevents or impoverishes delivery of service to customers, clients, pupils, parents, patients, etc as appropriate. Be as specific as possible.

• Resist the temptation to fight back

This is what the bully wants you to do. You will be given plenty of opportunities and are likely to be provoked on a daily basis. The game is "I can do it to you, but if you do it to me it's a disciplinary offence". Do not take up the opportunity to play the bully's game, as you will lose. You cannot - and will never - win when you play the bully's game. Indeed, the concept of "win" gives the game away. The bully sees it only as a win-lose situation. He would not play it unless he knew he was going to win every time. You can win by choosing not to play.

If you are ever tempted to think that you can win, the bully has an ace up his sleeve that you cannot or will not use. He cheats. As a victim, you, by definition, are an honest person. Even if you try to cheat, your lack of experience in behaving in an underhand manner will let you down.

One of the reasons for provocation is to give the bully an incident which can then be used against you. If you are ever goaded into responding, the bully will never let you forget how badly you behaved. He'll let everyone else know as well, and ensure it's put on your record. Should you ever respond inappropriately to this type of provocation, make sure in any subsequent disciplinary proceedings that the *reason* for your reaction is recorded and discussed. Ask why the bully chose to use provocation, why the bully feels it necessary to behave in this way, what the bully was hoping to achieve by it, how behaving like this contributes to the aims and objectives of the organisation, etc.

Respond assertively, with a prepared response, which, with practice, you can vary according to circumstance. See chapter 12 for ideas on assertive responses.

• Tackling the bully directly

If you feel sufficiently empowered to tackle the bully face to face, get specific and stay specific - the bully will wriggle and squirm, but stick to the facts and stick to your guns. The bully's response is to try to divert attention away from what you want to discuss, so be prepared to dig your heels in - if appropriate, use the *"I'm sorry you choose to divert attention away from what I wish to discuss"* approach. Beware though that some bullies, when rumbled, may go underground or change tack. Use assertiveness (*"I'm sorry you choose to think/act/feel/behave like that"*), with absolute terms (*"unacceptable"* rather than *"unfair"* or *"unjust"*). Expect any reaction, from abject humility, through conciliation, to aggression, even violence. *Never* trust a bully.

• Tell the bully what their behaviour is doing to you

Using as much assertiveness as you can muster, alert the bully to the effect their behaviour is having on you. Tell him it must stop. Use words like "unacceptable" rather than "unfair" or "unjust". Resist the temptation at this stage to threaten with grievance procedures, legal action, etc. This is likely to be perceived as provocative and antagonistic. Save these courses of action for later, should they be needed.

• Put your complaint in writing

Many people feel happier writing to the person who is bullying or harassing them; a letter can be modelled on a standard example, modified and polished till the writer feels happy with it. It also acts as a permanent record and can be copied to other parties. A further advantage is that you are seen to be taking the appropriate actions, whether or not you are recognised for doing so at the time. Keep the letter short - one page at the most. Six pages of pouring your heart out is more likely to give the bully the opportunity to confirm to everybody his side of the story; save your narrative for later.

You might like to use the following suggestion as a basis for your own letter; beware though that the vindictiveness and spitefulness of the average bully will mean that your situation may become worse - although in most cases, that will happen anyway. Replace the text in square brackets as appropriate:

Dear [formal title],

Over the last [period of time] you have chosen to behave towards me in the manner of a bully which I find threatening, intimidating, and unacceptable.

Specifically, you have
   [list three or four points briefly here]

Your criticisms have little or no validity and I believe you exhibit them solely for the purpose of control.

Your behaviour prevents me and others from undertaking our work and contributing towards the aims and objectives of [the employer]. I ask you to stop behaving like this towards me at once.

A copy of this letter will remain on file and I shall take further action if you choose not to stop bullying/harassing me.

Yours sincerely etc.

• Don't explain, elaborate, justify, apologise, etc

In doing so, you accept blame, and ultimately responsibility. Instead, focus on the intent behind the content, and the causes of your problems, not the problems themselves.

• Tape-recorded evidence

Although this smacks of espionage, it is one of the few ways in which the bully's Jekyll and Hyde nature can be revealed. It is particularly useful where the bully uses foul or offensive language when no witnesses are present. Once you have recorded a tape, make a couple of copies and keep them in separate locations. A transcript of the tape might also be a wise precaution.

You may wish to keep the tape until you have exhausted all official channels - this enables you to portray yourself as a conscientious person who has tried all the recommended avenues of approach; otherwise, the bully will claim that "you are out to get him", it's a "set-up", and that your behaviour is "untrustworthy" and you are "deserving of the actions being taken against you". In fact, everything the bully is guilty of.

When the bully finds out that you have tape-recorded evidence, you are likely to be charged immediately with disciplinary offences. You may be exposing deceit, lying, incompetence, collusion, negligence and liability - so fireworks are to be expected. A threatening and intimidating response can be seen as a consequence of fear - the bully fears that they have finally been caught out. It may mean all-out war from now on. You are also likely to be accused of all sorts, from gross misconduct and harassment to criminal behaviour. Probably treason, which is the time-honoured method by which dictators dispose of those they fear.

It is likely the bully will try and prevent the tape from being used as evidence. If so, ask publicly what the bully has to fear from hearing the tape. Some suitable extracts from the transcript might usefully be circulated at this juncture, although take care to act as responsibly and professionally as is possible in the circumstances. By the time things have got to this stage, you will probably have a solicitor involved.

• Defending yourself

In meetings, hearings etc, always try and focus on *intent* and *cause*. Rather than responding to the content of what the bully says and does, use an assertive defence "I'm sorry you choose to think like that" or "Thank you for sharing your views with me" as a way of both defending yourself and gaining valuable thinking time. Then highlight the intent and put the ball firmly back into the bully's court. Bite your lip, let the bully squirm for a change.

Each time reference is made to your state of health, especially mental health, draw attention to the cause of your state of health and who you believe is responsible for the state and position you now find yourself in.

• Assert your rights

In meetings etc, instead of asking permission (for example "can I have a representative present?") claim the right without assuming that you need to have the bully's approval ("I shall be accompanied by my representative"). Each time you ask for permission, you give the bully a chance to say no; in many situations, it may be more appropriate to assume your right, then when the bully objects, force the bully to justify, in writing, why he is trying to deny you your rights.

• Silence

In meetings, use the power of silence to keep the spot-light on the bully. You are not obliged to say anything unless you wish to. If you are dealing with a silent aggressive type, it is likely the bully will ask a question then remain silent whilst you talk at length. If necessary respond by turning the question round and reflecting it back. You may have to do this repeatedly, which, despite the bully's protestations, is an acceptable and necessary technique in the face of adversity. The more objections, the more success you are achieving and the more you are in control of the meeting.

You may need to maintain your silence for 10 or even 20 minutes or more. The temptation to speak may be overwhelming, but bite your tongue. If you've asked a question like "Why are you choosing to behave in this manner?" and the bully remains silent (note that a person of honest intent will rarely refuse to answer your question), maintain the silence for as long as it takes. Ensure your representatives are aware before the meeting that you may use this tactic so they don't unwittingly break the silence. If someone does, repeat the question and restart the silence.

• Negotiating tactics

Ensure that each point is discussed fully before moving on to the next. It is likely the bully will want to flit from point to point, issue to issue, allegation to allegation etc as away of pre-venting you from defending yourself, spreading confusion, and diverting attention away from the reason you are in this posi-tion and the cause of your difficulties - his behaviour. If the bully does this, draw attention to the fact that the bully is choosing to avoid answering each question then follow it with the reason the bully chooses to do this - to divert attention away etc.

Each time the bully refuses to answer, or responds with a counter-attack - which you can interpret as a sign of success - smile sweetly and repeat the question. On the third or fourth occasion, draw attention to the fact that this is the third or fourth time you have had to ask the question, and why is your adversary refusing to answer the question? What is it that he fears will be revealed if forced to answer the question? Regard every interaction like this as an opportunity to reveal intent.

• Projection

"Is it really me? Am I the one at fault?"

When making unjustified criticisms or unfounded allegations, it is likely that the bully is projecting his own weaknesses, shortcomings and failings on to you as a way of avoiding having to face up to them in himself, and as a way of diverting attention away from himself. Once alerted to this habit, each criticism or allegation can then be seen in a new light - as a revelation or admission. By recording what the bully says and does, it is possible to build up a picture of the bully as he wishes not be seen. Bullies who make repeated but unsubstantiated allegations of sexual misconduct, moral impropriety or criminal activity are worthy of special attention in this respect.

• Beware the mental health trap

This is a turning point, one on which you can assert control and begin your comeback. See chapter 8.

• Accident book

Record your psychiatric injuries in the accident book, which makes it a health and safety issue. This may improve your chances of making a successful claim later. Expect your employer to object, possibly vehemently.

• See your GP

The consequence of being bullied is stress. Stress causes a wide range of symptoms, both physical and psychological. Some are quite bizarre. Because bullying takes place over a long period, and perhaps because of other pressures in the workplace, the symptoms may not be noticed until they become severe. Consult the lists in chapter 8 - you may experience other symptoms, and be aware that stress may exacerbate previous or existing medical conditions.

Most GPs will be sympathetic, but if your GP is unconcerned, consider changing. Make discreet enquiries amongst family, friends, or through work for a GP who is understanding and knowledgeable about stress-related symptoms. Bullying has only recently been identified as one of the principal cause of stress, so it may take several years before this knowledge - and the solutions - percolate through the medical establishment to the sharp end.

There are several advantages of reporting to your GP, whether or not you receive a sympathetic hearing. One is that you are recorded as a statistic, and in according yourself this honour, you are taking direct action to address the problems of bullying and stress. The more people come forward to report their experience, the bigger the numbers. When fed back to the Department of Health, the figures will be converted into cost. The bigger the cost, the more likely people in high places are to be spurred into action. The government has a responsibility to manage the nation's taxes wisely, and embarrassment over huge and unnecessary expenditures can influence elections. Nothing moves a politician faster than the prospect of losing votes.

Another advantage is that you obtain a proper diagnosis of your illness (or rather, injury), which is essential if you wish to consider suing for personal injury later. It is vital that you obtain medical evidence of your injuries at the time it is happening; do not leave it until after you have left your employment, as you will be giving your employer the opportunity to refute liability on the basis that your injuries were sustained after your departure. You may wish to seek referral to a clinical psychologist (not a psychiatrist) whose report might include a diagnosis of (say) grievous bodily harm from psychological assault or PTSD caused by bullying.

• Occupational health

Larger employers have an occupational health department, with professional staff including a doctor and a nurse. These persons' remit is to safeguard the health and welfare of employees. If you don't feel able to broach the subject of bullying straightaway, you can use stress as your lead-in. Stress is topical, with high awareness of the effects; awareness of the causes is growing, and your case may contribute to furthering that understanding. Although the chief medical officer in an occupational health department has influence within the company or organisation, he or she may only be able to advise the employers, not decree or impose a course of action.

Staff in occupational health should be independent, and, once again, you may be surprised at their degree of familiarity with your problem. They may be able to refer you to an appropriate counsellor.

• Welfare and counselling

Many employers have a welfare department to whom employees can turn in times of need. Although the term "welfare" may imply poverty and low socio-economic standing, the department often advises clients on a wide range of personal problems, including bereavement, divorce, accident, injury, illness, etc. People feel a reluctance to accept help from such a source, believing that it is not for them; however, a counsellor can become your biggest ally. You may be surprised to discover how many other people are seeking help for the same problem, perhaps because of the same person. The more people who know about what is happening to you, and who is responsible, the better.

• Unions

Unions are a vital resource, especially in fulfilling their traditional role of helping those who, for whatever reason, are unable to help themselves. However, the high expectations of members at a time of great need, society's low awareness of how to tackle bullying, and the unions' convalescence from the wounds of over-zealous anti-union legislation have combined to produce a situation where many people feel they are not getting the support they need and for which they are paying.

A union's response to help in cases of bullying is also largely dependent on the individual representative, who, in many cases, may be in a difficult position himself. It must be remembered that union reps are ordinary people and usually ordinary employees as well, and their power and ability to act might be limited by virtue of their position, career prospects, professional obligations, even acquaintance or friendship with either or both parties.

In the UK, the MSF union has taken the lead and been actively tackling workplace bullying for a number of years. At the time of writing, other unions who are actively addressing bullying include the teachers' union NASUWT, and the finance sector unions and staff associations who come under the umbrella of the Financial Services Staff Federation (FSSF). Other unions are in the process of drafting anti-bullying policies, which is to be encouraged.

It's almost impossible to tackle a bullying situation successfully by yourself, as you are dealing with people who operate beyond the bounds of acceptable behaviour. Most bullying is carried out by a manager on a subordinate, and the majority of bullies survive by virtue of the fact that they receive either active or passive support from above. Even where the bullying is peer-peer or from a subordinate to the manager, bullies are such convincing liars that they inevitably convince superiors that theirs is the correct story. A victim on their own is normally on a hiding to nothing.

It should be superfluous to point out that addressing workplace bullying is in everybody's interests, especially the employers', who by choosing either to do nothing, or by backing the bully, are leaving themselves open to potentially costly legal action, adverse publicity and possible public relations humiliation.

One of the principal advantages of a union is the support you can gain, both practical and moral, if you have to take your employer to an industrial tribunal. Also, if you need to take your case to a higher court, then your union may be able to provide legal support and backing; given that a favourite tactic of a bullying employer is to threaten to sue the employee for legal costs, usually amounting to hundreds of thousands of pounds, the value of a union in these circumstances cannot be underestimated.

Your union representative may also be aware of other allegations of bullying, perhaps involving the same perpetrator; if so, you have corroboration for your claims, and whilst most bullies can discredit and demolish a single complainant, it's much more difficult to dismiss two independent witnesses.

If you do not feel that you have had the support you need and deserve from your local union representative, you are entitled to work your way up the union hierarchy, going right to the top if necessary. There may be other representatives within the union hierarchy, such as the Equal Opportunities Officer, with whom you can make contact. If you still feel dissatisfied and feel like cancelling your union subscription, do not undertake this step lightly, as once terminated, your membership may be difficult or impossible to reinstate, and you may be ineligible for subsequent legal assistance. It might be better to remain a member and work to raise awareness within the union - perhaps you might even consider becoming a representative yourself.

• Personnel

Your personnel department (often now called human resources (HR) - in the absence of a personnel department or personnel officer, the person in the organisation who is responsible for hiring and firing) will be able to advise you of your rights as an employee, and the procedures which you need to follow for pursuing a grievance. Bear in mind that personnel departments implement the rules and procedures on behalf of the employer; they often don't invent or write them. Ask for a copy of your employer's policy on bullying at work. Employers can be categorised (albeit simplistically) in terms of their attitude to bullying as follows:

- no anti-bullying policy at all
- a general harassment policy which is supposed to include bullying (if bullying is not addressed directly, it's not an anti-bullying policy and will be ineffective)
- an anti-bullying policy which has been drawn up as a window-dressing exercise but is wholly ineffective (sometimes the person designated as responsible for addressing bullying is the bully)
- an anti-bullying policy which has been carefully thought through, is genuine and has the full backing of the employer, is properly resourced, and has been intro-duced with the cooperation and agreement of all employees

If your employer comes into one the first three categories, this may be an opportunity for some more pioneering work; you may not benefit directly, but at least those who come after you can benefit from your experience - in most cases, once you are out of the picture, the bully will quickly turn his attention to the next victim. Once again, you can enjoy the altruistic feeling of doing something useful, even if you are not the beneficiary. Who knows, perhaps in a year's time, you might be asked to be a witness for your successor. Victims of bullying tend to be long-term thinkers.

• Remind your employer of their obligations

Whether or not the personnel department are helpful, this is an opportunity to make your employer aware of the moral and legal obligations with respect to the wellbeing of staff. If you are forced into tribunal later, this step is an important brownie point in your favour, as you will have demonstrated a professional and responsible attitude to resolving the situation.

• Be wary of bad advice

Whilst bullying is a behaviour practised probably since the inception of the human race, how to understand, tackle and overcome workplace bullying is a new subject. Despite being well-intentioned, advice is only as effective as the insight, knowledge or experience of the person giving it. In most cases, incorrect or inappropriate advice will make a bad situation worse.

As already mentioned, bullying can be seen as a form of psychological rape because of its intrusive and violational nature; thus the appropriateness of the following advice (which many victims have reported receiving) can be gauged by its relevance to a rape victim. Sufferers of depression may recognise some of the following too.

-   "Ignore it"
    In most cases, whatever course of action you take, including ignoring it, the bully's behaviour will get worse. It's a virtual certainty that the bully's behaviour will not improve of its own accord. Better to face up to the problem now rather than sustain further injury.
-   "Take no notice of him/her"
    Ditto.
-   "Keep your head down and get on with your job"
    Ditto.
-   "Don't let it worry you"
    Ditto.
-   "He's like that to everyone"
    Good. You've got more evidence and lots of independent witnesses to provide corroboration.
-   "She's very volatile"
    Then she's a liability to herself, other employees and the employer. How does volatility (which implies unpredictability, lack of control, self-discipline, etc) contribute towards achieving the aims and objectives of the organisation?

- "Pull yourself together"

  The classic answer by which the person giving it reveals that they have no knowledge or understanding of the problem. Alternatively, if they are aware of the problem, they may, by transferring blame onto the person suffering, be denying responsibility for facing up to it.

- "Shrug it off and get on with your life"

  If only one could.

- "Just forget about it"

  Ditto. If only the bully would. Pigs might fly.

- "Stand up to the bully"

  A sensible strategy, but only if you know how, *and* the employer demonstrates a genuine will to address the problem. The information in this book will help, but people of an empathic nature need to learn the skills of psychological self-defence and practice them regularly. Assertiveness training is a start, but it can take years of continuous learning and regular practise. The fly in the ointment is that bullies are content to lie, cheat, deceive, shift the goalposts continually, and if necessary abuse their position of power.

- "Take six/twelve/eighteen months' unpaid leave"

  You lose six/twelve/eighteen months' salary, plus benefits etc, and who pays the mortgage and all the other bills in the meantime? Your career suffers a setback, and you've a lengthy absence to explain to a future prospective employer. And when you do eventually return, your boss is still there, although he will probably have been promoted and replaced by someone of the same ilk.

- "Say sorry to the bully"

  In the same way that a victim of rape should apologise to her aggressor, or a victim of child abuse should apologise to their abuser?

- "Report him/her to senior management/personnel"

  Most bullies operate in a hierarchy, and personnel, more often than not, exist to implement and carry out the policies and procedures of senior management.

- "Take a stress management course"

  Bullying causes high negative stress, and the only answer to negative stress is to identify and eliminate the cause. And after you've been on the course, the bully is still there.

- "Imagine the bully wearing a silly hat"

  The person who reported this (after having been on an expensive interpersonal skills training course) confided that the effectiveness of the suggestion was increased dramatically by the addition of an axe through the middle of it.

• Grievance

Most employers have a procedure which can be invoked if an employee has a grievance. It has to be said that in many cases the procedure is structured in such a way that it favours the manager. However, the procedure can be used to air feelings, bring the bully's behaviour into the open, and gauge likely support from your employer. Any procedural meetings need to be administered or conducted by or in the presence of a third party who should be neutral and independent, usually a representative from the personnel or human resources department. You are entitled to have your own adviser or witness present, such as a union representative. Be suspicious and assertive if anyone tries to deny you that right.

Before you invoke the grievance, familiarise yourself with the terms of the procedure. When it relates to a bullying manager, you are well advised to do your homework before disclosing your intent.

If you decide to proceed, your journal will be your bible. Dates, times, places, records of conversations - you will need to be certain of your facts, as the bully is likely to challenge everything. The slightest mistake - or doubt - on your part will be seized upon. Be prepared for this with an assertive statement of the form "I'm sorry you need to make such a big fuss about that point" and stick to your guns. Bullies are aggressively persuasive, and will threaten the waverer into retraction or apology at every opportunity. Once the bully has done this three or four times, they have gained the upper hand and, by implication, can dismiss all your evidence as "unsafe", "flawed", "insubstantial", "inconsequential", etc.

If you feel unable to handle such intimidation, you can elect to take an ally with you for moral support, to ask questions for you, and protect you from the flak. Choose someone who is clued up on bullying, otherwise well-intentioned intervention can backfire, as bullies exude a divisive influence. The bully is likely to be less aggressive if there is an observer who understands what is going on.

You may not be able to rely on witnesses, as many of them will be too frightened to speak up, fearing retribution later, usually in the form of being selected for redundancy, not gaining promotion, being moved unnecessarily, or just having their lives made impossibly and unnecessarily difficult. From their point of view, they are unwilling to put their livelihoods on the line, even if they do passionately believe you are right. One can empathise, although the feeling of being the sacrificial lamb can be perturbing.

The grievance procedure, if followed through, has one advantage, albeit altruistic. A record should be made and kept on the bully's file. Take heed that some personnel departments will only make an entry on the bully's record if your grievance is successful; often the action is not, given that the grievance procedure, having been defined by management, is often tilted in favour of seniority, as well as being inappropriate for dealing with bullying. Remember also that bullying is usually hierarchical.

Even if you are unsuccessful, there is documentary evidence which, if another action is initiated later, increases the likelihood that a victim's testimony will be believed. Also, the word will be out, and sometimes other victims may come forward to corroborate your report. At any rate, the bully has been publicly identified, and the employer's hand becomes visible to all.

If your case goes to tribunal, the fact that you followed your employer's grievance procedure is another point in your favour, as well as denying the respondent the opportunity to win sympathy by claiming that the procedures for dealing with your situation were there but you didn't follow them.

• Don't sign anything you disagree with

The bully often uses the opportunity for intimidation and threat to coerce their victim into signing (and therefore accepting) an inappropriate annual appraisal. You are within your rights to refuse to sign anything which you believe is inaccurate; however, this abuse of power is very difficult to fight. Involve your union representative and make a clear and concise statement of everything you disagree with, as well as adding achievements, duties and responsibilities fulfilled, testimonials received, etc which have been omitted. This can also be an opportunity to bring the bullying behaviour out into the open.

• Fighting disciplinary proceedings

Once the bully has begun proceedings against you, you have an uphill struggle in front of you, especially if the bully's managers and personnel join forces. Hearings have the distinct feeling of foregone conclusion, and in these circumstances proceedings often court comparison with kangaroos rather than justice.

The best you can usually hope for is to make everybody involved painfully aware of the unacceptability of their behaviour. This may be of altruistic value to your successors. You might like to consider the following:

> Inform as many people as possible what is going on and why - bullies like to keep their activities secret, it helps them get away with it.

> Occasionally, the bully is so confident that they will tell you in advance that the purpose of the meeting is to give you a verbal or written warning. You might find the following helpful in rebutting this tactic:

"You have stated openly that the purpose of the meeting you have requested on [date] is to issue me with a [verbal/written warning etc]. In my view, your unwillingness to allow me a fair hearing represents a foregone conclusion and confirms by example the allegations of bullying that I have been forced to make. In choosing to behave in this manner, you are admitting that are bullying me."

> If you are charged with insubordination, point out assertively that in choosing to use this term, the bully is

acknowledging the reason why he has chosen to get rid of you - you have a right not to be subjugated. In expressing the need to subjugate you, the person is admitting that they are a bully. An assertive defence of this charge might go along the lines of:

"In choosing to concoct a charge of insubordination you are acknowledging that I have asserted my right not to be treated in the manner in which you have chosen to behave towards me. In doing so, you are drawing attention to the unacceptability of your behaviour and also to the fact that you are now abusing the disciplinary procedure for your own purposes, that is, to get rid of me because I have had the courage to reveal and defend myself against your bullying behaviour."

> Occasionally, the bully will initiate proceedings, then subsequently alter or add to the charge when it appears it's not going to stick. If this happens, seize on the opportunity:

"In altering the charge at this late stage you are admitting to your lack of evidence and unsound judgement in making an insubstantial allegation in the first place. In my view, this amounts to an admission that you are abusing the disciplinary procedures for your own ends."

If the bully persists in altering charges, insist that each change requires the bully to restart disciplinary proceedings from scratch. Record the number of times this happens and make it an issue each time. Draw attention to the fact that fiddling the charges to fit the purpose shows poor management, lack of competence - and reveals the true purpose of the bully's action.

> If you are one of the department's or company's top performing staff, highlight aggressively the fact that the bully is choosing to get rid of the best employees, and this is contrary to the aims and objectives of the company. You align yourself with the employer and isolate the bully, forcing him to justify why he is acting against the interests of the employer.

> If the bully persists in pursuing disciplinary proceedings, then the following defensive approach might be appropriate:

"In choosing to pursue disciplinary proceedings you are, in my view, bringing into discredit yourself, your staff, your department, and your employer. Having revealed your behaviour and asserted my right not to be bullied, I understand how expedient it is for you to abuse the employer's disciplinary procedures in order to get rid of me. Because bullying is a compulsive and addictive habit, it is highly likely that once I am out of the way, you will select a new victim and start again. Whilst you may be able to hoodwink the employer into backing your behaviour in my case, you will be causing the employer to incur liability in my successor's case. I therefore ask you to (a) withdraw all proceedings immediately, (b) acknowledge and agree to treat me with the respect and dignity to which all employees have a right, and (c) undertake not to behave in this manner towards me again."

• If you are a teacher...

Contact REDRESS, the bullied teachers' network, from whom you can gain detailed information regarding the legal position of teachers - whose terms and condition of employment are determined by various Education Acts. The procedures, processes, composition of bodies, etc are defined in Statutory Instruments.

The 1988 Education Act defines the terms and conditions under which a teacher shall be employed and cease to be employed. Teachers are treated differently from other employees, and knowing the difference can make all the difference.

Anyone in distress can also consult the 1993 Education Act. You can call the DfEE on ☎ 0171 925 5000 and ask either for the Teachers' Branch, or the Governors' Advice Branch. The latter is subdivided into *grant maintained* and *locally maintained*, and you can gain advice on what governors can and cannot do, in lay terms. The Governors Guide to the Law, available from the Publications Department, contains regulations pertaining to discipline etc.

In state schools, a case can only be made on disciplinary,

competence or grievance grounds. If the governors decide to sack, the case must be referred to the LEA, and salary shall be paid until such time as the LEA has reviewed the case. In a grant-maintained school, both panels are within the school. In independent schools, the provisions of the 1986 Consolidation Act apply.

A teacher cannot be dismissed on ill-health grounds until a medical hearing has sat, examined the case and adjudicated. To dismiss without this hearing is a breach of contract.

Any decisions and actions which do not conform to the rules and regulations are deemed ultra vires (beyond legal authority), that is, flawed and therefore nullified.

• If you are a nurse or GP...

You may find it useful to refer to Section 8 of Whitley, which covers harassment at work. Whitley defines the terms and conditions of doctors and nurses.

• Don't underestimate the bully

The bully is a person who is happy to operate outside the bounds of accepted behaviour; the more you stand up to such a person, the worse their behaviour often becomes. The most common mistake in fighting back is to underestimate the lengths to which the bully will go to be rid of you. Whereas male bullies tend to be overtly aggressive and hostile, females tend to be especially manipulative, devious and spiteful. Do not go it alone.

> *"I thought I could handle it. I've dealt with unpleasant people many times before, but I was totally unprepared for the barrage of lies and obnoxious behaviour to which I was subjected. She even tried to turn my family against me. I've been in the workplace for over 25 years and I've never had an experience like it. I still can't believe it."*

• If forced out then...

If you are forced into resigning, voluntary redundancy, ill-health retirement or early retirement, make it clear to your employer in writing that you have been forced into this position through desperation/bullying, and that you had no other alternative - this will improve your chances if you go to tribunal or court later. Seek legal advice before signing anything - explain to your solicitor that you are being bullied (beware that many solicitors have no experience of handling bullying cases yet).

• Check accreditation

If your employer is applying for, or has gained, Investors in People accreditation, then there is a commitment from senior management to look after, and develop its employees. At present (1996) IiP doesn't address bullying, but it may be useful to point out the incongruence of a publicly stated commitment and what is actually happening on the shop or office floor. IiP is administered by the local Training and Enterprise Council (TEC).

• Self-help groups

Wherever injustice rears its ugly head, or where there is pain and suffering which is not fully realised or addressed, self-help groups spring up to fill the need for information, advice and support. Frequently, a campaign or network of like-minded contacts fulfils the role of a self-help group. Some people report that a self-help group alone has been of more value in their recovery than all the professional services combined. This is particularly so in the early stages of awareness of a social ill or evil.

Making contact with and talking to individuals who have been through an experience similar to yours is one of the fastest ways to getting oneself back on the rails. Although full recovery from bullying may take years, talking to someone who has "had the experience" is a turning point and may be the single most important step towards making a return to good health and normal life. See the resource section for details of how to start or make contact with self-help groups.

• Focus on yourself

People who are bullied tend to think instinctively about other people and other people's needs, sometimes to the detriment of themselves. Now is the time to think about yourself, to put yourself first for a change. This is not selfishness, but a recognition of both rights and needs in the current situation, and constitutes an appropriate redrawing of the dividing line between oneself and others. In general, empathic people draw this line too far away from themselves, and in an ideal world, this would not matter. However, bullies place the line too close to themselves, and readily take advantage of others' generosity, empathy and willingness to share.

For empathic people, the knowledge that their line has to be redrawn can be both enlightening and challenging. However, one can console oneself with the knowledge that it is a necessity in the harsh world of reality; also, once control has been reasserted, a more astute judgement of self and others can be appraised.

Behaving assertively is a key component to achieving this objective, and in learning to differentiate between the needs of self and others, one learns that one does not have to take responsibility for other peoples' actions, behaviour and needs. We are all responsible for our own behaviour; this includes bullies, who through their actions absolve themselves of that responsibility. In that respect you are now forewarned and forearmed.

• Look after yourself

Now is the time to rest and recuperate, although there is often little or no opportunity to do so; seeking justice and another job becomes an obsessive necessity, the urgency often taking precedence over recovery of health. This might be the moment to relinquish other obligations, for example voluntary work, especially those that involve guilt. Decisions made on the basis of guilt tend to be poor. This is the time to put yourself first for a while - for a change, perhaps?

• Reassure partner and family

Partners, children and families are the unseen victims of bullying, and sometimes become direct victims as their spouse, parent etc releases the pent-up frustrations from their workplace by transferring the behaviours on to those around them. Lack of sympathy all round adds to the resentment, making behaviour worse. Frequently, this is unwitting, though whether by choice or not, the effect is the same. It is vital that bullying is recognised as the cause of the individual's behaviour, for only then can an appropriate course of action be followed.

One of the symptoms of bullying is obsession - with resolving the situation, dealing with the bully, getting back to normal, raising awareness generally, fighting injustice, etc.

Although the obsessiveness declines with time, partners and families look on helplessly, hopelessly and with increasing resentment and boredom as their loved one is consumed in a battle which appears as arcane as it is unfathomable. Patience, tolerance, support and understanding are required, although as this phase may last several years, relationships and family life take one hell of a battering.

In some cases, a crisis such as bullying drives a wedge between family members and relationships break down. Occasionally, the bully encourages this by contacting partners and family directly and giving each person a different story. However, in many cases, the predicament causes loved ones to rally round and rise to the challenge. If all family members, including children, can be made aware of the nature of the emergency and understand its causes, then a successful resolution is much more likely. Older children can benefit from the parent's experience and thus later enter the world of work suitably enlightened.

• Get a good night's sleep

One of the early symptoms - and clues - to bullying is an inability to sleep. The individual who is being bullied can find no respite from their dilemma, no solution to their problem, no way out of the situation in which they feel helpless and trapped. Only identifying and addressing the cause of the inability to sleep will result in the rest and recuperation that is urgently required. Now that you are enlightened as to the causes of bullying - and if you are a victim, the reasons for your being bullied, as well as the practical steps you can take to resist it - try the following techniques:

Deep relaxation: with no distractions, lie comfortably on your back, take a long slow deep breath in, preferably through the nose, hold it for a couple of seconds (as long as you feel comfortable), then breathe out gently through the mouth. Pause for a couple of seconds, then repeat the process. As you breathe out, relax a part of your body. Start with the toes, then your feet, ankles, shins etc, until you reach the top of your body. Pay particular attention to all the muscles in the head, face, neck, ears, etc. Imagine waves of calm enveloping your body. This procedure is similar to Yoga breathing exercises, and you can modify it to suit your needs.

With practice, you may find that just thinking about the exercise is enough to get you off to sleep.

Visualising the problem solved: all problems resolve themselves eventually, either by being addressed and worked out, or by losing their relevance over time. Lie down comfortably and visualise yourself in the position of your problem having been resolved. Do *not* attempt to think about *how* the problem was resolved, just bask in the freedom that resolution has brought. By using a visualisation of this nature, you are both relieving anxiety and employing the power of your subconscious mind to help you move forward. For maximum effect use this technique in conjunction with the deep breathing exercise already described.

- Look at the position from a third person/neutral/alien point of view

The obsessive and all-pervading complexion of bullying overwhelms the individual to the point where it becomes difficult, if not impossible, to think objectively. One way of countering this manic zeal is to put yourself in the position of an independent observer who is far enough away, both physically and emotionally, to analyse and ponder the behaviours of all parties. To gain enough distance, I sometimes adopt the topical viewpoint of an alien observing with both bewilderment and dismay the bafflingly self-destructive antics of the species known as the human being. Distance lends perspective, and if you were an adviser to the human race, what would you recommend?

Looking at yourself from the position of a third party is a technique commonly employed by many famous, talented and successful people. In fact, visualisation and the ability to activate vivid visual imagery crop up regularly in the study of success, talent, genius and giftedness. People who are bullied often display high levels of creativity and imaginativeness, so your inherent skills already stand you in good stead.

- Voluntary counselling opportunities

Counselling is a resource from which everyone can benefit. As well as a form of support in times of need, counselling can be used to enhance performance - you don't have to be "ill" to qualify.

You may be able to obtain counselling through your employer, but if not, you may be able to obtain it through your GP. If neither of these avenues are open to you, there are a number of counselling services available, ranging from private (for which one might expect to pay around £30 for a 50-minute session) to voluntary. Your GP's surgery, Citizens Advice Bureau, Library, Adult Education Centre, Methodist Church etc are good sources of information.

• Take a break

Bullying situations, including recovery, are often measured in years rather than months, and during the time that you are preoccupied, it is likely that breaks and holidays have been few and far between. Perhaps they have been non-existent. Now might be the time to recharge your batteries, soak up some summer - or even winter - sunshine, and treat yourself to a welcome and well-deserved rest. Once suitably re-energised, you can attack your situation with renewed vigour and enthusiasm.

• Learn defensive strategies

Whilst one should be able to walk the streets and corridors without fear of being attacked, the reality is that danger is ever present. Statistically, the chances of being physically attacked are extremely small - except for those who are. Unfortunately, the chances of being verbally and professionally abused in the workplace are now about 50/50. Regardless of whether you believe you should have to go to these lengths to protect yourself, it makes sense to be proactive.

Assertiveness training is the best defence, and although assertiveness alone will not resolve a bullying situation, it will at least prevent you from being seriously hurt. Many employers are ironically supportive of assertiveness training, and you may be able - indeed I would urge you - to take advantage of this opportunity. Otherwise, Adult Education Centres offer both day and evening classes at considerably less cost than commercial training organisations. The mix of informality and local involvement can add to the effectiveness of this type of training. Assertiveness is a big subject, and I recommend you seek out more than one training opportunity to gain different viewpoints. I also recommend Gael Lindenfield's books (see resource section).

When the threat of physical or verbal attack is present on a daily basis, one naturally feels vulnerable, particularly if job and health are at risk. Learning assertive behaviour has the added benefit of reducing feelings of vulnerability.

• Inform the site union

If you are not a union member, but there is a union presence, it may be worth contacting the principal union who represents employees in your organisation. Although they will probably not be able to help directly, they may be aware of similar cases from the past, or even currently in progress. One of the things bullies fear most is for victims to start talking to each other. Even if no help is available for you, at least you have made someone aware, which may be of use to your successors or others in the same boat.

• Attend training/conferences on how to handle bullies

As awareness and understanding of bullying gains momentum, you will find an increasing number of seminars and workshops being developed to offer advice on how to handle bullying situations. You may be able to take advantage of these. Similarly, there is at least one conference a year on the subject, and whilst attendance may be too expensive for the individual, one can make the calling notice or other advertising material available to one's employer, personnel department or other interested parties.

• Write to your councillor

If you're employed in the public sector, write to your local councillor and alert him or her to your present situation.

• Write to your MP

Members of Parliament are elected to represent the voters of their constituency, as well as contribute towards the workings of the government of the day. With estimates of the cost of bullying ranging from £1-12 billion, the government needs to be made aware of the opportunity for improvement to the performance of the economy which overcoming workplace bullying will occasion.

You can contribute to this process by writing to your MP, highlighting the enormous cost to employers and the State, the self-defeating nature of bullying, the waste of time, effort and resources, etc. Ask your MP to support the Dignity at Work Bill if it has not yet become law.

If you can highlight and articulate your injustice, you may be able to persuade your Member of Parliament to take up your case, or even intercede on your behalf, particularly if your employer is government funded. Needless to say, some MPs may be more accessible and supportive than others.

• Write to your MEP

Despite a certain reluctance to conform to the consensus of justice of Greater Europe, Britain is obliged to conform to European law.

• Write to the Secretary of State for Employment

Bullying is an employment issue, and the government has direct responsibility for minding the circumstances of the nation's workforce.

• Write to the Secretary of State for Education

If you're in the education sector, write to the appropriate minister, highlighting the outrageous waste of public funds that bullying entails.

• Write to the Secretary of State for Health

Ditto if you are employed in the health sector. In any case, write and highlight the cost to the State in sickness benefit and other social security payouts which are unnecessary and avoidable.

• Write to the Home Office, if appropriate
Ditto.

• Write to the Prime Minister
Ditto.

• Write to opposition MPs
Ditto.

• Write to influential people

You can also write to appropriate union leaders, your bishop or other church leaders, local chamber of commerce, anyone else you can think of who may be, or should be, interested in workplace bullying and its effects.

• Citizens Advice Bureau

Your local CAB is an important port of call, as you may be able to gain advice on many aspects of employment, representation, rights, benefits, etc. You might be surprised how many other people in your area are seeking similar advice. The CAB can also advise you on Free Representation Units (FRU) and The Law Centre.

• The Law Centre

The CAB provide free advice of a general nature, but if you need specific legal advice, you may be able to gain this from your local Law Centre. If you are unable to afford a solicitor, or are seeking to verify the viability of your case, your Law Centre may be able to advise you appropriately.

• Free Representation Unit

The FRU is a bank of solicitors with general qualifications in law who wish to increase or broaden their experience. They may be able to provide you with legal advice either at a reduced fee or possibly free.

The advantages are that you gain access to a solicitor at reduced cost who may have an interest in advising or taking on your case; the disadvantages are that you may be a guinea-pig for a solicitor who has little expertise in the area of law that relates to your case. If you cannot afford the services of a solicitor, this may be an avenue worth exploring. Contact the CAB for further information.

• Recourse to law

See chapter 14.

• Get it out into the open

Abuse is sustained by taboo and silence; by bringing the issue of workplace bullying out into the open at every opportunity, you are contributing to changing the climate within your organisation. The more people know about the subject, the less acceptable the behaviour and the more isolated the bully (and supporters) become.

• Make it an issue

If the employer is a publicly quoted company, holding shares (even the minimum quantity) entitles you to attend the AGM and ask questions. Refusal to tackle bullying is an indication of poor management, and shareholders and investors may decide to withdraw or withhold investment where the consequences (on performance, productivity, profitability, as well as legal) of not tackling bullying may seriously affect future financial performance.

• Compensation

Some victims of bullying might consider an application to the Criminal Injuries Compensation Board. Although designed primarily for the victims of violent criminal behaviour, it is useful to note that awards can be made on the basis of mental as well as physical injury. There are a number of qualifying criteria, including the need to report the offence to the police "without delay". To make a claim, obtain an application form from the CICB (see resource section).

• Benefits to which you may be entitled

Whether or not you are forced into ill-health retirement, you may be able to claim sickness benefit if you do not have a job and are unfit to work. Many people feel guilty about receiving benefit, but if you've paid your contribution, you are entitled to receive it - that's your right. Take it and use the interim period to rest and recover. After six months, if you are still eligible, you move on to incapacity benefit, although the DSS will probably ask you to undergo a medical. Keep a journal of all your symptoms for this purpose.

If health is not sufficiently impaired (or rather visibly impaired) to qualify for sickness benefit, you may be able to claim unemployment benefit. However, if you are not at full strength, the treadmill of having to spend much of your week applying for jobs which may be unsuitable, may require you to move house or work away from home or travel long distances every day, and which you probably have little chance of getting anyway, just to stay within the bounds of eligibility can seem to some like a continuation of the bullying process. The new job seekers allowance has eased the problem of finding the right job by forcing claimants to take any job regardless of suitability. We await the effects of this conservatively cultural revolution with interest.

• Resignation

As discussed previously, resigning and leaving may be the only sensible option. Bullying involves abuse of power and you face a situation over which you do not have control. It is the bully's choice to behave like a bully, and given that bullies tend to pick on people who are both good at their job and popular with people, feelings of failure are inappropriate.

If you do resign, inform your employer in writing, perhaps through your solicitor or other competent witness, of the reasons why you believe you have been forced into resigning.

• Join the Campaign Against Bullying At Work

The Campaign Against Bullying At Work (CABAW) has been formed with the backing of the MSF union and under the chairmanship of Lord Monkswell. The principal aim of the Campaign is to introduce legislation to outlaw workplace bullying in the same way that racial and sexual discrimination are covered by acts of Parliament. It is hoped that the campaign's proposed Dignity at Work Bill 1996 will receive the support of Parliament. See resource section for details of the Campaign.

• Beware vindictiveness

Once a person adopts a bullying approach, and selects a victim, there is a predictable course of events, usually leading to termination of employment of the victim. The bully's behaviour deteriorates in direct proportion to the psychiatric injuries sustained and exhibited by the victim; the process is hastened by the victim's realisation and understanding of what is happening to them. By the time matters reach court, the bully, often aided and abetted by the employer, is displaying a vindictiveness of such intensity that one wonders if the Mental Health Act should be invoked. Unfortunately, the Jekyll and Hyde nature comes to the fore, and frequently it is the victim who remains in the spotlight.

• Harassment

Many victims of bullying find themselves harassed, sometimes for years after they have left their place of employment. If you are in this position, it is essential that you record each instance, no matter how trivial.

Provisions in the Criminal Justice and Public Order Act (1994) make it a criminal offence to cause alarm or distress by threatening, abusive or insulting words or behaviour.

Harassment can take many forms; if there is a physical, racial or sexual slant, the law is in place to deal with it. Verbal allegations without written evidence may also constitute harassment. You may wish to avail yourself of the latest developments in anti-stalking legislation.

If you receive nuisance, anonymous, threatening, intimidating or abusive phone calls, contact the telephone service provider. Making malicious calls is a criminal offence, and the service provider may be able to work with you, and the police if necessary, to trace the caller.

If you are experiencing this type of harassment, do not speak to the caller at all; put the phone to one side and replace it later. Most telephone exchanges are now digital, so tracing calls is much easier. On a BT line, you may be able to ascertain the caller's number by dialling 1471 immediately after the call. A caller can withhold their number by preceding their call by dialling 141. BT provide a free leaflet on malicious calls which can be obtained from Phone Shops or by dialling 150 for BT Customer Service. For full details, refer to your telephone directory.

• Coming out

Bullying stimulates the sense of injustice to such an enormous degree that many want to tell their story to the widest possible audience. Some feel they are prepared to go to prison in order to reveal the injustice they have suffered. Whilst it may not be much comfort to those suffering in modern-day society, it's nevertheless interesting to note that many of the world's greatest reformers (for example Gandhi, Pankhurst, Mandela, etc) have spent time in prison for their beliefs and activities, and as a precursor to challenging and changing the status quo which was the agency of their respective injustices.

Many people who are bullied feel shame, embarrassment and guilt, and are stimulated in this by the bully. These are strong encouragements to keeping quiet; abuse thrives on silence. After reading this book, of course, you will know that there is nothing shameful or embarrassing about being picked on, and the degree of guilt endured is inappropriate.

This is a major step in your life, and not to be taken lightly. For some people, it gives them a sense of purpose, and they draw on their innate resourcefulness to bring the injustice to the attention of society. Motivation, enthusiasm, rebellion, evangelism, public speaking, satire, and many more, if used wisely, maturely, and with control, can be harnessed to persuade, influence and overcome almost any inequality or injustice.

There are countless examples of where an unpleasant experience, or trauma, or loss have stimulated an individual to work tirelessly to bring about change or justice. In fact, this happens so often that one is tempted to ask with hindsight whether this was the reason one came into the world, whether through the experience one has discovered one's purpose in life. If this strikes a chord, books listed in the resource section under "miscellaneous" may be of interest.

If you are the sort of person whose outrage at injustice makes you want to do something about it, coming out is the first step in your campaign. Alternatively, if you shun the limelight, there are countless self-help groups, societies, clubs, or informal gatherings where you can contribute in less obtrusive but just as important ways. All groups, campaigns, initiatives etc have a founder - perhaps this is your calling?

• Using the media

In my experience, the media have been very kind and supportive to cases of bullying, offering and maintaining anonymity where appropriate. In many cases, those working in programme production or article writing have either personally experienced of witnessed the behaviours being described. If you decide to use the media but don't wish to reveal your identity, request anonymity at the outset. If you are still employed, you might need to seek legal advice on whether and how to take part in any media activity. When speaking publicly, remember to focus on behaviours and intent, rather than the personalities.

• Changing hearts and minds

"The pen is mightier than the sword"

Many discover the truth of this cliché and a written articulation, whether through feature articles, poetry, fiction, personal story or self-help book reaches a possible worldwide audience. It's worth noting that many writers choose their medium wisely because they recognise that they are not effective speakers.

People who are bullied also tend to be artistic, imaginative and creative; many already have a book inside them. Personal experiences make excellent topics for soap operas (which cover moral issues of the time), dramas, comedies, sitcoms, satires and film scripts.

A best-selling book could run into millions of long-lived copies in many languages. If successful, the royalties could provide a new source of income for life. On the other hand, if you have an evangelist streak which you can harness, then radio, TV and personal appearances are your platform. Worldwide terrestrial and satellite TV give you a potential global audience.

• Voluntary work

If you are in the position of being unable to work, either through still suffering severe psychiatric injury, or not being able to obtain suitable employment, many people find that voluntary work aids the recovery process, helps rebuild confidence and self-esteem, and is something positive to put on the CV. You also begin to build up contacts with people and potential employers. You can initially limit your hours to match your stamina, then build up as you feel able. If the people you work with are reminiscent of your former place of employment, you can withdraw quickly and find another voluntary organisation - one where they treat people as people. If you are prepared to work without pay for a short while, the opportunities are almost limitless.

• Review career goals

This may seem premature, but think about turning this potentially disastrous situation to your advantage; define or reassess your goals in life - is there anything you've always longed to do? Might this be the time to make that move in a different direction? Could the financial boost of a redundancy payment be the opportunity to pursue what you've really always wanted to do? This is not a time for knee-jerk decisions, especially as your objectivity (or rather the baseline of your objectivity, and against which you assess your objectivity itself) may not be at its most stable or reliable. Think carefully, think long-term, seek advice and support if you plan major changes. Some people have found that being bullied out of their job is life's way of helping them find their true purpose in life.

• Retraining

One of the benefits of being unemployed or on sickness benefit is that you can gain financial help with training courses. In some cases, you may be able to get training free.

Many training programmes and academic courses, especially if they lead to a recognised qualification, can be very demanding, requiring sustained stamina and concentration, which are often limited by the severe psychiatric injuries of bullying. Nevertheless, some people find this is the opportunity to study a subject that secretly they wished to but never expected to. If you qualify for free enrolment, so much the better.

Whilst longer courses, especially those leading to a recognised qualification, might also require substantial investment in text books etc, you may fortuitously find your impoverished circumstances entitle you to a student grant.

• Forgiveness

Finally, a word about forgiveness. You may feel the experience is too horrific - and too close - to consider this important step. You may also feel that even the suggestion of forgiveness is insulting. However, you will need to embrace the concept one day; indeed, understanding the role and importance of forgiveness now may bring that day closer.

Using the knowledge gained from this book, you can now see that bullying is a human behaviour which we all exhibit from time to time; it is unfortunate that a small number of people choose to exhibit these characteristics all the time.

Forgiving someone does not mean that you have to subsequently like that person, and you don't have to tell them that you have forgiven them. You can choose not to come into contact with them again. You don't even have to respect them, if you choose not to. You can choose never to have anything to do with them ever again.

Forgiveness comes in two forms, external and internal. In the former, the stimulus to forgive results from a genuine apology from the perpetrator, accompanied by appropriate reparation or recompense. From an employer, this might mean a compensation payment (perhaps in the guise of a redundancy package), an excellent reference and a letter of apology. After such an action, the healing process can begin in earnest. However, given the insensitivity of bullies and the attendant denial, an apology is unlikely to be forthcoming.

The second type of forgiveness is internal. It means letting go - in your mind - of another person's behaviour. Simply decide to let go of the past, put the unpleasant memory in its proper place, remind yourself that it was the bully who chose to behave like that, not you, that the likely reasons for attracting the bully's attention were your ability and popularity, then embrace the good (that is, learning) that has come from the experience. Otherwise, the experience becomes part of the baggage that we collect throughout life, weighing us down, holding us back, preventing our achieving the ultimate goal of fully mature behaviour skills.

Not letting go means that you are choosing to allow the bully to continue to control you through the bitter memory of your experience. Forgiveness is therefore an essential component of breaking the bully's hold and refusing to let that person control you beyond the experience. Realising that it is the bully who has the problem and not you is like cutting the fetters of control.

Whether you let the bully know you have forgiven them is up to you. In some circumstances, this may be appropriate, perhaps beneficial. In others, it could reopen old wounds. There is no obligation to tell your tormentor, and your decision will be based on both your circumstances, and how good you feel about yourself. Most people will probably feel that it is inappropriate to make any approach; given the insensitivity and selfishness of bullies, such a course of action is likely to be embraced by the bully as an opportunity for one last attack on you.

Nothing can change the past, and you may find it helpful to use counselling as a way of putting the experience in its proper place - behind you. If this encounter has stirred up other traumas or unpleasant experiences in your life, then therapy may also be appropriate. Until recently, these techniques have been taboo subjects, society fearing (through ignorance) that they are only for people who "have something wrong in the head". It is a pity that counselling and therapy are often only available after the damage has been done. In fact, counselling is a resource which empowers and enables, encouraging and supporting individuals through self-learning and self-discovery. For counselling to be successful - and many people have discovered the benefits - it is essential that you have an excellent relationship with your counsellor (or therapist), and that such people have a sympathetic understanding of bullying and its effects.

With a counsellor, clients derive solutions by themselves for themselves - one of the most powerful and cathartic types of problem-solving known. Therapy is a yet more powerful technique, of growing necessity to helping to maintain stability in an increasingly complex and stressful world.

Negotiating a settlement

If, having tried every approach, your employer is still unwilling to address the problem of bullying, and is still seeking to be rid of you, then there are a number of areas on which you can base a negotiated settlement. It's a wise idea to have moral, physical, professional and legal support before entering into negotiations, as you may be dealing with people who play dirty. It is indeed a shame that one may have to go to the lengths described here in order to gain a just settlement; nevertheless, if the employer chooses not to face up to the reality of a bully, then that is the employer's choice.

In many cases it appears to be the *threat* of legal action combined with the inevitable publicity which will bring forth a settlement, rather than the court appearance itself.

Having exhausted internal procedures, or having been precluded from following them, some have found the following approaches productive:

- enlighten the employer as to the areas of law that bullying transgresses
- highlight the bully's characteristics, including specious behaviour and self-interest
- portray the bully as he truly is - not an asset, but a liability being carried by those he bullies, hiding behind and using the employer for his own ends
- point out that the bully is loyal only to himself, not to the employer, nor colleagues, customers, etc
- state that bullying is compulsive and addictive - the bully is likely to have a history of victims, as well as a future - and now that the employer has been made

aware, the employer must fulfil their moral and legal duties and responsibilities
- bullying and its effects are predictable and foreseeable
- there may be skeletons in the employer's closet with respect to the bully - now's the time to begin to air them
- in many cases, there may be skeletons in the bully's closet, which the employer may know about; a little digging could reveal sufficient evidence to convince an employer that public knowledge of such information might make a settlement a more attractive option; for example:
  - because of the compulsive and addictive nature of bullying, most bullies have a history of victims; check the bully's employment record with present and previous employers
  - look for sudden, unexpected or unexplained moves of job by the bully, especially from a high-paid position to a lower-paid position
  - do you have any colleagues who worked or still work for the bully's previous employer and who could provide information about the bully's departure?
  - could your union representative contact the previous representative who might have been aware of the circumstances at that time?
  - records of industrial tribunals are available for public inspection - see chapter 14
  - bullies often have marital, personal and financial difficulties - whilst highlighting these would in normal circumstances be considered unethical, the circumstances are not normal, but have been created and are being driven by the bully; it is likely you are in the process of being eliminated, after which another victim will be selected
  - if the employer knows about the bully's history, there are questions of complicity and liability
  - if the employer does not know about the bully's history, there are questions of competence and negligence
  - the employer may not wish to be seen employing (perhaps harbouring) such a person

- highlight the enormous waste of money that bullying entails; shareholders, investors, customers and auditors may be interested to know just how much the employer is spending on supporting or defending bullying
- point out that the publicity which bullying cases now command ensures a wide audience, including the Internet
- quote case law, including *Walker* v. *Northumberland County Council*, plus any other cases that have succeeded since

Settlement terms

Most employers, having got themselves this far entrenched, are unwilling to back down and leaving is often the only option. Any agreement at this stage needs to have legal backing, and word-of-mouth promises are most unlikely to be fulfilled. For many victims of bullying, a suitable settlement would probably consist of at least the following:

- a financial settlement commensurate with injuries sustained, opportunities denied, interruption to career, recovery for up to five years, etc
- an excellent and unconditional reference, lack of which is often the greatest bar to further employment
- a written agreement not to harass or intimidate the victim further
- no gagging clause - most employers insist on this as a way of keeping the victim quiet

Summary

A question many people ask after having been bullied out of their job is "Could I have done better?". The simple answer is "No". To stand up to a bully and overcome the behaviours exhibited requires high levels of interpersonal skills, high behavioural maturity, high degrees of assertiveness, superb communication skills, knowledge and insight from a previous similar experience, plus the financial independence to put your job and career on the line by standing up for yourself in the face of someone who is prepared to abuse their position of power to maintain dominance over you.

14   Recourse to law

This chapter is a simplified introduction to the current legal situation vis-à-vis bullying and should not be regarded as an authoritative guide to the law. For more detailed information on Industrial Tribunals, readers should refer to "Industrial Tribunals Procedures" (there are three separate booklets covering England & Wales, Scotland, and Northern Ireland), available free from the Industrial Tribunals Helpline. In all legal matters, the services of an appropriate professional adviser or representative are recommended.

For many victims of bullying, this is their first encounter with the legal system. At the time of writing, the law does not specifically address bullying, and the law as it relates to unfair dismissal and intolerable working conditions is so complicated that you are well advised to seek legal advice; your union is one potential source.

The principal areas of law relevant to bullying are listed below. Contraventions of the first three, Employment Protection (Consolidation) Act 1978, Sex Discrimination Act 1975 and Race Relations Act 1976, are likely to be heard in an industrial tribunal (IT), whose function is to settle disputes concerning employment. Criminal actions are likely to be heard in a Magistrates' Court, although the more serious criminal cases may be heard in a Crown Court. Civil claims which fall outside the remit of industrial tribunals are likely to be heard in a County Court, whilst more important civil cases (and those where damages exceed £50,000) may be heard in the High Court. The (simplified) hierarchy of the English court system is shown in Figure 1. Each higher court may overrule decisions of a lower court:

If the decision of an industrial tribunal is appealed, it will be heard by an employment appeal tribunal (EAT); however, the EAT can only look at questions of law. Appeals from EAT, County Court and High Court will be heard in the Court of Appeal. Ultimately, one may appeal to the House of Lords if it

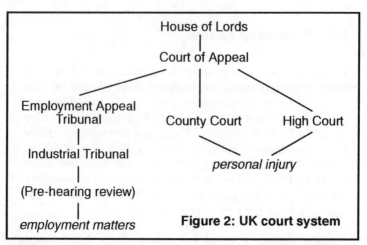

Figure 2: UK court system

can be shown to involve a point of law of public importance; in this case, leave to appeal needs to be gained from the lower court or from the Appeal Committee of the House of Lords. Beyond this there is the European Court. It should be noted that where there is a discrepancy between UK and EC law, then Community law takes precedence.

Employment Protection (Consolidation) Act 1978

Tribunals are concerned principally with alleged infringements of employment law. Until there is legal redress for bullying, you will have to hang your case on the nearest peg; typically, this means unfair dismissal (including constructive dismissal), sexual or racial discrimination.

Where a case of unfair dismissal is to be presented to an industrial tribunal, a successful outcome for the applicant depends on satisfying four criteria:

1. the employee must fall within the rules of eligibility for unfair dismissal (eg must have been employed by the same employer for 104 continuous weeks)
2. the employee must establish that they have been dismissed by the employer; this includes constructive dismissal where the employee feels they have no alternative but to resign
3. the reasons for dismissal were not "fair"
4. the employer has not acted reasonably (ACAS publish

codes of practice which provide general guidelines on what is "reasonable")

Unfair dismissal: an employee meeting the criteria for eligibility who believes they have been unfairly dismissed may take their case to an industrial tribunal. The employer must be able to justify the dismissal and show that the reasons for sacking were "fair", for example misconduct, drunkenness, violence, etc. Other reasons include:

-> swearing - in cases of bullying where the victim has been humiliated in front of others, especially where foul language was used, the inconsistency of the employer in sacking the victim but retaining the perpetrator could be highlighted;

-> ill-health - this is an opportunity to highlight assertively the *cause* of ill-health, ie *"as a direct consequence of the behaviours exhibited towards me by [the bully] over the period [dates]"*. Medical and other reports from your GP, psychologist, occupational health department, consultant etc may be required.

"Fairness" is defined in section 57(3):

"the determination of the question whether the dismissal was fair or unfair, having regard to the reason shown by the employer, shall depend on whether in the circumstances (including the size and administrative resources of the employer's undertaking) the employer acted reasonably or unreasonably in treating it as a sufficient reason for dismissing the employee and that question shall be determined in accordance with equity and the substantial merits of the case."

With unfair dismissal, the onus is on the employer to prove that it was not unfair, whereas with constructive dismissal, the onus is on the employee to prove that the action of the employer went to the root of the contract.

Constructive dismissal: where the employer makes conditions so intolerable that the employee is left with no option but to resign, a claim of constructive dismissal can be made to the industrial tribunal. Section 55 (2)(c) states that

"an employee shall be treated as dismissed by his employer ... if the employee terminates that contract with

or without notice in circumstances such that he is
entitled to terminate it without notice by reason of the
employer's conduct."

It is not so much the unacceptable behaviour of the employer
which is the legal basis for constructive dismissal, rather it is
a major breach of the employment contract; in practice this
means a breach of trust and confidence which is implied in
the contract. In many cases, the bully makes it impossible for
the employee to carry out their duties, and it is this which
can be presented as constituting a major breach of trust and
confidence. It is essential that a diary of events be kept, with
all correspondence, and that the employer be given an
opportunity to address and correct the situation. You will also
need to demonstrate that the action which precipitated your
decision to resign was "the last straw".

Other: employees have various other rights in relation to
dismissal or suffering detriment, including refusing to work
on Sundays, pregnancy, maternity leave, return to work,
trade union membership, and time off in relation to safety or
public duties.

Sex Discrimination Act 1975
Where there is a sexual element to bullying, a case can be
taken to an industrial tribunal. The two-year qualifying
period does not apply. Contact the Equal Opportunities
Commission for further information. A Guide to the Sex
Discrimination Act is available from Employment Service Job
Centres. Liz Curtis's book "Making Advances" covers the
subject well (see resource section).

Race Relations Act 1976
Where an employee suffers abuse, victimisation or discrimination as a result of race, colour, cultural background etc, a
case can be taken to an industrial tribunal. The two-year
qualifying period does not apply. Contact the Commission for
Racial Equality for more information. A guide to the Race
Relations Act is available from the Home Office.

Disability Discrimination Act 1995
Where an employee suffers discrimination, victimisation or
believes they have been treated less favourably than other
employees as a result of disability or impairment, an action

can be brought at an industrial tribunal under this new act which came into force in December 1996.

Health and Safety at Work Act 1974
Action may be appropriate where the employer has not taken reasonable steps to ensure the safety and wellbeing of employees. Attention is being directed to ensuring that this Act applies to psychological as well as physical wellbeing. Information from industrial tribunals can be fed into the Health and Safety Executive who can bring an independent criminal prosecution.

Wrongful dismissal
Any dismissal in breach of the contract of employment is classed as wrongful dismissal. Where there is a procedure for dismissal for disciplinary offences, the procedure constitutes part of the contract of employment. If, in dismissing the employee, the procedure is not observed or followed, wrongful dismissal may be claimed. This type of case is dealt with by the courts rather than tribunal. It should be noted that a court may consider only whether the procedure has been followed, not whether the procedure itself is fair.

Criminal Justice and Public Order Act 1994
A case can be brought under this new act if one person acts, with intent, to cause another person harassment, alarm or distress by the use of threatening, abusive or insulting words or behaviour. This is classed as a criminal offence and handled by the Crown Prosecution Service.

EC law
Under European law, employers have a moral and legal obligation called a duty of care to ensure the safety and wellbeing of their employees.

Personal injury/illness
Where an employee suffers injury or illness as a result of bullying - and the injuries experienced through sustained bullying are serious and often life-threatening - a claim for personal injury may be pursued.

It is important to see a solicitor as soon as possible. The law now permits solicitors to take on personal injury cases on a no win, no fee basis (also called conditional fee basis), so you only pay your solicitor's fees if you win. If you lose you

may have to pay the other side's costs, but it is now possible
to take out insurance against this. If the solicitor is a member
of the Law Society Personal Injury Panel, the cost of
insurance at time of writing is a very modest £85. In the
event of your claim succeeding, you need to be reasonably
certain that any amount awarded will exceed your legal bill,
or else you could still end substantially out of pocket.
However, your solicitor may offer you a guarantee that your
legal fees will not exceed 25% of any amount you win. You
also need to check for any other hidden fees, disbursements,
expenses, etc.

Your solicitor will need medical reports, so keep your GP
informed of what is happening to you at work. Many people
are reluctant to tell their doctor, or see a psychologist for fear
of being labelled as having a "mental health problem". This
fear will prevail until society is able to distinguish clearly
between mental illness and psychiatric injury.

Industrial Tribunal
Tribunals make legally binding decisions in a number of
areas of employment-related law.

The idea of industrial tribunals is to make it possible for
individuals to have their cases heard without the necessity
(and time, cost and risk) of going to a higher court. It is
possible for the individual to prepare and present their own
case without the services of a solicitor, and whilst there have
been notable successes in this respect, it is not an activity for
the faint-hearted; winning a case of constructive dismissal (or
any form of unfair dismissal) is not easy. The amount of
effort, preparation, research and knowledge required should
not be underestimated, nor the potential effects of prolonged
stress and expectation on physical and psychological
wellbeing. Also, the law is changing and evolving all the time,
as is its application.

If you are still recovering from the severe psychological
injuries of being bullied, the challenge is that much greater;
you will have to consider whether you will be able to relive
your nightmare. Whether or not you have broken free from
the bully's control or influence, you will face the unpleasant
task of cross-examining him and perhaps his cross-examining
you. You will also face the hostility of the employer's

solicitors, whose threatening and intimidatory tactics, whilst acceptable in court, lie outside the normal etiquette of daily life. These people are being paid money - often quite a large amount - to represent your employer and fend off your claim. They have no interest in you or your situation, and their behaviour on the day - and often in advance - can appear unscrupulous to the uninitiated and inexperienced. However, they are only doing what they are paid for.

It is common for the bully, the employer, and the employer's solicitors to hound you into believing that you "don't have a leg to stand on", your case is "doomed to failure", and that "the employer/solicitor/tribunal has better things to do than listen to your pathetic case". However, the need to behave like this is stimulated by fear, and the extent to which this harassment takes place can be seen as directly proportional to the employer's belief in their liability and guilt. For those whose sense of injustice has been turned up abnormally high, it might also be worth remembering that even if you don't succeed, it doesn't mean the case isn't worth hearing. Some tribunals involving bullying have been lost on a technicality, but with the tribunal chairman sympathising with the loser and castigating the victorious employer.

If you decide to use a solicitor, remember that solicitors are people bound by their profession. If when you read this book there is still no law decreeing bullying illegal, your solicitor can only act for you according to the law as it presently stands; this alone is what you are paying him or her for. The injustice you have experienced will have heightened your need and expectations of having your particular injustice addressed accordingly; however, your solicitor is unlikely to be a campaigner or reformer, nor can one reasonably expect your paid legal representative to champion your case by challenging the law. That said, it does occasionally happen.

You are unlikely to make history in an industrial tribunal, especially as the panel will rely heavily on case law, that is, previous judgements in similar cases. It is usually in the High Court that social injustices are addressed and landmark decisions taken, although unfortunately this course of action is beyond the reach and resources of most. Nevertheless, it is likely that we shall see solicitors (and barristers) increasingly taking on cases, perhaps with this and similar books in hand, and pursuing justice on the basis of health and safety, harassment, personal injury and employment law.

For most cases involving workplace bullying, an industrial tribunal has been the next logical step after termination of employment. The tribunal is an independent judicial body consisting of a legally qualified chairman and two lay members; in some circumstances, the chairman may preside without the two panel members. Reports of tribunal panel attitudes vary considerably, from "strongly biased against my case at the outset" to "incredibly supportive and perceptive". Given the duplicitous, deceitful but persuasive nature of bullies, it can be very difficult for a third party to make accurate judgements in all cases. Nevertheless, most people can expect to receive a fair hearing, but as with solicitors, the tribunal can only make judgements according to existing law, no matter how much they may sympathise with your circumstances. Any judgement not in accordance with existing law will be overturned on appeal.

As the person bringing the action, you are known as the "applicant"; the person or body defending the action is the "respondent". Whether you are going to industrial tribunal or pursuing a claim in the courts for personal injury, it can be a wise move to cite the employer as the first respondent and the bully (or bullies - cite all if there are two or more) as the second respondent. This makes it harder for the employer to abdicate responsibility by claiming the individuals were operating by themselves without the knowledge or consent of the employer.

The maximum award that a tribunal can make is around £17,000, although the average is usually below £3,000. Legal Aid is not available for tribunal hearings. You might well find that your legal fees exceed the compensation awarded, although many people feel that airing their grievance in public is more important than any sum awarded. If the case culminates in victory, there is added vindication.

The applicant fills in form IT1, so when completing the this, make your statement as clear, specific and concise as possible. Focus on actions, behaviours and consequences, not on personalities. Do not use exclamation marks, which tend to trivialise and solicit disbelief, thereby diminishing gravity and damaging credibility. If you don't feel happy writing the statement yourself, seek legal or professional advice, or the assistance of someone who understands workplace bullying. Your trade union, the Citizens Advice Bureau or local Law Centre may be able to help.

When you apply for your case to be heard, the tribunal will inform ACAS, who act independently to see if an agreement can be reached between the parties. The services of ACAS are free, and you can contact them in advance of tribunal.

At the tribunal, each party is responsible for their own costs, and if you lose, you should not have to pay the expenses of the other party. However, the tribunal has the power to order you to pay costs if it is felt you have acted "frivolously, vexatiously, abusively or disruptively or otherwise unreasonably". Needless to say, the respondent (or more usually the respondent's lawyers) may intimidate you into believing that you are acting in this manner as a means of getting you to withdraw your claim. This alone is good reason for having legal representation. Nevertheless, if you are threatened in this way, record it and if necessary report it at the tribunal; if stuck for words, you might find the following theme useful as a basis for your rebuttal:

"On [date], you stated your belief that in bringing this action I was acting [quote words if possible] and that you would pursue a counteraction forcing me to pay your legal expenses. In my belief this constitutes threatening and intimidating behaviour, and as such, represents an abuse of the tribunal system. I am sorry that you choose to pursue such a course of action, but in so doing you reveal the extent of your fear with regard to the action. If you genuinely believed in the validity of your position, you would not need to employ such tactics. In the circumstances, the fear you have expressed could be interpreted as an admission of guilt."

The tribunal may insist on a pre-hearing review if it is felt that either party has a weak case. Either side may also request a review, although the tribunal has the final word. This process was introduced in 1993 with the aim of weeding

out and discouraging those cases which, in the chairman's
view, have little prospect of success, thereby avoiding the cost
of a full tribunal.

The chairman of the pre-hearing review may order the
applicant to pay a deposit of up to £150 if it is felt that their
case is weak; however, with this order comes the threat of
incurring the respondent's costs should one lose the tribunal,
and it is this potential liability (which is theoretically
limitless) which acts as the strongest deterrent to continuing.
Furthermore, this will all take place shortly after the IT1
form has been submitted (that is, within the three-month
time limit) and will be experienced by the litigant as yet
another abusive experience whereby the courts apparently
join in with the general condemnation and denial. Many
victims of bullying will find themselves alone without union
or lawyer with a fragile grasp on employment, home, health
and emotions and may withdraw embittered and resentful at
this first hurdle.

Whilst the order to pay respondent's costs can only be
made at the request of the victors, and at the discretion of the
chairman, most victims of bullying are, not surprisingly,
unwilling to assume this risk. The behaviour of the
respondents at this time could be seen as an attempt to
frighten the applicant into withdrawing their case, and as
such could be interpreted as an abuse of the legal process and
even perhaps as an attempt by the bully to pervert the course
of justice.

There is hope however as decisions at pre-hearing reviews
have to date failed to be challenged. This is about to change
with the case of *Jones* v. *Borough Council of Calderdale* in
which the litigant in person appealed against the review
decision on the basis it was conducted incorrectly and in
contravention of the guidelines which state that no evidence
shall be considered at pre-hearing review.

The applicant's desire to proceed against all odds was
fuelled by the fact that the original decision to impose a
deposit was made apparently on the basis of the chairman
allegedly having looked at only one page of evidence out of
345 pages, the page in question being the only document
which portrayed the applicant in a bad light, the other 344

supporting the applicant's allegation of abuse through bullying, victimisation, harassment, sexual harassment and denial of equal opportunities. With other anomalies and the tribunal's decision to strike out the case despite an appeal being notified to them, this formed the basis of an appeal to the employment appeal tribunal and subsequently to the Appeal Court who in July 1996 granted leave for Miss Jones to appeal. Ironically, if the tribunal rules against her, she may still incur the other side's costs, but now facing loss of her house as well as her job and career feels she has nothing more left to lose.

Tribunals have the power to order an employer to reinstate an individual, but this rarely happens, and having got as far as tribunal, relations between employee and employer make this option impractical. Employers might also ignore an order for reinstatement, which may involve further costly legal action. If the reason for going to tribunal is bullying, and the bully is still in position, then going back into the company or organisation will be impossible, especially if the management have closed ranks behind that person. Defeat at tribunal for the employer will lead to further entrenchment, and the vindictive nature of bullies will become apparent.

Whether you have representation or not, it is a good idea to attend some tribunals in advance of your own - they are open to the public - to see what goes on and find out the form. Unlike the exciting courtroom dramas depicted on television, tribunals are often long-winded, with significant periods of waiting around with nothing apparently happening. Many cases are settled "out of court", often whilst the tribunal chairman is waiting for proceedings to begin, so you must expect your journey and time to be wasted occasionally.

You will need to put together all the paperwork which is relevant to your case; the technical term for this is a "bundle". It will probably include copies of letters between yourself and your employer, as well as memos, minutes, etc, which is why it is important to gather and keep as much documentary evidence as possible. It is a good idea to number all the pages so that individual pages can be referred to quickly, effortlessly and reliably on the day. A one-page summary sheet showing all important dates and actions in chronological order (for example grievance procedures initiated, appeals, resignation date, application to tribunal etc) can also be a wise move.

The tribunal panel need to see clearly the sequence of events, and the presentation of a case can be severely impeded by confusion over dates, missing documents, etc. Respondents will usually seize on any tiny opportunity such as these to confuse, distract and deflect attention. If any documents are known to be missing (for example the employer has chosen not to provide you with copies), include a sheet at the relevant point noting the omission.

Many applicants find that their bundle extends to several hundred pages, and even the most diligent panel may baulk at the prospect of having to read every sheet. Cases involving bullying are often complex, convoluted and confusing, which is all to the bully's advantage. You might find it helpful to separate the bundle into two or more piles, with the plums (the most incriminating documents containing the clearest evidence) extracted and highlighted for the panel to see, read and comprehend quickly and easily. It is likely these documents will form the basis of your case and be those which are discussed at length during proceedings. Ensure that each group of documents is labelled separately (eg A, B, C, etc) and can be referred to quickly and easily.

When it's time for your case to be heard, present it as concisely and clearly as possible; many applicants fail not for want of a good case, but for lack of presentation. Bear in mind also that the panel are there to interpret and apply the law as it presently stands; the fact that your injustice is obvious may not be enough by itself. You must present it in a manner that makes the existing law applicable.

When attending the tribunal, dress conservatively. If in doubt, err on the side of caution, or wear the same style of clothes that you expect your employer's representatives to wear. If it's your professionalism that has been called into question, don't give the bully a head start by appearing inappropriately dressed.

In the days prior to tribunal, and especially on the preceding afternoon, it is possible you will be contacted by the employer's solicitors. This is especially likely to happen if you are representing yourself. The purpose of this call will ostensibly be to see if an amicable or acceptable settlement can be reached without the necessity of going through with the tribunal. In reality, the purpose may have to do more with intimidation and threat than any intention of settlement. The degree of perceived threat might also be commensurate with the strength of your case. If this type of call is anticipated, you might consider recording it or having a witness present. As with all conversations which are of significance, ask assertively for it in writing; reluctance should be noted.

Many employers are keen to obtain a settlement to avoid publicity. In cases of bullying, the person exhibiting the behaviour often has a history of behaving in this manner, and it may not be the first time that the employer has been involved in legal proceedings because of this individual. Unfortunately, and especially with larger employers, the bully's managers and personnel join forces to prevent the legal action from becoming public knowledge. If an employer behaves like this once, then they are more likely to do this on subsequent occasions - if it becomes known that the individual has destroyed one or more previous members of staff, and the employer knows this, then the employer leaves themselves open to legal action in relation to all cases.

No wonder then that some employers go to enormous lengths to keep the lid on the situation, often threatening the employee all the way to tribunal, and beyond. The lid in this type of settlement usually consists of a "gagging" clause whereby in return for an agreed cash settlement (often quite paltry), the applicant is prohibited from saying anything to anyone about the case. Given the compulsive, addictive and repetitive nature of bullies, the need to silence those who testify comes as no surprise.

County or High Court

If you have been through industrial tribunal and employment appeal tribunal, or if you are seeking compensation for personal injury, you may move to a higher court. The costs and timescales escalate, as does your need for a lawyer who understands bullying and can fight your case successfully.

Legal aid is difficult, sometimes impossible, to obtain at the moment for this type of action. In one case, the excuse given for not granting legal aid to fight a bullying case is "there's never been a case based on bullying for which legal aid has been granted, therefore we can't grant you legal aid". Remember though that solicitors are now able to act on a "no win, no fee" basis in a personal injury case.

For cases where stress is involved (and bullying causes extreme and sustained negative stress), you may wish to familiarise yourself with the case of *Walker* v. *Northumberland County Council* [1995] IRLR 35 (High Court, Queens Bench Division). The case was settled on appeal in mid-1996 with the award of £175,000 to John Walker. It should be noted that the verdict was given on the basis of his second nervous breakdown. Other cases are in the pipeline.

European court
If you've worked your way through the UK legal system but still have not obtained the verdict you believe is right, you can take your case to the European Court. Be prepared for a very long battle, maybe in excess of five years, and potentially astronomical legal and other costs.

Time limits
Applications to industrial tribunal must be made within ninety days of the date of dismissal. It is wise to submit the application well before the limit to avoid unexpected delays and legal wrangling over actual dates of dismissal. Applications after this time may still be accepted, but only at the discretion of the panel, and only where it was "not reasonably practical" for the employee to apply within the prescribed time. There are other admissible circumstances, but the rules tend to be enforced strictly.

For highly traumatised victims of bullying, it may be possible to submit an application within the time limit but defer the actual date of tribunal until such time as health, strength and stamina have returned. You need legal advice in order to use the system in this way.

In cases of personal injury, the time limit, called a "limitation period", for starting proceedings is three years. However, the clock doesn't start to tick until the injured party has understood the nature of the misdeed, the significance of the injury and who caused it. This has particular relevance to the severe psychiatric injuries sustained by bullying. In addition, the court has a discretion to override the three-year limit.

Past tribunal decisions

Records of tribunal decisions going back to the mid-sixties are kept at the Central Office of the Industrial Tribunals at Bury St Edmunds in Suffolk (see resource section). A record is kept even where cases have been struck out (that is, an application was made to tribunal but was not heard, for example a settlement was reached in advance).

This Register, required by law, is available for inspection by any member of the public. The records consist of the names of applicants and respondents and decisions of the tribunal (although in cases of sexual harassment or national security the names may not be available). The respective bundles are not available. The IT1 and IT3 forms are held at regional offices, although these are not public documents.

The system is computerised for decisions dating from mid-1993; prior to that, a manual search is conducted. For recent cases, it is possible to locate a case using the applicant's and respondent's name (you may need both); for earlier cases, a case number is required. Copies of decisions are available for a small charge from the Office; ring the Industrial Tribunal Helpline for further information. If your employer has been taken to tribunal before, especially if the same person was involved, then the employer cannot use the excuse they didn't know. Knowledge of a former case (even if it was not heard) may aid you in either winning your case or achieving a more satisfactory out-of-court settlement.

Case law

The tribunal panel will often rely heavily on judgements given in previous cases, and a record of judgements can be found in the Industrial Relations Law Reports (IRLR); although rather heavy reading, familiarity with these cases could be a useful investment. The relevant sections of Croners Employment Law and similar publications might also be worth a browse. If you can't find these in public libraries, specialist (for example university or company) libraries may keep copies to which you can gain access.

Cases likely to be referred to are listed below, with extracts from either the court's decision (known as *ratio decidendi*, or just *ratio*) or the judge's comments on their decision (known as *obiter dicta*); the *obiter* have no legal bearing on the case itself, but may be influential in later cases, sometimes assuming a greater importance than the opinion itself.

Western Excavation (ECC) Ltd v. *Sharp* [1978] IRLR 27 (Court of Appeal)
This is the lead authority on constructive dismissal. In his comments on the court's decision, Lord Denning, then Master of the Rolls, defined the "Contract Test" in paragraph 15:

> *"If the employer is guilty of conduct which is a significant breach going to the root of the contract of employment; or which shows that the employer no longer intends to be bound by one or more of the essential terms of the contract; then the employee is entitled to treat himself as discharged from any further performance. If he does so, then he terminates the contract by reason of the employer's conduct. He is constructively dismissed. The employee is entitled in those circumstances to leave at the instant without giving any notice at all, or alternatively, he may give notice and say he is leaving at the end of the notice. But the conduct must in either case be sufficiently serious to entitle him to leave at once. Moreover, he must make up his mind soon after the conduct of which he complains; for, if he continues for any length of time without leaving, he will lose his right to treat himself as discharged. He will be regarded as having elected to affirm the contract."*

A Garner v. *Grange Furnishing Ltd* [1977] IRLR 206 (Employment Appeal Tribunal)
Whilst resignation may follow a single incident, the employer's repudiation (refusing or ceasing to acknowledge or recognise) of the contract of employment can be as a result of a series of incidents, as in Justice Kilner Brown's judgement:

> *"Whilst an employer's conduct to fall within para 5(2)(c) [of Schedule 1 of the Trade Union and Labour Relations Reform Act] has to be such as to amount to a repudiation*

*of the contract, conduct amounting to a repudiation can
be a series of small incidents over a period of time. If the
conduct of the employer is making it impossible for the
employee to go on working, that is plainly a repudiation
of the contract of employment."*

Lewis v. *Motorworld Garages* [1985] IRLR 465 (Court of Appeal)
Commenting on their decision, Lord Justice Glidewell
summarised the principles in paragraph 36:

*"a) In order to prove that he has suffered constructive
dismissal, an employee who leaves his employment must
prove that he did so as a result of a breach of contract by
his employer, which shows that the employer no longer
intends to be bound by an essential term of contract.*

*b) However there are normally implied in a contract of
employment mutual rights and obligations of trust and
confidence. A breach of this implied term may justify the
employee in leaving and claiming he has been
constructively dismissed.*

*c) The breach of this implied obligation of trust and con-
fidence may consist of a series of actions on the part of the
employer which cumulatively amount to a breach of the
term, though each individual incident may not do so. In
particular in such a case the last action of the employer
which leads to the employee leaving need not itself be a
breach of contract; the question is, does the cumulative
series of acts taken together amount to a breach of the
implied term? This is the 'last straw' situation.*

*d) The decision whether there has been a breach of
contract by the employer so as to constitute constructive
dismissal of the employee is one of mixed law and fact
for the Industrial Tribunal. An appellate court, whether
the Employment Appeal Tribunal or the Court of
Appeal, may only overrule that decision if the Tribunal
has misdirected itself as to the relevant law or has made
a finding of fact for which there is no supporting
evidence or which no reasonable Tribunal could make."*

Lord Justice Glidewell went on to say:

*"This case raises another issue of principle which, so far
as I can ascertain, has not yet been considered by this*

court. If the employer is in breach of an express term of a contract of employment, of such seriousness that the employee would be justified in leaving and claiming constructive dismissal, but the employee does not leave and accepts the altered terms of employment; if subsequently a series of actions by the employer might constitute together a breach of the implied obligation of trust and confidence; is the employee then entitled to treat the original action by the employer, which was a breach of the expressed terms of the contract as a part - the start - of a series of actions which taken together with the employer's other actions, might cumulatively amount to a breach of the implied terms? In my judgement, the answer to this question is clearly 'yes'."

Martin v. *MBS Fastenings (Glynwed) Distribution Ltd* [1984] IRLR 198 (Court of Appeal)

Constructive dismissal, and the issue of whether there was a dismissal, was commented upon by Lord Donaldson; in paragraph 15 he states:

*"Whatever the respective actions of the employer and employee at the time when the contract of employment is terminated, at the end of the day the question always remains the same: 'Who **really** [Judge's emphasis] terminated the contract of employment?'. If the answer is the employer, there was a dismissal within paragraph (a) of section 55(2) [of the Employment Protection (Consolidation) Act 1978]. If the answer is the employee, a further question may then arise, namely 'Did he do so in circumstances such that he was entitled to do so without notice by reason of the employer's conduct?' If the answer is 'Yes' then the employer is nevertheless to be treated as if he had dismissed the employee, notwithstanding that it was the employee who terminated the contract."*

Woods v. *W M Car Services (Peterborough) Ltd* [1982] IRLR 413 (Court of Appeal)

The relationship of trust and confidence was described in his comments on their decision by Lord Denning, then Master of the Rolls:

"It is the duty of the employer to be good and considerate to his servants. Sometimes it is formulated as an implied term not to do anything likely to destroy the relationship of confidence between them... But I prefer to look at it in this way: the employer must be good and considerate to his servants. Just as a servant must be good and faithful, so an employer must be good and considerate. Just as in the old days an employee could be guilty of misconduct justifying his dismissal, so in modern times an employer can be guilty of misconduct justifying the employee in leaving at once without notice. In each case it depends on whether the misconduct amounted to a repudiatory breach as defined in Western Excavation (ECC) Ltd v. Sharp."

Walker v. *Josiah Wedgewood and Sons Ltd* [1978] IRLR 105 (Employment Appeal Tribunal)
With constructive dismissal, it is important that the tribunal be satisfied that the reason for resignation is the unacceptable behaviour of the employer, and not that the employee is resigning simply in favour of another job. Justice Arnold stated in his comments at paragraph 19:

"We think for our part that it is at least requisite that the employee should leave because of the breach of the employer's relevant duty to him and that this should demonstrably be the case. It is not sufficient, we think, if he merely leaves - at any rate in any circumstances at all similar to the present. And secondly, we think it is not sufficient if he leaves in circumstances which indicate some ground for his leaving other than the breach of the employer's obligations to him."

Bashir v. *Brillo Manufacturing Company* [1979] IRLR 295 (Employment Appeal Tribunal)
Affirmation was addressed by Justice Slyn in his comments at paragraph 17:

"Accordingly here it seems to us that the Industrial Tribunal, although quite rightly seeking to apply the decision of the Court of Appeal in Western Excavation v. Sharp, have attached too much to the mere passage of time. What they really had to consider was whether he

not having worked, there were other factors which could be taken as showing an election to affirm the contract as varied. On the very special facts of this case, where the employees was absent sick for some two-and-a-half months after the act of the employer which is relied upon as a repudiation, and where the employer was also pressing the man to take the new job, realising that he was refusing it, but going on to pay him sick pay, it seems to us that Mr Bashir was still entitled, at the end of the period, to say when he was ready, or apparently ready, to go back to work that he accepted the repudiation."

W E Cox Toner (International) Ltd v. *Crook* [1981] IRLR 443 (Employment Appeal Tribunal)

Justice Browne-Wilkinson dealt further with the issue of affirmation; in his comments at paragraph 13 he said:

"It is accepted by both sides (as we think rightly) that the general principles of the law of contract apply to this case, subject to such modifications as are appropriate to take account of the factors which distinguish contracts of employment from other contracts. Although we were not referred to cases outside the field of employment law, our own researches have led us to the view that the general principles applicable to a repudiation of contract are as follows. If one party ('the guilty party') commits a repudiatory breach of the contract the other party ('the innocent party') can choose one of two courses: he can affirm the contract and insist on its further performance or he can accept the repudiation, in which case the contract is at an end. The innocent party must at some stage elect between these two possible courses: if he once affirms the contract his right to accept the repudiation is at an end. But he is not bound to elect within a reasonable or any other time. Mere delay by itself (unaccompanied by any express or implied affirmation of a contract) does not constitute affirmation of the contract; but if it is prolonged it may be evidence of an implied affirmation. Affirmation of the contract can be implied. Thus if the innocent party calls on the guilty party for further performance of the contract, he will normally be taken to have affirmed the contract since his conduct is only con-

sistent with the continued existence of the contractual obligation. Moreover, if the innocent party himself does acts which are only consistent with the continued existence of the contract such acts will normally show affirmation of the contract. However if the innocent party further performs the contract to a limited extent but at the same time makes it clear that he is reserving his rights to accept the repudiation or is only continuing so as to allow the guilty party to remedy the breach such further performance does not prejudice his right subsequently to accept the repudiation.

It is against this background that one has to read the short summary of the law given by Lord Denning, Master of the Rolls, in the Western Excavation case. The passage 'moreover he must make up his mind soon after the conduct of which he complains: for if he continues for any length of time without leaving he will lose his right to treat himself as discharged' is not and was not intended to be, a comprehensive statement of the whole law. As it seems to us, Lord Denning was referring to an obvious difference between a contract of employment and most other contracts. An employee faced with a repudiation by his employer is in a very difficult position. If he goes to work the next day, he will himself be doing an act which, in one sense, is only consistent with the continued existence of the contract, he might be said to be affirming the contract. Certainly when he accepts his next pay packet (ie further performance of the contract by the guilty party) the risk of being held to affirm the contract is very great. Therefore if the ordinary principles of contract law were to apply to a contract of employment, delay might be very serious, not in its own right but because any delay normally involves further performance of the contract by both parties. It is not the delay which may be fatal, but what happens during the period of the delay."

W A Goold (Pearmak) Ltd v. *McConnell* [1955] **IRLR 516**

The question of proper grievance procedures were considered by Justice Morison, who said at paragraph 11:

"It is clear therefore that Parliament considers that good industrial relations requires employers to provide their employees with a method of dealing with grievances in a proper and timeous fashion. This is also consistent, of course, with the codes of practice. That being so, the Industrial Tribunal was entitled, in our judgement, to conclude that there was an implied term in the contract of employment that the employers would reasonably and promptly afford a reasonable opportunity to their employees to obtain redress of any grievance they may have. It was in our judgement rightly conceded at the Industrial Tribunal that such could be a breach of contract.

Further, it seems to us that the right to obtain redress against a grievance is fundamental for very obvious reasons."

Liability

Bullying causes both enormous stress and severe psychiatric injury, and whilst the person suffering these consequences is in no doubt of the reality and severity, as are the people supporting the victim, convincing a tribunal or court is a different matter. Liability, negligence, etc are covered in the book *Stress and Employer Liability* (see resource section).

Another hurdle is establishing "foreseeability". The employer will claim that the injuries sustained by a person suffering from stress were not "foreseeable", and therefore the employer cannot be held liable. For example, "I had no idea this person was going to have a nervous breakdown as a result of their work, therefore I'm not liable". Refusal to accept responsibility for the consequences of one's behaviour towards others is a familiar theme. However...

-> people who bully often have a history of exhibiting the behaviour - the longer the bully has been in post, the more employees (ie witnesses) will have been subjected to that person's behaviour

-> the employer will probably know - or should know (if not, there is a question of competency) - from the circumstances of the departure of your predecessor(s) that a factor in their leaving was the unacceptable behaviour of an individual, or group of individuals (this is one reason for reluctance to implement exit interviews). Knowing or choosing to ignore reasons for departure, especially when disciplinary proceedings, ill-health or early retirement are involved, could render the employer liable the next time it happens. The same applies when the employer is taken to tribunal for wrongful or constructive dismissal or to court for any other claim involving injury caused by the unacceptable behaviour of another employee - the circumstances and behaviours are documented.

Predecessors

You may find it worthwhile to find out what happened to your predecessor(s). On many occasions, they will have left in questionable circumstances, and successions of enforced or reluctant resignation, early retirement, or ill-health retirement (eg following nervous breakdown) crop up with alarming regularity. It may be worth your while making contact, although this needs to be handled tactfully, possibly through a third party - sometimes people don't want to be reminded of their nightmare, and their decision not to become embroiled must be respected. Alternatively, they may welcome the chance to see justice done at last. The world has moved on significantly since their demise.

Preparing your case

Once you have collected and collated your paperwork, the documents can be scanned for evidence which can be turned to your advantage. This is why it is important to obtain as much clarification and justification in writing as possible.

A common tactic by employers is to make it difficult for the employee to obtain copies of all the relevant paperwork. When requested material is supplied, frequently, important documents, letters etc are missing. Make sure your requests for the documents are in writing, and if they haven't been supplied, draw attention to the omission by asking in writing why the employer has chosen not to make them available.

If you are writing an important letter to your employer, you may wish to send it by recorded delivery so that there is documentary evidence of the letter having been received. Or you may wish to fax the letter and keep the transmission slip.

Although bullies appear not to exhibit any sense of guilt, it seems that even the most devious and manipulative of bullies betray themselves through "inadvertency". This is an unintentional revelation, or clue, and seems to be a safeguard of humanity by which even the most heinous of criminals disclose their guilt and invite detection. Following are a few ideas which you can use a guide - they can be used in any meetings or proceedings.

One of the most fertile areas for revealing the bully is their attempt at empathy, which appears through the occasional apparent gesture of concern or uncharacteristic and prominent apology. The purpose of this has less to do with the wellbeing of their victim and more to do with self-interest and self-protection.

During the period when the victim is on sick leave, the bully will often write a letter which includes a phrase along the lines of "...we have great empathy with your recent illness...". The content of this statement appears innocuous, but closer inspection reveals an intent at variance with the content, eg:

Who is "we"? Is the bully empowered to speak for the employer? Is the bully trying to hide behind the employer when their victim's injuries are under discussion?

What is "great empathy"? Often, the bully does not visit their victim whilst in hospital when recovering from psychiatric injury or breakdown, makes no enquiries as to their health or progress in recovery, has not otherwise written, sent a card or flowers or made any attempt to establish the facts. In other words, the bully's behaviour is at variance with the caring image they are trying to portray.

The word "illness" can be seen as an attempt to portray the victim as "mentally ill". This becomes an opportunity to ask questions such as:

"Why does [the bully] need to portray me as mentally ill?" and "'Is it not the case that [the bully's] attempts to portray me as mentally ill are in fact (a) an attempt to divert attention away from the cause of my illness, that is, his behaviour towards me during the period [dates], and (b) an abdication and denial of responsibility for the fulfilment of his duties and responsibilities for his [position] particularly in respect of his legal obligation to ensure the safety and wellbeing of employees in his care?"

"Is it not the case that [the bully's] frequent use of the term 'mental illness' is an attempt to portray me as 'unstable' and is it not more likely that [the bully's] attempts to designate me as 'mentally ill' are actually an unwitting projection of his own psychopathic behaviour?"

"If I was mentally ill, as [the bully] repeatedly claims, why did [the bully] nevertheless choose to continue to behave in such an unacceptable manner? Is it not the case that [the bully] is trying to have it both ways - portraying me as "mentally ill" *and* abdicating responsibility for his behaviour?"

"Will [the bully] please explain how, if I really am the "mentally unsound" person he wishes to portray me as, I have been able to research, prepare and present such a convincing case?"

A bully is a person who denies responsibility for the effect of their behaviour on others. A line of questioning here might include "Are you a responsible person?" If yes, then the bully is admitting responsibility for the effect their behaviour has had on their victim. If no, then...

Other challenging questions could include, where appropriate:

"Will [the bully] please explain how his behaviour in making life difficult for [the victim] contributes towards achieving the aims and objective of [the employer]?"

"Will [the bully] please explain why [the victim's] career is marked by glowing testimonies from former bosses, customers and colleagues, whilst [the bully's] is characterised by resignations, early retirements, ill-health retirements and nervous breakdowns?"

On this subject, it may be useful to find out how often the bully has resorted to using the disciplinary procedures in the past: "Will [the bully] please explain why he has been involved in disciplinary procedures [number of times] over the last [period of time]?" The more times the procedures have been used, the more opportunity you have to ask the employer "Why do you choose to support [the bully] in his regular use of the disciplinary procedures rather than to investigate his need to use them on such a regular basis?" and "Is it not more likely that a manager who needs to resort to invoking disciplinary procedures frequently is demonstrating an inability to manage - or is it that he shows poor judgement in selecting staff?"

The respondent's industrial tribunal form, IT3, can often be a gold mine of opportunity, for example (this applies to other documents as well):

- establish the authorship of the justification for dismissal - frequently it is the bully's words with the chief personnel officer's signature - you may need to compare style, content and phraseology with other documents written by the bully; if the person signing is not the author, then cross-examining the signatory could produce discrepancy, inconsistency and evasiveness which can all be highlighted. There may also be other documents to which this applies.

- use of archaic or slang or vernacular English - contrast the seriousness of the situation and lack of professionalism

- look for discrepancy between reasons for dismissal (eg incompetence, misconduct) and documented achievements, notable successes and appraisals which are at odds with the opinions now being expressed

- identify amateur diagnoses (eg manic depression, psychotic behaviour) and challenge the validity, origin, intent and purpose, especially if you have a GP's or psychologist' s statement to the contrary

- if the basis of justification is "insubordination", turn it to your advantage by stating that in your view, the employer's choice of the word insubordination is a recognition that you were unwilling to submit to the bully's domineering and subjugating behaviour - by this stage you may have already drawn attention to the fact that the bully's behaviour is not commensurate with the achieving the aims and objectives of the employer, that the constant criticisms have no validity and indicate unsound judgement, and that the bully's behaviour has more in common with a psychopathic personality than with management; your resistance was an unwillingness to fall in with this type of behaviour which was exhibited and sustained through an abuse of power

- question whether the justifications, excuses, allegations or other "reasons" quoted constitute justifiable and reasonable grounds for dismissal
- where the justification is based on a trivial incident, draw attention to the triviality and that in choosing to base their case on such a trivial incident, they are drawing attention to the fact that their case lacks substantive evidence
- if phrases like "irrational and emotional behaviour" are used, point out that in choosing to use these words, the employer is correctly identifying the principal symptoms that a victim of bullying exhibits - likewise "crying", "tearfulness", "irritable", "angry outbursts"; ask assertively why the employer chose not to investigate the *cause* of this behaviour

Any letter or document by the bully's hand, as well as minutes of meetings, dismissal and appeals procedures are also fertile ground; look for, and draw attention to, the use of sarcasm, guilt, threat, intimidation and provocation. Also any remarks which are patronising, belittling, demeaning etc, especially if used on a regular basis. Ask why the perpetrator felt it necessary to use these devices.

In minutes of disciplinary meetings, look for evidence of interrogation - for example where questions are fired or statements made by members of the panel without the opportunity for reply. In this type of situation, the bully's interjections often have little or no relevance to the flow of the discussion or objectives of the meeting. The bully's utterance is for intimidation and control - you can draw attention to this tactic. Look also for evidence of the chairman not being in charge of the meeting, for example allowing "open season" for anyone to fire questions at random. Perhaps the bully is in control of the proceedings instead of the chairperson?

Another tactic of bullies is to confuse statements and questions. "You have poor relations with customers then" is a typical example in which the syntax (words used and structure of sentence) is a statement, but the tone of voice clearly indicates a question. Draw attention to this practice each time it is used and seek clarification as to whether it is a statement or question. If the former, you might highlight that use of this tactic indicates a foregone conclusion, and that asking it reveals an intent (designating the individual as having a trait) in conflict with content (seeking clarification or confirmation as to whether the individual has the trait).

Talking of foregone conclusions, most meetings with the bully are conducted with that sole aim. Sometimes bullies will be quite brazen about this, for example stating openly that "the purpose of this meeting is to give you a verbal warning". It may be possible to show from minutes and records that there is little or no evidence of impartiality and genuine desire to establish facts, but that the tenor and tone of the meeting indicate a predetermined outcome. An absence of positive language with an abundance of negative language and negative expectation are also indicative of inevitable result.

In many cases, the lack of real evidence forces the bully to focus on trivial incidents, often blowing them out of proportion. Each occasion is a chance to draw attention to the fact that by placing so much emphasis and reliance on such a trivial incident, the bully is drawing attention to the lack of substantial evidence.

Often, the bully will be so keen to diagnose mental illness that he will ascribe the cause to an event or illness in the victim's past. Documentary evidence (for example from a GP) can be used to refute this claim, and the opportunity can be taken to spotlight the fact that the bully's eagerness to falsely attribute their victim's current mental state to an unconnected former event is an attempt to divert attention away from the real cause, which is the bully's behaviour etc.

Documentary evidence of resistance to seek medical help (for example counselling) is often highlighted by the bully as evidence of mental instability and unsound judgement. This can be turned round by describing the mental health trap, as well as stating your belief at the time that once you were off the premises (for example on sick leave) you would not be allowed back. Sometimes later correspondence or actions confirm this fear.

Occasionally, in the haste to despatch their victim, the bully will choose not to investigate any of the claims of victimisation or persecution. This lack of care, uninterest or refusal to consider any version of events except their own can be portrayed as unprofessional, unreasonable and unacceptable. Unwillingness or inability to exercise reasonable skill or take reasonable care might also be deemed as negligent.

An uneasy mixture of formality and informality is also characteristic of the bully. Sometimes a letter will be addressed informally, for example "Dear Susan" or even "Dear Sue", at other times formally for example "Dear Mrs Smith". This inconsistency could suggest the bully distancing himself from the seriousness of the situation he has created, which could suggest abdication and denial of responsibility. It might also suggest untrustworthiness, duplicity and hypocrisy.

In any bundle, there are likely to be memos, letters and reports written by the bully. Sometimes, as the moment of dismissal approaches, the bully unwittingly shies away from the responsibility of carrying out the final act. In one case, the bully's signature changed from full name (which was how she normally signed letters) to initials, and on the letter that announced dismissal her signature was absent. One could intimate that a criminal psychologist might suggest that in omitting to sign such an important document, the bully could not bring herself to commit the final deed, which might perhaps constitute an unwitting admission of guilt.

In many cases, as the dismissal looms, the amount of paperwork flying around increases. It can be useful to locate and emphasise those documents which are not copied to the victim, especially if they contain comments or matters of import. The "reasonableness" of drawing conclusions and taking decisions without informing the subject of those decisions can be questioned. Also, at this time, the bully sometimes unexpectedly becomes meticulous in documenting every step, action or decision. This discrepancy between recording very little and suddenly recording everything is suggestive of someone covering their back - for what purpose?

Another tactic of the bully at the time of dismissal is to garner support from people in positions of authority, for example director of personnel. Once again, it seems to indicate a desire to cover his back rather than serve any legitimate purpose. Sometimes the bully will even involve the police with claims of harassment; this is reminiscent of the coward who, having committed his evil deed, runs to and hides behind an authority figure for protection. Many will recall a playground experience where the school bully, having eventually provoked their victim into an aggressive response, then runs to teacher in floods of tears claiming they are being bullied. Unaware of the months of preceding torment, the victim is then punished for their violent behaviour.

At tribunal or in court, the compulsive lying of the bully may be believable, and you need to have done your homework on your facts and details. Superficially, the bully's answers can be very convincing, however, you might feel it appropriate to use the words "specious" (plausibly deceptive), "evasive" (choosing to avoid answering the question) and "insubstantial" (illusory, lacking in substance and credibility).

Often, the bully, and the employer, will hide behind their solicitor or legal team, who will protect their client from any question or line of investigation which could lead to their unmasking. If appropriate, you could try turning this to your advantage; in response to an interjection with a statement of the form *"Mr X, we all understand your need to protect your client, and I note your objection/interjection every time the discussion threatens to reveal the behaviour of your client. In future, I shall assume that your instinct to object is stimulated by fear of revelation and I shall therefore deem every subsequent interjection by default as a potential admission of guilt"*. If you feel the circumstances warrant it, you could use the pronoun "we" instead of "I" to add authority.

After verdict

Whether you win or lose, there is a very high probability that within a short time, perhaps as little as forty-eight hours, the bully will start to exhibit familiar behaviours. If the bully has won, there will be gloating and smugness; otherwise, there will be a sour grapes and blame, for example "our solicitor didn't do his job properly".

Either way, contrition and remorse are likely to be absent; for these, one needs a conscience.

15　Moral issues

One of the reasons why society has ignored bullying may be because in addressing the behaviour, several moral issues are raised. Bullying is a societal problem, and if society is to tackle and overcome bullying, then these issues have to be aired and a decision or consensus derived.

Self-defence in the workplace

A lot has been said about a person's right - and especially a woman's right - to be able to walk the streets at night without being attacked or raped. The "sensible" attitude is not to go out alone, even in relatively safe areas, but only in a group of people - or only if one is trained in self-defence. Whilst the utopian ideal is for everybody to be able to walk freely at any time of day or night in any area, the reality is that some people will be attacked. Statistically, such attacks are extremely rare - except to those people who become victims.

A survey in 1994 by Staffordshire University Business School found that out of more than a thousand people interviewed, over half had either experienced or witnessed bullying in the workplace. Given that bullies never admit to the behaviour themselves, the figure is probably higher.

With bullying at work such a commonplace occurrence, the moral question is, should one have to have the psychological equivalent of a karate black belt simply to be able to get on with one's job?

As with the threat of physical attack, the answer is probably that one shouldn't have to take such precautions, but training in assertiveness, interpersonal skills and behavioural maturity, a commitment to work for better conditions in the workplace, combined with union of staff association membership and a knowledge of employment law are a wise precaution.

Acceptability

Strong management styles - or bullying, for it's often only a question of whether you're on the receiving end - have been the preferred and predominant way of conducting employee relations from as far back as anyone can remember. Not only is this macho style of man (sic) management (sic) tolerated, it is frequently encouraged and rewarded. The only way to get on in an organisation with this management climate is to emulate the behaviour. Like recruits like, like promotes like, and deviation from the accepted management style will preclude advancement. Creativity and imagination are stifled, and employees with these characteristics tend to leave, as do those with strong people skills. Over a period of time, a mandatory non-people-focused management style reigns.

With the excesses of workplace bullying receiving increasing exposure, society is starting to ask whether this really is the best way to conduct business. As awareness rises of the awful consequences of such behaviour, often with either tacit or active approval of management, questions like "how does this behaviour contribute to the profitability/ efficiency of the company/organisation?" are being asked more openly and more regularly. The proposed Dignity at Work Bill to place bullying in the same category as other forms of discrimination and sexual harassment could open the floodgates to a deluge of claims.

Take a manager who has a bullying style and who has received the encouragement and backing of management (and, until recently, society) and been rewarded (for example by promotion) for behaving in this manner. Suddenly, because of a change in attitude by society, with the introduction of a new law, this manager is the subject of disciplinary proceedings, and perhaps a criminal prosecution, for behaving in a manner which until recently was condoned. The moral question is: to what extent is a manager in this position entitled to feel aggrieved?

What did I do to deserve it?
One of the most insulting and offensive questions that victims of bullying are asked is "what did you do to bring this on yourself?". There are parallels here with victims of rape and other forms of abuse.

It is the bully's choice to behave in the way they do, and also their choice to abuse their position for the purpose of self-gratification. Low   assertiveness,   indecision, susceptibility to guilt and dependency, as well as the exhibition of approval-seeking behaviours through the need to be valued should not, in my book, be deemed as acceptable excuses for bullying. A good rule of thumb might be to take the line that by default, the abused person is never to blame for the abuse committed by another individual who has chosen to act in an abusive manner.

My own moral standpoint is that any person who takes on a supervisory or managerial role or position of authority and trust with respect to the care of other people must accept the responsibility for the safety and wellbeing, both physical and mental, of the individuals in their charge. This is a mandatory and unavoidable prerequisite for acceptance of the position, as well as a legal obligation. Unwillingness to accept and fulfil that responsibility should automatically preclude an individual from deriving any benefit arising from the position, including remuneration by way of salary, privilege, etc. Furthermore, an individual should be relieved of and denied their position until such time as they are able and willing to accept that responsibility.

Workplace bullying is both a common and complex problem, and if this ruling were to be applied immediately across the board, there would be many vacant positions. Social change cannot be wrought overnight, and an appropriate start to the process might be a public commitment from the managing director, chief executive etc to an anti-bullying policy, backed up by independent counselling, mentoring and training for all.

A precedent for this type of "amnesty" has been set recently by the non-white peoples of South Africa. If justice were to be done for all the iniquities and horrors of apartheid, then probably more than half the population would be in jail - many for a very long time. The resulting vacuum would be a mecca for unscrupulous and irresponsible elements to take over, resulting in chaos, anarchy and the possible breakdown of society altogether.

The achievement of the greater goal of having faced up to, tackled and overcome a particular social evil means that individual injustices may have to be set aside (except perhaps for the most severe), otherwise the cycle of alternating violence/vengeance perpetuates itself. Indeed, it may not be possible for total justice, and giving up one's own pursuit of justice in exchange for creating a better world for one's children may be an acceptable trade-off.

Reconciliation in a climate of genuine remorse, rebuilding, fairness and forgiveness, backed up by support, training and investment are the way forward of the mature mind. The opportunity to contribute to and participate in the planning and creation of one's own future is often sufficient, in most cases, to keep attention off the past and on the desired long-term result.

Whistleblowing

A person who observes or discovers their colleagues, managers or employer acting in a manner which is legally or morally unacceptable (for example committing criminal acts such as fraud, flouting health and safety regulations which may put peoples' lives at risk, or breaching professional codes of conduct) finds themselves in the moral dilemma of "should I tell or keep quiet"? In the former, dismissal through victimisation, bullying or redundancy will inevitably result; with the latter, others may lose their jobs, including (or especially) those not directly involved.

A climate needs to be engendered where it is no longer deemed unseemly, for whatever reason, to report unacceptable behaviours, especially those in breach of the law. In addition, the person reporting the offence needs the protection of the law.

Right to provide

Everyone has the right to have the opportunity to work to earn income and support themselves and their family. Conversely, no-one has licence to deny others that right. Presently, employers - and society - are supporting many of those who choose by their behaviour to deny others the opportunity to work.

Responsibility

Research on behaviour and behaviour styles indicates that when a person acts like a bully, that person is not discerning or comprehending the consequences of their behaviour on others.

With a physical assault, there will be blood, bruising, perhaps broken bones which are revealed on X-rays. Plaster casts, bandages, crutches, etc provide further visual evidence. All these are obvious, even to the untrained eye. With bullying, the assault is a psychological one, only rarely spilling over into physical attack, and even then leaving few traces.

Because psychological assault leaves no obvious external injuries, the assumption is that there are no injuries. However, as discussed in chapter 8, the injuries are many and long-lived, frequently resulting in impairment of ability to undertake basic functions such as employment.

The moral question is, to what degree is one responsible for one's behaviour, and the consequences of one's behaviour? Have bullies never learnt, or been taught, to recognise the consequences of their behaviour on others - or have they chosen to ignore the consequences?

An important point to note is that many bullies are quick to complain and assert their rights (often quoting or running to the law) when bullying behaviours are exhibited upon them by other people. In articulating their belief in the unacceptability of these behaviours whilst denying responsibility for the consequences of their own (same) behaviour, the bully is drawing attention to, and implicitly acknowledging, their abdication and denial of responsibility.

Mitigation
Behind most bullies there's an unhappy childhood or unsatisfactory upbringing, which may include abuse, neglect, constant absence of approval, denial or lack of love. To what extent then are the privations of one's upbringing to be taken into account when adjudicating the behaviour of a bully? To what extent should one feel sorry for the bully? To what extent should one feel sorry for the people like Hitler?

Society deems that when people reach a certain age, they are judged as being responsible for their behaviour. Whilst the specific age may vary from country to country, it can safely be assumed that by the age of 17, and certainly by 21, a person, unless physically or mentally impaired in some way, is responsible and culpable for their actions. This is particularly so if the person is being paid by way of salary, and such remuneration is accepted as the ostensible reward for fulfilling the duties and responsibilities of that position.

Furthermore, if the perpetrator foresees harm as a result of their choice of actions, the word "reckless" is used. If the perpetrator did not foresee the harm, but society thinks they should have, the term "negligent" is employed. The only accepted defences to this consensus are diminished responsibility, insanity and delusion.

Given the severe psychiatric injuries that bullying causes, the repetitive, cyclic and predictable nature of the behaviour, against what standard should bullying be adjudged?

Acceptance of the moral standpoint that any person over a certain age *is* responsible for their behaviour, then it might be appropriate to treat this type of petition in two separate parts: firstly, judgement for the behaviours exhibited and the injuries and damage caused, then, after - and only after - judgement, action to address the asserted mitigating circumstances.

Personal and professional development

If an employee performs well in the fulfilment of their duties, but otherwise demonstrates (for example) poor or limited communication skills, to what extent is that person's manager responsible for addressing or overcoming the interpersonal skills aspects or shortcomings, given that the person's work is satisfactory?

This appears to be one area where disabled people, especially those with speech difficulties, and those for whom the language of the workplace (for example English in England) is not their first language, seem to face particular prejudice. It is also the area where a manager may choose to bully when he is not sufficiently mature to understand and handle the behaviour style which includes low assertiveness, guilt, deference and approval seeking.

To what extent is it incumbent on the manager, or the employer, to help that person develop such skills, even when those skills may not be strictly necessary for completion of the tasks for which that person was recruited?

Rehabilitation

When a criminal offence is committed, the perpetrator is hunted down, caught and prosecuted. A guilty verdict leads to the imposition of a punishment, the type and severity of which being determined by the rules and guidelines of the law of the day. This punitive approach meets the current needs of society, although a heretic might consider the penal system little more than a sanitised form of revenge, assuaging society's lust for retribution. The more horrifying the crime, the greater the lust and the greater the satisfaction of punitive and penal forms of sentence. "Short sharp shock", "bring back the birch", "restore corporal punishment", "reintroduce capital punishment" - macho fighting talk may win votes (as Home Secretaries know), but are hardly tough on the causes of crime.

In severe cases, an element of punishment is clearly necessary, but does locking a person up for long periods in the company of convicted and experienced felons address the reason why that person chose to commit that crime in the first place? Are not prisons really universities of crime? How does heaping on guilt combined with fear of further imprisonment on reoffence contribute to understanding, tackling and resolving the cause of that person's behaviour? One begins to suspect that the short-term expedient of locking people up is much cheaper than the cost of discovering the cause of people's choice to commit crime, than addressing and resolving that cause. Being more popular with the general public, it is likely to win more votes. But I wonder which approach is likely to be more effective in the long term?

The issue is even more sensitive when it concerns abuse, particularly sexual abuse, especially of children. The natural revulsion that all right-minded citizens feel when the details of such crimes are revealed stirs the desire for revenge in us all. But a moment's pause for reflection reveals a flaw in society's approach. Locking up a child abuser prevents the offending individual from committing his vile act for the duration of his sentence. But the law, which is the consensus of society, deems that such a crime merits only a limited custodial sentence, following which, the person is released back into society. Child abuse, being a deviant sexual behaviour primarily of the male species, is highly compulsive, and unless the source of the compulsion is tackled and overcome, the individual *will* reoffend.

The hope is that the infused sense of guilt, combined with the threat of further imprisonment, will prevent the person from reoffending. But we know that sexual abuse is a compulsive behaviour linked to the male sex drive, whose engulfing potency is well understood, and therefore the likelihood is that without treatment, the individual will eventually reoffend. The moral dilemma is this: is society ignoring the consequences of its actions by allowing its judgement to be clouded by revulsion and desire for revenge? Thus enlightened, it is only a small step to saying that society, by preferring punishment to therapy (addressing effects rather than causes, adopting short-term fixes rather than long-term solutions), is unwittingly condoning repetition of the offence.

Bullying behaviours are present behind most crimes, and the secretive nature of child sexual abuse is a classic case of the dominance, betrayal of trust and abuse of power of one individual over another.

The moral issue is this: in the face of the devastating psychiatric injuries caused by a bully's behaviour, what degree of help should bullies themselves be accorded to help them overcome their compulsive behaviour?

16 Taking action - the way forward

"I don't want anyone to have to go through what I've been through or suffer what I've suffered."

Stories of victims let down by the management, employer, personnel, legal system, occupational health department, GP and union still occur, but is noticeable that whilst writing this book, there has been a marked improvement, especially in the latter three categories. Most unions are now actively drafting policies on bullying, many GPs are now sympathetic to stress and stress-related injuries and illnesses, and occupational health departments are also reported as being very helpful. There are encouraging signs that personnel departments are beginning to question their role in times of change, particularly with respect to the way employees are sometimes summarily despatched. There are even a few employers who, having survived the distractions of recession, adaptation and survival, are beginning to realise the benefits of valuing their staff. This is a trend which must be encouraged and rewarded.

Articles on bullying now appear on an almost weekly basis on radio, television, and in magazines and journals. The taboos surrounding the subject of bullying are slowly lifting as the subject is brought out into the open. Several survivors of bullying are thinking of writing books of their experiences.

Employers and society need to recognise and acknowledge the unacceptability of bullying and there are encouraging signs that the pace of change is quickening; the process is now irreversible.

Backlash

As more and more cases of workplace bullying come to light, so we shall see more and more successful tribunals and court cases. Employees who have put up with abuse, in often appalling circumstances, perhaps for many years, will refuse to accept such intolerable working conditions any longer. Employers who continue to ignore the growing demands for reform will find themselves increasingly in the dock, and on the wrong end of verdicts.

In times of acute job shortage, employees have little choice in respect of their employer, but as the country, and the world, moves out of recession, there will be greater job opportunity for everyone. In the workplace, those who are best at their job will progressively consider leaving if their employer refuses to value them or treat them with respect and dignity. Also, any employer who does not value staff will have difficulty recruiting; the best staff will only work for the best employers. Fulfilment of obligations in respect of wellbeing of employees will be used increasingly as a major criterion by job applicants when selecting prospective employers. Interviewees who currently ask about equal opportunities will in future enquire about anti-bullying policies, perhaps requiring to see evidence of effectiveness.

Over recent years, consumers have been flexing their collective muscles by using positive discrimination to choose where they spend their money. Shops, businesses and suppliers are preferred as much on the basis of environmental policies (for example attitude to pollution, conservation, sustainable resources, recycling, responsible suppliers etc) as on product and service quality. Companies that don't conform to customers' ecological criteria find they are boycotted.

The financial markets are also now witnessing the introduction of "ethical investing", where portfolios comprise only those companies which meet designated moral criteria such as no involvement in weapons manufacture and trading, no connection with tobacco or drugs, etc. Already there are promising signs that this new ethical awareness is being extended to exclude those manufacturers who exploit the cheap labour markets, especially those of Asia.

Although caution is necessary to distinguish between those businesses who genuinely comply with the principles they espouse, and those who are simply jumping on the bandwagon, the trend is encouraging. First ethical consumerism, then ethical investment; from here, it is only a small step to extend the idea to encouraging trade and custom with those employers who genuinely value and look after their staff, and excluding those organisations which abuse their workforce.

Why should employers take action now?

With the incidence of bullying increasing and awareness accelerating, the potential for conflict between employees and employers grows daily. Small incidents become flash-points for the release of tensions of employees abused by years of change, uncertainty, devaluation and downsizing. Whilst there will no doubt be many more court cases, when matters turn legal, for things to have got this far the battle is already lost.

In war, whichever side may call itself the victor, there are no winners, but all are losers."
Neville Chamberlain, 1938

A tribunal or court case will typically appear to have a winner and a loser, although a moment's reflection reveals the true cost - whoever wins, there are always two losers. If the injured party loses, the bully carries on and because of the compulsive and addictive nature of the behaviour, and the employer will soon find themselves in court again. If the employer loses, then the victim is likely to leave anyway, taking with them the benefit of training, experience, etc. Regardless of the outcome, the employer's reputation will be dented by the necessity for legal action. Either way, once the legal dust has settled, the underlying problem - bullying and the need to bully - has remained unaddressed.

Employers have to recognise that bullying is not "tough management", and that a bully uses their Jekyll and Hyde persona to convince their employer that they are "doing a good job" when in truth they have only one interest - themselves. The bully will do anything - to anyone - to ensure their own survival, not matter the cost. Employers have to understand that such behaviour represents a cost and a liability, one that will receive increasing prominence.

With workplace bullying now featuring regularly in the media, employees who are being bullied are able to recognize that what is happening to them is not their fault; it is the bully who chooses to behave in a manner which is reprehensible. With greater access to self-help books, training and other materials, victims are feeling increasingly empowered to stand up and fight back. Unions are finding that the sudden upsurge in demand for help in bullying situations provides an opportunity to regain membership, status and some of the powers eroded over recent years. The interest that surrounds cases of workplace bullying now ensures the widest publicity, and media attention is soon likely to include the Internet.

Soon, employers will not wish to be seen harbouring or encouraging bullies. Furthermore, following publication of this book, employers are on notice that

a) "bullying" and "management" are separate activities
b) bullying is compulsive, addictive and therefore predictable and foreseeable
c) the effects of bullying in terms of the severe psychiatric injuries are also predictable and foreseeable

On the legal front, a campaign has started to bring about the introduction of legislation to outlaw bullying at work. For employers, the discomfort of facing up to and tackling bullying now will be nothing compared to the pain and penalties which await those who deny and delay. Do it now, for short-term pain is long-term gain.

Finally, employers already have an obligation under EC law, called a duty of care, to ensure the wellbeing of their employees. Those who continue to refuse to fulfil their obligations will be increasingly and expensively called to account.

Helping the victim

As with other forms of abuse and assault, it is essential that the victim is given the opportunity to tell their story in a forum which is supportive and independent. Using the information in this and similar books, it should be possible in most cases to determine quickly and accurately the veracity of the experience being related. The traumatising effect of sustained psychiatric injury means that the victim may take several days, weeks, months, or even years to recall the whole experience. The act of recalling may generate intense feelings of anger, frustration and resentment which for the listener necessitates the use of counselling skills.

Where the employer does not provide any opportunity for victims of bullying to report their experience (which includes many smaller companies and organisations), there needs to be a helpline that victims can call to gain information and initial support. It is hoped that soon a national support service can be set up; in the meantime, those helplines now operating appear in the resource section.

Victims of bullying also need to feel that they can call on the protection of the law when they assert their right not to be bullied, in the same way that people who experience discrimination and harassment on grounds of race, sex or disability now enjoy the backing of legislation. There is another important aspect to criminalisation of a behaviour: the law is a consensus and judgement of society, so the presence of appropriate Acts of Parliament is evidence of society's attitude towards that behaviour. Absence of law can, in some quarters, be interpreted as tacit approval for the behaviour.

The isolating nature of bullying means that many victims remain unaware of what is happening to them, so the rising tide of awareness needs to become a flood. For many victims, by the time realisation dawns, the damage is done and tribunal or court is the only option for justice and redress.

The symptoms and effects of bullying, which are often misdiagnosed or misattributed, need to be identified, understood, and traced back to their cause. A feature of bullying which is generally not appreciated is that in the months (which may exceed a year) which immediately follow cessation of employment (whether through termination or ill-health absence) the traumatised victim is often physically unable to touch anything which reminds them of their experience. Many victims report the strange feeling of sitting in front of large piles of evidence, knowing the ease with they formerly handled paperwork, but feeling paralysed, unable to touch, read or process any of it. Despite an intense desire to see justice done, the traumatised victim is clearly going to be incapable of completing their IT1 and constructing their bundle within the twelve-week time limit for applying to tribunal.

The effects of workplace bullying on the home environment are currently not recognised, and time off for partners and other affected family members could significantly help recovery. Many victims of bullying have reported the benefits of counselling; in many cases, that benefit could be extended to include partners and families.

Knowing that the average person who is bullied is selected on the grounds that they are good at their job and popular with people, and that the typical victim's profile contains qualities such as honesty, trustworthiness, conscientiousness, etc, then it is clear that the shame, embarrassment and guilt that victims feel is misguided. In selecting a victim, the bully is ironically paying that person a backhanded compliment. With this in mind, perhaps victims, rather than feeling constrained by their victim status, should parade their battle scars with honour and pride.

Helping the bully

This is a contentious issue which has already been touched on in chapter 15. Being a part of the survival mechanism, bullying is a behaviour common to all human beings, and therefore exhibited by everybody on occasion. Workplace bullying is a severe and particularly destructive form of the behaviour which involves, among other things, abuse of power by individuals who are apparently born without empathy, and who have never learnt to recognise the consequences of their behaviour on others.

"Father, forgive them, for they know not what they do."

You may be getting the feeling that being bullied by those in authority who are denying the consequences of their behaviour is not a new difficulty.

Bullying appears to be an immature form of leadership, and those who are born with this behaviour style predominant feel irresistibly drawn to positions of power; for most, this means management. Such people have an increased, sometimes overwhelming desire to lead, and are irresistibly drawn towards positions of management, control, trust, authority, etc. When the demands of position exceed the maturity of behaviour skills, bullying ensues.

Of course, not everybody with this predominant behaviour style is a bully, just as not every one who bullies has this behaviour style predominant. However, my research, experience and observation suggests that in the workplace at least, there is a high correlation between predominant behaviour style plus low self-confidence and low behavioural maturity, and bullying.

Adult bullying can be seen as one of the principal scars of an unhappy childhood. The bully often appears to have a lot of internal anger, and an inability to express love. Whether or not they were loved as a child, confirmation of being loved was probably scarce, possibly absent. A child brought up in this environment is less likely to develop empathy and respect, and may find in later years they are unable to relate to others in terms other than by bullying. Lack of approval throughout childhood translates into an inability to give approval in adulthood. It is difficult to give what you have never received, and you cannot display what you have never learnt. It would also seem that a bully is a person who is born without guilt, and who has never been taught how to feel guilty.

Empathy is absent, and occasional overt attempts at caring for others can be seen, on closer inspection, to have their motivation in self-protection and self-interest. Not so much "how are you?" but "is your injury serious enough for there to be ramifications for me?".

Some of the avenues which could be explored and from which bullies might benefit include:
- mentoring - the mentor becomes counsellor, adviser, confidant, teacher, etc and could be seen as fulfilling a parental role, especially in
  - being able to recognise effects of behaviour on others
  - development of sensitivity
  - development of empathy and caring
  - the building of confidence and esteem
  - learning to differentiate between acceptability and unacceptability
- supervision - to ensure that patterns of behaviour are changing and improving, that bullying is not

continuing covertly, and that the bully is genuinely
committed to change and development

- recognition of different behaviour styles - people vary
  in style, expectation and the way that they react; the
  workplace is about teamwork, and everybody has
  something to contribute
- removal of pressures, including temporary suspension
  of responsibility for staff

Employer's action

For the most serious cases, the provisions of the Mental
Health Act may apply. For those cases where the bully's
behaviour borders on the psychopathic, but there is
insufficient evidence to warrant action, then the most
appropriate course may be early and perhaps compulsory
retirement. The cost and length of period of treatment may
preclude the benefit of converting the individual into a
responsible person. Whether this is the employer's
responsibility is also open to question, although if the person
remains in position, especially with managerial
responsibility, then the employer clearly has both a duty and
a legal obligation.

We are all responsible for our behaviour, and the
consequences of our behaviour on others; if an individual
refuses to accept this responsibility, especially after being
alerted, then ending of employment may be appropriate. If
employees have suffered at this person's hands, then redress
may also be appropriate.

For the majority of managers, a combination of
awareness, commitment to progress, climate of
unacceptability, openness, and training for everybody is more
likely to bring about the desired results, although this does
require enlightenment, courage, faith, investment and long-
term thinking. In the last decade of the twentieth century,
there seems to be a world shortage of these.

The bullying manager is likely to have a history of
behaving in the manner described, and such actions are
likely to have been rewarded by promotion - perhaps more
than once. Honour and recognition by superiors are the
strongest reinforcement of the habit, which is why changing
the ethos of the whole company or organisation - from the top

down - is a prerequisite for success in tackling and overcoming bullying.

Because of the moral issues, simply firing a bullying manager may be inappropriate, especially if it comes out of the blue. The manager will be able to claim, with some justification, that the dismissal is unfair. If employers fail to take action now, it is likely that when the law is extended to exclude bullying, there will be some cases of a manager promoted one day and arrested or sacked the next.

Moving the bully may also be inappropriate; what is needed is training, help, encouragement - and supervision. Bullies are often born with the skills of leadership, but immaturity precludes their development and deployment. However, where a manager is unable to fulfil the duties and responsibilities of position, especially in respect of treatment of staff, it may be necessary to take away that person's powers, for the time being at least. If bullying is an overdominance of the self-protection mechanism and survival instinct, this step requires strong and mature leadership and could be equivalent to taking a bone away from a Rottweiler.

A reprimand by itself is also unlikely to bring about permanent change; what is needed is counselling in an employer-wide anti-bullying climate.

Because of the contentiousness of the issue, and the opportunity for conflict, an employer needs considerable courage to take hold of this nettle. Many cases will suddenly come out of the woodwork, and managers who were formerly praised and promoted will suddenly find themselves vilified. Those who recruited or promoted such individuals will also find themselves in the spotlight. From the employer's point of view, it is important that this doesn't become a "management-bashing" exercise, but is seen as a genuine commitment to change.

One way to tackle this hurdle might be to declare some kind of "amnesty". The employer, after consultation with unions or other workers' representatives - it's essential that this is not done in secret, for abuse thrives on secrecy - produces an honest, open and jargon-free statement along the lines of:

1. bullying is a problem of society which until recently has been poorly understood and overlooked
2. it is in everybody's interests to tackle and overcome the problem, and as a responsible employer, we are taking an early lead in this respect
3. in consultation with unions, workers' representatives, etc, a comprehensive anti-bullying policy is being introduced, which includes independent investigation and counselling
4. a training programme is being initiated which covers awareness, ways of tackling bullying, interpersonal skills and confidence building; all employees, including the chief executive, will receive appropriate training over the next twelve months

The employer will need to tackle the thorny problem of managers who have a history of bullying, but who until now have been tolerated and supported. Once the problem of bullying is acknowledged openly, it is likely that a number of new cases will come to light, with victims having high expectations of appropriate action. One way forward might be for existing bullying cases to be investigated and graded, eg:

1. where a person has exhibited psychopathic or criminal behaviour, they shall be subject to legal proceedings
2. in very serious cases, action shall be taken according to the employer's disciplinary procedures
3. in serious cases, where the cost of retraining would be too high for the benefits gained, the individual shall be "retired"
4. where the degree of bullying is classed as moderate, the person shall be subject to programme of training, counselling, supervision; a move with suspension of responsibility may also be appropriate
5. cases of mild bullying will be written off subject to compliance with the anti-bullying policy and appropriate training

Setting up a non-bullying policy

The principal requirement of an effective anti-bullying policy is that it must be endorsed, implemented and followed wholeheartedly, genuinely and enthusiastically from the top down. Everybody must be committed to and subject to the code - without exception.

Behaviour percolates down, and people who choose to behave in the manner of a bully will always, consciously or unconsciously, select a role model whose example can be quoted if challenged to justify their behaviour. "The boss doesn't follow the rules, so why should I", "If it's good enough for the Chief Executive, it's good enough for me - look where it got him" and other excuses are trotted out.

The primary tenets of the policy are that bullying is wholly unacceptable, and that anyone guilty of behaving in this manner will be subject to predetermined procedures, which, if the case is proved, mean the offending individual will be liable to disciplinary action. This could range from a verbal warning to dismissal, depending on the circumstances and severity of the offence. Most employers already have a policy for harassment, including sexual or racial harassment, and in many cases, bullying can be slotted in - provided that it remains its separate identity, and is not lost amongst the terminology.

The second strand of an effective anti-bullying policy is free and unrestrained access to an independent counsellor or investigator who is trained to recognise bullying. Any employee who feels they are being bullied (or victimised, etc) can seek independent advice, information, and if necessary, counselling, without fear of further victimisation simply for having sought advice. If the complaint is found to have validity, the person whose alleged behaviour triggered the complaint can be moved or suspended pending a full investigation.

Thirdly, there needs to be a clear set of procedures for investigating any complaint fairly and impartially, which will result in certain specified courses of action depending on the outcome of the investigation. In other words, bullying shall be treated in the same manner as any other criminal or disciplinary offence.

A point that employers need to note is that an effective policy will take time to implement and time to become fully effective. It requires a long-term view, and a couple of years may need to be regarded as the minimum period for the majority of existing cases to come forward and attitudes at all levels of the workforce to complete their transition from disbelief and denial to open rejection.

To be effective, however, an anti-bullying policy needs not only to be reactive - that is, it is up to the individual who feels they are being bullied to take action and initiate investigation - but to be proactive as well. With the majority of cases of bullying involving a line manager, the annual appraisal system may need revision, for who is going to criticise or implicate the very person on whom your career progression depends?

Other ways include independent and anonymous staff surveys, close cooperation with unions on individual cases, and exit interviews.

In a wider context, an anti-bullying policy is not just about catching bullies, it's about fostering a climate of dignity and respect by and for all employees at and between all levels; in other words, making respect a way of life for every employee when in their interactions with colleagues, bosses, subordinates, customers, clients, pupils, students, patients, charges, contractors, sub-contractors, suppliers, the public, and so on. In most cases, this will lead to a handsome return on investment through productivity and performance gains combined with loyalty from one's patrons.

In summary, the employer's action needs to include:
- statement of policy, preferably by the chief executive, managing director or person at similar level
- timescale for implementation of policy
- production of a written policy
- liaison on development and implementation of policy with unions, works councils or workers' representatives
- implementation of policy and associated procedures
- incorporation of anti-bullying measures with existing anti-harassment and discrimination procedures
- review of grievance procedures
- training of personnel and human resources department
- training of occupational health staff
- provision of a welfare and counselling service for victims of bullying

- opportunities for counselling for families of victims
- independent and continuing review of disciplinary and legal actions against the employer
- facilities for independent monitoring of the procedure and its effectiveness
- use of exit interviews to catch otherwise elusive cases

Employer recognition
Some employers institute outplacement programmes following redundancy announcements; here, a specialist company runs an intensive programme of helping those made redundant to find and apply for another job. Whilst these programmes can certainly be of great benefit (placement rates are often as high as 70-80%), they can also sometimes be seen as too little too late, especially with those employers with a poor record in caring for their staff.

Many employers now have an continuing employee assistance programme (EAP) whereby employees gain continuing support in both personal and professional needs, and are encouraged to keep their skills and training up to date so that in the event of redundancy they are well placed to obtain another job quickly. In more enlightened programmes, the EAP covers training in personal, interpersonal and behavioural skills and is linked to the employer's staff development procedures and programmes, which include bullying and harassment policies.

It seems likely that those employers who will prosper in the new millennium are likely to be those who have defined, published and implemented a non-bullying policy, where staff feel cared for and valued. Customers will vote with their wallets, and deal only with employers that have a no-bullying policy. This has already happened with the green-environmental issue. Shareholders and investors will begin again to look at safer and more profitable long-term investments as the current short-term greed becomes increasingly unstable and unacceptable. Ironically, it may turn out that those employers which have the best EAPs are the ones who are least likely to need them.

Law
Where human behaviour is concerned, and especially if money is involved (as in business), attitudes will only change

if acceptable standards of behaviour are backed up by law. It is sad that it is only through heavy financial penalty or the prospect of imprisonment that many employers will be persuaded to accept and fulfil their legal and moral obligations in respect of the wellbeing of their employees. Promises, undertakings, codes of practice etc are used by some unscrupulous employers to enable them to carry on behaving in the proscribed manner whilst appearing to agree and conform; some obstinate employers may need to be placed in the position of feeling the embarrassment of exposure.

The Employment Protection (Consolidation) Act 1978 needs amending and updating as follows:

- the twelve-week time limit for applying to industrial tribunal needs to be extended to at least two years if bullying is involved, with further extension in very serious cases
- the two-year qualifying period for unfair dismissal needs to be abolished; instead, rights should be automatic on start of employment for all employees, including those who are part-time, on fixed-term contract, short-term contract, flexible hours and zero hours contract, casual labour, temping, homeworking, teleworking, etc
- the Act (and others relating to employment) needs to apply to people working in a voluntary capacity
- the Act needs to address and proscribe bullying specifically such that claims for constructive dismissal on this basis are more likely to be successful
- the limits on compensation awarded at tribunal need to be raised to a more effective level, eg £50,000 or more.
- in cases of bullying, the employer's liability shall be unlimited
- the Act needs to make the bully personally liable as well as the employer

The Health & Safety at Work Act (1974) needs to be amended to ensure that bullying and its effect on health are addressed directly.

Sweden has already taken the initiative on bullying and adopted in September 1993 an "Ordinance of the Swedish

National Board of Occupational Safety and Health containing
Provisions on measures against Victimization at Work". An
English translation is published under ISSN 0348-2138. The
term victimisation here covers "adult bullying, mental
violence, social rejection and harassment, including sexual
harassment". Not only is workplace bullying illegal in
Sweden, the authorities recognise the enormous harm that
the behaviour causes and the cost to the State of supporting
or subsidising victims, perhaps for the rest of that person's
life. With a recognised irony, a former mental asylum has
been converted to a place of recovery where victims receive
treatment and support to enable them to become productive
and return to working life in a relatively short time.
Employers are obliged to foot the bill.

Society's way forward

Although exhibited by individuals, bullying is a problem of
society; resolution requires that society:

a) acknowledge that bullying exists

b) recognise what bullying is

c) state unequivocally its rejection of bullying and that
   such behaviour is wholly unacceptable

d) recognise the cost to

   i) the employer

   ii) the individual

   iii the family

   iv) the State

e) create a climate of unacceptability by exposing bullies
   who abuse their position to line their pockets and
   ensure their survival through the destruction of others

f) take positive action to

   i) ensure procedures (laws) exist to deal with bullying
      when it happens

   ii) raise awareness and understanding of bullying at
       every level

   iii) provide training and education into behavioural
        skills (eg parenting, school, workplace)

   iv) provide support for all involved in addressing
       workplace bullying

With bullying ingrained in human nature, a strategy for its
eradication requires a mixture of immediate action and
longer-term planning, which might encompass:

a) short-term action
  -> establishment of a network of self-help groups
     organised by geography, occupation and skills
  -> establishment of groups to campaign for change, to
     lobby Parliament and to support victims of bullying
     through the legal process
  -> forging links with other pressure groups whose
     interests include bullying and harassment (see
     resource section)
  -> mounting seminars, conferences and discussion
     forums to raise awareness
  -> ditto programmes on TV and radio, articles and
     features in newspapers and magazines
  -> regular opportunities for all for training, courses
     and workshops on all aspects of bullying
  -> independent and influential intervention and
     arbitration by individuals who understand bullying

b) medium-term action
  -> establishment of a fully-resourced national
     confidential helpline
  -> sponsorship of further research on bullying
  -> more books on bullying from all perspectives,
     including victims
  -> introduction of accountability of employers,
     managers, etc
  -> making whistleblowing acceptable, perhaps
     mandatory
  -> outlawing or restricting the use of gagging clauses
  -> extension of existing laws to cover bullying
  -> development of codes of practice to incorporate
     bullying
  -> upgrading of accreditation schemes (IiP, ISO9000/
     BS5750) to incorporate bullying
  -> establishment of a restart scheme for abused
     employees to rebuild their lives
  -> the establishment of a recovery centre for severely
     traumatised victims (as in Sweden)

c) long-term action

-> whilst recognising the democratic stability resulting from the censorious and adversarial nature of society, developing a more mature and cooperative basis for interaction, consensus and government

-> inclusion of interpersonal skills and behavioural maturity on the national curriculum

-> the incorporation and growth of confidence building and behavioural skills in nursery education

-> facilities and support for the enhancement of parenting skills to recognise the importance of building confidence and esteem

Conclusion

In the workplace, bullying is a largely valueless and obsolete behaviour which is being visited upon individuals with increasing frequency. Only by working together at every level of society can the problem be recognised, tackled and overcome.

Although the problem seems currently to be getting worse, in the run-up to the new millennium this could be seen as an opportunity. Whilst only a small number of individuals bully, there are few victims, little perceived cost and insufficient objections to the behaviour; only when a sufficient number of people are affected will the problem be properly addressed, tackled and overcome. The escalation of denial and increasingly vindictive measures being taken to threaten and intimidate those who dare to stand up and proclaim the injustice can be taken as a sign of a threshold for change in society's attitude. The critical mass appears to be nigh.

The apparent increase in bullying at work provides an opportunity to observe, analyse, and understand a previously ignored, deep-seated, violent and increasingly superfluous side to the human species. As we prepare to herald the new millennium, insight and understanding of the true nature of bullying could be seen as a prerequisite for the next step in human evolution. In the meantime, it will take courage, maturity and all our combined efforts to overcome the behaviour.

Together we can crack it.

Resources
Helplines
Bullying at work
IMPERATIVE bullying support line, ☎ 0181 885 1677 (Mon-Tues 7 pm-9 pm, Saturday 9.30 am-11.30 am)

IMPERATIVE bullying support line, ☎ 01983 856379 (Mon-Fri 8 pm-10 pm)

Workplace bullying advice line, ☎ 01235 834548 (office hours)

In Scotland: Bullying information line, ☎ 01505 615990 (Tuesday 7 pm-9 pm and Sunday 10 am-12 noon)

For details of local contact points or self-help groups in your area, or if you want to start one, write to the author via the publisher (please enclose sae):

Success Unlimited, PO Box 77, Wantage, Oxon OX12 8YP, UK

Bullying in school
ChildLine, ☎ 0800 1111 (24-hour freephone for children)

Advice and information
Raising awareness of bullying through research and development, training and education, and spreading ideas of how to recognise, combat and deal with bullying:

Andrea Adams Trust, c/o Lyn Witheridge, Shalimar House, 24 Derek Avenue, Hove, East Sussex BN3 4PF, ☎ 01273 417850, Fax 01273 417075

Issues of harassment:

National Harassment Network, University of Central Lancashire, Preston PR1 2HE, ☎ 01772 893398

PCAW provides free advice and help to employees & others with serious concerns about public dangers and malpractice, including fraud, whistleblowing, abuse, corruption, health and safety:

Public Concern at Work, Lincoln's Inn House, 42 Kingsway, London WC2B 6EN, ☎ 0171 404 6609, Fax 0171 404 6576

Freedom to Care campaigns in areas of accountability, bullying, whistleblowing and gagging clauses:

Freedom to Care, PO Box 125, West Molesey, Surrey KT8 1YE, ☎ 0181 224 1022

UK Work-Stress Network: addressing stress at work, understanding the causes and campaigning for effective health and safety measures. Part of the European Work-Stress Network:

Dave Jones, Convenor, UK Work-Stress Network,
  28 Haywood Crescent, Waters Edge, Norton, Runcorn,
  Cheshire WA7 6NB, ☎ 01928 716389

REDRESS, the bullied teachers' network:

Jenni Watson, Secretary, Bramble House, Mason Drive,
  Hook, Goole, Humberside DN14 5NE, ☎ 01405 764432

Books & publications
Bullying
Andrea Adams, *Bullying at Work - How to Confront and
  Overcome It*, Virago, 1992

Policy documents
MSF, *Bullying at Work: How to Tackle it - A Guide for MSF
  Representatives and Members*, August 1995, price £10 to
  non-members: MSF Health and Safety Office, Whitehall
  College, Dane O'Coys Road, Bishop's Stortford,
  Hertfordshire CM23 2JN

NASUWT, *No Place To Hide: Confronting Workplace Bullies*,
  April 1996, available for a nominal p&p charge to non-
  members: NASUWT, Hillscourt Education Centre,
  Rednal, Birmingham B45 8RS, ☎ 0121 453 6150,
  Fax 0121 457 6208/9

Health, stress and mental illness publications
C Cooper & S Williams, *Creating Healthy Work
  Organisations*, Kogan Page

C Cooper & R Payne, *Causes, Coping and Consequences of
  Stress at Work*, John Wiley & Son

J Earnshaw & C Cooper, *Stress and Employer Liability*, IPD, 1996

M Napier & K Wheat, *Recovering Damages for Psychiatric
  Injury*, Blackstone Press

R Greenhalgh, *Industrial Tribunals*, IPD, 1996

R Jenkins & N Coney (ed), *Prevention of Mental Ill Health in
  the Workplace*, HMSO

U Markham, *Managing Stress: the Stress Survival Guide for
  Today*, Element Books, 1995

M Reddy, *The Manager's Guide to Counselling at Work*, Routledge

V Sutherland & C Cooper, *Understanding Stress*, Chapman
  and Hall

Richard L Gregory (ed), *Oxford Companion to the Mind*,
  Oxford University Press, 1987

You and Your Rights, Readers Digest, 1991

John Pritchard, Helen Garlick et al, *The New Penguin Guide to the Law*, Viking Books, 1992

Procedures, Industrial Tribunals (free - call the IT Helpline)

Working for Your Health, CBI

A Guide to Mental Health in the Workplace, Department of Health

Mental Illness - What Does it Mean? Department of Health

Stress at Work - A Guide for Employers, HSE

Mental Distress at Work - First-Aid Measures, HSE

Health Education Authority, *Action on Stress at Work*, HMSO

Health and Employment, ACAS

Discipline at Work, ACAS

Effective Organisations, ACAS

Statement on Harassment at Work, IPD

Croner's Employment Law, Croner Publications Ltd, refer to the copy in your local library

Childhood and upbringing

The following resources are useful for your children, and for reviewing your own childhood:

Rosemary Stones, *Don't Pick on Me - How to Handle Bullying*, Piccadilly Press, 1993

Gael Lindenfield, *Confident Children*, Thorsons, 1994

Michele Elliott, *501 Ways to be a Good Parent*, Hodder & Stoughton, 1996

Kidscape, 152 Buckingham Palace Road, London SW1W 9TR, ☎ 0171 730 3300 (send large sae for free booklet on child bullying)

Sexual harassment

Liz Curtis, *Making Advances*, BBC Books, 1993

Recovery

Benjamin Colodzin, *How to Survive Trauma*, Station Hill Press, 1993

David Kinchin, *Post-traumatic Stress Disorder*, Thorsons, 1994

Dr David Muss, *The Trauma Trap*, Doubleday, 1991

Dr William Wilkie, *Understanding Stress Breakdown*, Millennium Books, 1995

Robert Priest, *Anxiety and Depression*, Vermilion, 1996

Confidence building

Wayne Dyer, *Your Erroneous Zones*, Arrow

Gael Lindenfield, *Superconfidence*, Thorsons, 1992

Self-improvement

Dr Harry Alder, *The Right Brain Manager*, Piatkus, 1993

Dr Eia Asen, *Family Therapy for Everyone - How to Get the Best out of Living Together*, BBC, 1995

Tony Buzan, *Use Your Head*, Ariel Book BBC, 1982

Dale Carnegie, *How to Win Friends and Influence People*, Cedar Books, 1991

Gael Lindenfield, *Self Esteem*, Thorsons, 1995

Gael Lindenfield, *Managing Anger,* Thorsons

Gael Lindenfield, *The Positive Woman*, Thorsons

Gael Lindenfield, *Assert Yourself,* Thorsons, 1995

Dr Patricia Love & Jo Robinson, *Hot Monogamy*, Piatkus, 1994

Allan Pease, *Body Language*, Sheldon Press, 1981

David J Schwartz, *The Magic of Thinking Big*, Thorsons, 1984

David J Schwartz, *Maximize Your Mental Power*, Thorsons, 1986

Robin Skynner and John Cleese, *Life and How to Survive It*, Methuen, 1993

Robin Skynner and John Cleese, *Families And How To Survive Them*, Methuen, 1983

Napoleon Hill and W Clement Stone, *Success through a Positive Mental Attitude*, Thorsons, 1990

Miscellaneous

Wayne Dyer, *You'll See It When You Believe It*, Arrow, 1990

Betty J Eadie, *Embraced by the Light*, Thorsons, 1992

Robin Norwood, *Women Who Love Too Much*, Arrow Books, 1985

James Redfield, *The Celestine Prophecy*, Bantam Books, 1994

James Redfield & Carol Adrienne, *The Celestine Prophecy: An Experiential Guide*, Bantam Books, 1995

Virginia Satir, *Peoplemaking*, Souvenir Press, 1978

Richard Tedeschi & Lawrence Calhoun, *Trauma and Transformation: Growing in the Aftermath of Suffering*, Sage, 1996

Media

Dan Poynter and Mindy Bingham, *Is There a Book Inside You?* Exley Publications, 1986

Judith Appelbaum and Nancy Evans, *How to get Happily Published*, Plume, 1982

Peter Finch, *How to Publish Yourself*, Allison & Busby, 1987

John Kremer, *1001 Ways to Market your Books*, Ad-Lib Publications, 1989

Ian Linton, *Writing for a Living*, Kogan Page, 1985

Judith Butcher, *Copy Editing*, CUP, 1992

Writers' and Artists' Yearbook, A&C Black, annual

Writers' Handbook, annual

William Parkhurst, *How to get Publicity and Make the Most of It Once You've Got It*, Times Books, 1985

Training and Counselling

Counselling, consultancy and training services for individuals and organisations - specialising in workplace issues:
Centre for Personal & Professional Development, The Mill, Shawford, Winchester, Hampshire SO21 2BP,
☎ 01962 715838, Fax 01962 715160

Positive action to stop aggression in the workplace:
Mabruk Training, Shalimar House, 24 Derek Avenue, Hove, East Sussex BN3 4PF, ☎ 01273 417850, Fax 01273 417075

Caring for the personal safety of all people:
The Suzy Lamplugh Trust, 14 East Sheen Avenue, London SW14 8AS, ☎ 0181 392 1839, Fax 0181 392 1830

Confidential counselling and welfare service for employees and individuals, especially stress and bullying counselling, and assertiveness to combat aggression:
Chilton Counselling Ltd, Building 455, Curie Avenue, Harwell, Didcot, Oxon OX11 0RA, ☎ 01235 433061, Fax 01235 432816

Personal & organisational stress and bullying in the workplace:
Gillian Graveson Associates, Wintonlea, Watt Road, Bridge of Weir, Renfrewshire PA11 3DL, ☎ 01505 614046

Stress management and good citizenship training:
Jacky Kennedy Associates, 31 Greenway, Braunston, Daventry, Northants NN11 7JT, ☎ 01788 891994, Fax 01788 890997

Personal & professional development, interpersonal skills etc:
The Industrial Society, Peter Runge House, 3 Carlton House Terrace, London SW1Y 5DG, UK, ☎ 0171 839 4300

One of the UK's largest providers of EAP programmes dealing with workplace problems, including stress and bullying:
PPC UK Ltd, Florence House, St Mary's Road, Hinckley, Leicestershire LE10 1EQ, ☎ 01455 890011

British Association of Counselling, 1 Regent Place, Rugby, Warwickshire CV21 2PJ, ☎ 01788 578328

Organisations

ACAS Advisory Service, 27 Wilton Street, London SW1X, 7AZ

ACAS Regional Offices:

Northern Region:, Westgate House, Westgate Road,
Newcastle upon Tyne NE1 1TJ, ☎ 0191 261 2191

Yorkshire and Humberside Region: Commerce House,
St Albans Place, Leeds LS2 8HH, ☎ 0113 243 1371

Eastern & Southern Region: Westminster House, 125 Fleet
Road, Fleet, Aldershot, Hampshire GU13 8PD,
☎ 01252 822566

South & Western Region, 27a Regent Street, Clifton, Bristol
BS8 4HR, ☎ 0117 970 6269

Midlands Region, Leonard House, 319/323 Bradford Street,
Birmingham B5 6ET, ☎ 0121 666 7576

Nottingham Office, Anderson House, Clinton Avenue,
Nottingham NG5 1AW, ☎ 0115 985 8253

London Region, Clifton House, Euston Road, London
NW1 2RB, ☎ 0171 396 0022

North West Region, Boulton House, 17-21 Chorlton Street,
Manchester M1 3HY, ☎ 0161 237 1790

Merseyside Office, Cressington House, 249 St Mary's Road,
Garston, Liverpool L19 0NF, ☎ 0151 427 8881

Accrington Office, 1st Floor, Bradshawgate House, 1 Oak
Street, Accrington, Lancs BB5 1EQ, ☎ 01254 871996

Wales: Phase 1, Ty Glas Road, Llanishen, Cardiff CF4 5PH,
☎ 01222 762636

ACAS publications: ACAS Reader Ltd, PO Box 404,
Leicester LE4 9ZZ

Anti-Bullying Campaign, 10 Borough Hill Street,
London SE1 9QQ

Audit Commission, 1 Vincent Square, London SW1P 2PN

CABAW, Campaign Against Bullying At Work: write to
MSF/CABAW, 33-37 Moreland Street, London EC1V 8BB,
☎ 0171 505 3000, Fax 0171 505 3030

CBI, 103 New Oxford Street, London WC1A 1DU

Citizens Advice Bureau - see local phone book

Commission for Racial Equality, Elliott House, 10-12
Allington Street, London SW1E 5EH, ☎ 0171 828 7022

Criminal Injuries Compensation Board, Whittington House,
19 Alfred Place, London WC1E 7LG, ☎ 0171 636 2812

Department of Health, Richmond House, 79 Whitehall,
London SW1A 2NS, ☎ 0171 210 5150/1/2/3

Department of Health publications: Cambertown Ltd,
8 Commercial Road, Goldthorpe, Rotherham, S Yorks S63 9BL

Equal Opportunities Commission:
  England: Overseas House, Quay Street,
  Manchester M3 3HN, ☎ 0161 833 9244
  Wales: Caerwys House, Windsor Lane, Cardiff CF1 1LB,
  ☎ 01222 343552

Faculty of Occupational Medicine, 6 St Andrews Place,
Regents Park, London NW1 4LB, ☎ 0171 487 3414

Freedom to Care, PO Box 125, West Molesey,
Surrey KT8 1YE, ☎ 0181 224 1022

Health Education Authority publications: Customer Services
Department, Marston Book Services Ltd, PO Box 87, Osney
Mead Industrial Estate, Oxford OX2 0DT

Health Information Line, Dept of Health, ☎ 0800 665544

HSE publications: HSE Books, PO Box 1999, Sudbury,
Suffolk CO10 6FS, UK, ☎ 01787 881165, Fax 01787 313995

Health and Safety Executive public enquiry point: HSE
Information Centre, Broad Lane, Sheffield S3 7HQ,
☎ 0114 289 2345, Fax 0114 289 2333

Home Office, 50 Queen Anne's Gate, London SW1H 9AT

Industrial Tribunals: Central Office of the Industrial
Tribunals, 100 Southgate Street, Bury St Edmunds, Suffolk
IP33 2AQ, ☎ 01284 762300

Industrial Tribunals Helpline: ☎ 0345 959775

Industrial Tribunals (England and Wales):
  London (South): Montague Court, 101 London Road, West
  Croydon CR0 2RF, ☎ 0181 667 9131
  London (North): 19-29 Woburn Place, London WC1 0LU,
  ☎ 0171 273 8575
  Bedford: 8-10 Howard Street, Bedford MK40 3HS,
  ☎ 01234 352306
  Birmingham: Phoenix House, 1-3 Newhall Street,
  Birmingham B3 3NH, ☎ 0121 236 6051
  Bristol: The Crescent Centre, Temple Back, Bristol
  BS1 6EZ, ☎ 0117 929 8261
  Cardiff: Caradog House, 1-6 St Andrews Place, Cardiff
  CF1 3BE, ☎ 01222 372693
  Leeds: 3rd Floor, 11 Albion Street, Leeds LS1 5ES,
  ☎ 0113 245 9741
  Manchester: Alexandra House, 14-22 The Parsonage,
  Manchester M3 2JA, ☎ 0161 833 0581

Newcastle: Plummer House, 3rd Floor, Market Street East,
Newcastle-upon-Tyne NE1 6NF, ☎ 0191 232 8865
Nottingham: 7th Floor, Borkbeck House, Trinity Square,
Nottingham NG1 4AX, ☎ 0115 947 5701
Southampton: Duke's Keep, 3rd Floor, Marsh Lane,
Southampton SO1 1EX, ☎ 01703 639555

Institute of Personnel & Development, IPD House, Camp Road,
London SW19 4UX, ☎ 0181 971 9000, Fax 0181 263 3333

Lesbian and Gay Employment Rights, St Margaret's House,
21 Old Ford Road, London EC1 9PL, ☎ 0181 983 0696
(general enquiries and gay males), ☎ 0181 983 0694 (lesbians)

MIND, Granta House, 15-19 Broadway, London E15 4BQ,
☎ 0181 522 1728

National Association of Citizens Advice Bureaux,
Myddelton House, 115-123 Pentonville Road,
London N1 9LZ, ☎ 0171 833 2181, Fax 0171 833 4371

National Anti-Stalking & Harassment Support Group
(NASH), Bath Place Community Venture, Leamington Spa,
Warwickshire CV31 3AQ

NHS Executive Headquarters, Department of Health,
Wellington House, 135-155 Waterloo Road, London SE1 8UG

Parents at Work, Long Hours Campaign, Fifth Floor, 45
Beech Street, Barbican, London EC2Y 8AD, ☎ 0171 628 3565

RELATE, Herbert Grey College, Little Church Street, Rugby,
Warwickshire CV21 3AP, ☎ 001788 573421

Samaritans - see telephone directory for local numbers

Society of Occupational Medicine, 6 St Andrews Place,
Regents Park, London NW1 4LB, ☎ 0171 486 2641

The Tavistock Clinic, 120 Belsize Lane, London NW3 5BA,
☎ 0171 435 71111

The Samaritans, 10 The Grove, Slough, Berkshire SL1 1EY,
☎ 01753 532713

Trades Union Congress, Great Russell Street,
London WC1B 3LS, ☎ 0171 636 4030

Victim Support Scheme, National Office, Cranmer House,
39 Brixton Road, London SW9 6DZ, ☎ 0171 735 9166

Westminster Pastoral Foundation, 23 Kensington Square,
London W8 5HN, ☎ 0171 937 6956

Women Against Sexual Harassment (WASH), 312 The
Chandlery, 50 Westminster Bridge Road, London SE1 7QY,
☎ 0171 721 7592

Scotland

ACAS, Franborough House, 123-157 Bothwell Street,
Glasgow G2 7JR, ☎ 0141 248 1400

Equal Opportunities Commission, St Andrew House, 141
West Nile Street, Glasgow G1 2RN, ☎ 0141 332 8018

Industrial Tribunals (Scotland): ☎ 0141 204 0730
  Central Office of the Industrial Tribunals, St Andrew
  House, 141 West Nile Street, Glasgow G1 2RU,
  ☎ 0141 331 1601
  Office of the Industrial Tribunals, 124-125 Princes Street,
  Edinburgh EH2 4AD, ☎ 0131 226 5584
  Office of the Industrial Tribunals, 2nd Floor, 13 Albert
  Square, Dundee DD1 1DD, ☎ 01382 21578
  Office of the Industrial Tribunals, 2nd Floor, Inverlair
  House, 84 West North Street, Aberdeen AB9 1AL,
  ☎ 01224 643307

Scottish Institute of Human Relationships, 56 Albany Street,
Edinburgh EH1 3QU

Scottish Trades Union Congress, 16 Woodlands Terrace,
Glasgow G3 6DF, ☎ 0141 332 4946

Northern Ireland

Equal Opportunities Commission for Northern Ireland,
Chamber of Commerce House, 22 Great Victoria Street,
Belfast BT2 2BA, ☎ 01232 242752

Fair Employment Commission, Andras House, 60 Great
Victoria Street, Belfast BT2 7BB, ☎ 01232 240020

Health & Safety Agency, 83 Ladas Drive, Belfast BT6 9FH,
☎ 01232 251333

Industrial Tribunals:
  Office of the Industrial Tribunals and the Fair Employment
  Tribunal, Long Bridge House, 20-24 Waring Street,
  Belfast BT1 2EB, ☎ 01232 327666

Labour Relations Agency, Windsor House, 9-15 Bedford
Street, Belfast BT2 7NU, ☎ 01232 321442

Legal Aid Department of the Law Society of Northern
Ireland, 3rd Floor, Bedford House, 16-22 Bedford Street,
Belfast BT2 7EL, ☎ 01232 246441

Redundancy Branch, Department of Economic Development,
Netherleigh, Massey Avenue, Belfast, ☎ 01232 529900

Index

Bully in sight

Comments and feedback

The author welcomes feedback, comments, amendments, advice and information for possible inclusion in future editions.

Please send to:

Success Unlimited
PO Box 77
Wantage
Oxfordshire OX12 8YP
UK

Thank you for your comments

This page may be photocopied <small>C1.0-041296</small>

Bully in sight

Order Form

Please send me .... copies of **BULLY IN SIGHT** at £12.95 per copy.

I understand that if I am not completely satisfied I may return the book(s) in good condition within 30 days for a full refund of the purchase price - no questions asked.

Tick if you would like your book(s) signed by the author ☐

Name (BLOCK LETTERS)...

Address...

....

....

Postcode ....

Postage and packing: UK customers (including BFPO) please allow £1.20 for first book, plus £1 for the second book, plus 50p for each subsequent book up to a maximum of £7.20.

Overseas customers (including Ireland) please allow £2.50 for the first book, plus £1.50 for the second book, plus £1 for each additional book. For air mail outside Europe please add an extra £1.00 per book.

I enclose Postal Order/IMO/Cheque for ....

(sterling only please) payable to "Success Unlimited".

Send to: Success Unlimited, PO Box 77, Wantage, Oxfordshire OX12 8YP, UK

Please photocopy this page for more copies

01.0-041296